Previous books by Hilde Larsen.

From HELL to Inspired

Know the Truth and Get Healthy

No More BULLSHIT

Power Up and Grow Free—You Are the Only One You Have Been Waiting For

HILDE LARSEN

iUniverse

NO MORE BULLSHIT

Power Up and Grow Free—You Are the Only One You Have Been Waiting For

iUniverse books may be ordered through booksellers or by contacting:

iUniverse
1663 Liberty Drive
Bloomington, IN 47403
www.iuniverse.com
1-800-Authors (1-800-288-4677)

Because of the dynamic nature of the Internet, any web addresses or links contained in this book may have changed since publication and may no longer be valid. The views expressed in this work are solely those of the author and do not necessarily reflect the views of the publisher, and the publisher hereby disclaims any responsibility for them.

Any people depicted in stock imagery provided by Thinkstock are models, and such images are being used for illustrative purposes only. Certain stock imagery © Thinkstock.

Photography by Trevor James Samborski.

ISBN: 978-1-5320-1416-1 (sc)
ISBN: 978-1-5320-1565-6 (hc)
ISBN: 978-1-5320-1415-4 (e)

Library of Congress Control Number: 2017902645

Print information available on the last page.

iUniverse rev. date: 03/14/2017

DISCOVER WHAT YOU HAVE
BEEN WAITING FOR.

THE TIME IS NOW!

Dear reader,

By awakening to who we really are, we're able to let go of everything that has been holding us back. By truly connecting with our inner source, God and Creation, we're able to effortlessly flow through life with a renewed passion and enthusiasm. This natural passion for living and creating, is a part of every breath that we take.

My love for life itself has led me to explore the amazing abundance and love that we are all a part of. Pain is inevitable, but suffering is a choice. Love is the ultimate language of the Universe, and anything not thereof is an obstruction of the flow of life.

Who you really are, and the power you hold within, is stronger than any agony or despair.

You are worthy of a life in abundance and joy, as you choose to awaken to your true essence. You are amazing, and through letting go of your clutter and old programming you will set yourself free.

Hilde

CONTENTS

PART 1   YOU ARE THE ONLY ONE YOU HAVE BEEN WAITING FOR

Chapter 1 The same old story..3

Chapter 2 You are the only one.. 12

Chapter 3 False beliefs.. 21

Chapter 4 The power of ignorance.................................40

Chapter 5 Fear, the ultimate challenge..........................48

PART 2   POWER UP AND GROW FREE

Chapter 6 The true story...59

Chapter 7 The truth will set you free.............................76

Chapter 8 No more resistance 91

Chapter 9 What is your excuse? 99

Chapter 10 De-clutter and Grow FREE.......................... 112

Chapter 11 Authentic investments................................135

Chapter 12 Finding your purpose..................................147

Chapter 13 Your power and beyond 157

PART 3   STEPPING INTO THE GRACE

Chapter 14 Guidance and signs.. 169

Chapter 15 Which comfort zone? 179

Chapter 16 Gratitude and the gift of nature.................................... 189

Chapter 17 How can I serve 202

Chapter 18 Letting go of the outcome.. 212

Chapter 19 From knowledge to wisdom 224

Chapter 20 How dare you?.. 238

PART 4   MASTER YOUR BLESSINGS

Chapter 21 Are you allowing greatness?.. 247

Chapter 22 Spread your wings 258

Chapter 23 Spiritual awakening.. 266

Chapter 24 True abundance 273

Chapter 25 Your life manifesto 280

AFTERWORD.. 293

NOTES And Reading Suggestions... 295

ACKNOWLEDGEMENTS

This book was energetically written long before *From HELL to Inspired* and *Know the truth and get Healthy*. Our inner power is the ultimate foundation of any healing and awakening path. My strong and firm connection with Source and Mother Nature, has been my lifeline, my inspiration, and my greatest blessing through my earthly experiences. I have been constantly guided and directed. I have been shown the way, and intuitively and spiritually awakened on my path.

I honor God, the Creator, for this path and experience, and I thank Mother Earth for her abundance and comfort. No part of my life has been without amazing value, and I expect the same for the future, in all of creation.

By letting go of the bullshit, I was able to see the truth in a way that is both freeing and empowering.

Without all the great healers that have walked before me, I would not be able to share this truth. They are many. They have changed, and *are* changing this world. Thank you Dr. ND Robert Morse, Dr. Wayne

Dyer, Bruce H. Lipton, Dr. Colin Campbell, Arnold Ehret, Bernard Jensen DC, PhD, Paul Twitchell, Joe Vitale, Norman W. Walker, Dr. Douglas Graham, Dr. Sebi, Og Mandino, Steve Jobs, Joel Fuhrman, Dr. Max Gerson, Herbert M. Shelton, Dr. Masaru Emoto, Louise L. Hays, Andreas Moritz, Deepak Chopra, Echart Tolle, Nick Vujisic, Zig Ziglar, Napoleon Hill, Neal Donald Walch and Tony Robbins.

Thank you, Nature for blessing us with everything that we need to thrive. I am humble to have been shown the way. I am humble to be able to harvest from your abundance, and to dance in your energy.

To all that have given me the opportunity to guide and support them on their journey back to health. Thank you! *You* are who inspires me! *You* who are willing and eager to take charge of your own destiny.

To everyone that listens to my talks, my podcasts and who reads my articles, thank you. You Inspire me to keep walking my talk, and to keep bettering myself.

Thank you, truth and helpers, for shining your light for me to see.

Again, thank you!

ABOUT THE AUTHOR

Hilde Larsen, known as the one that Inspires, is the owner and founder of http://inspiredbyhilde.com/. She is a certified Health and Success Coach, a Raw Food Teacher, an Author and a certified Detox Specialist. Her glowing enthusiasm for health and vitality, has the leading role in her work.

Hilde Larsen is also an Inspirational media speaker, a blogger, and has her own YouTube channel. She is the author of three published books:

> From HELL to Inspired.
> Know The Truth and Get Healthy.
> No More Bullshit.

She creates online video programs, and has her own membership site Inspired Members.

Her interest for healing and spiritual growth also led her to become a Reiki Healer. She is highly intuitive, and has a strong connection to Mother Earth and the spiritual world.

Born and raised in Stavanger, Norway, she and her husband of 28 years have a second home in Florida, USA. She is a proud mother and grandmother, and a tree hugger at heart. Called by nature and spirit, she is inspiring many to take back their power.

Her career started as an interior architect, designing cruise ships and hotels. Being athletic all her life, she was the co-owner of an aerobics and spinning studio for many years. She closed her interior design and building company *Kolage*, in 2004, due to her severe illness. She then went on to studying journalism, and was guided to the path of healing and regeneration.

In her first book "From HELL to Inspired", Hilde shares her full story. A heartfelt gripping journey about her struggles from bedridden to living her dreams. Her second book "Know the Truth and get Healthy", is a step-by-step guide to true health and vitality.

Hilde now spends her time travelling between Norway and Florida, exploring health, healing and the human connection to nature. She also values her quality time with her close family and friends.

To request to work with Hilde, visit the website www. inspiredbyhilde.com.

PREFACE

Let's cut the crap and get real. What in the world has taken us so long? Why is it that we keep on living as if nothing is wrong, when the whole World is upside down? Have you noticed? If you are searching for the good life, for the typical abundance, health and happiness, I am happy you have ended up right here. Right here at the very beginning. You see, the celebration of life starts when we return to the hard-core causes of disconnect. We need to revisit ourselves, bullshit free.

As we dig deeper into life and its meaning, we are bringing forth everything not worthy of our light and true essence. Let us smoke it out, and set ourselves free. Fear nothing, and search for real truth. True freedom is knowing that the power is within us, and that we are the ones in charge of our own lives and experiences. We, us, the God force and creation, all one as we serve to grow and expand. At the same time, all we can do is simply to be.

If you've read my two previous books, *From HELL to Inspired*, and *Know the Truth and Get Healthy*, you know the importance of living in sync with Mother Nature; How everything we eat, think and live affects our lives. How our health is in our hands, and how chronic and disease is an illusion. To walk down the road of cleansing and rejuvenation is often the first step to empowerment, as it will set us free from the bondage of pain and suffering. At the same time, it is only the beginning. It is only a small part of this true and authentic path to our own perfect life on this Earth and beyond.

There is no glory in giving up, and there is no glory in staying sick. Life is about living the very best way that we know how, and to realize that suffering does not have to be a part of it. Pain is inevitable, but suffering is a choice. In my first book, *From HELL to inspired*, I take you with me on my own journey from feeling completely lost and sick, to living the life that I love. I have shared my experience on living with a so-called chronic illness, and my encounters with our so-called health care system. I am happy and honored to be able to share my path and my knowledge, and I am confident that if you are in the need of healing, on any level, you will find truth between those covers.

In my second book *Know the Truth and Get Healthy*, I show you step-by-step how to accomplish amazing health. It is a guide to true health and vitality. Health is simple, change is hard. The bullshit of our programming, our conditioning and our society is cluttering our judgment, and playing games with our subconscious mind.

When I was at my sickest, my all-time low, the one thing that never left me, was the willingness to fight for what I believed was possible. I knew that being ill was not who I really was. From being bedridden, and sick as a dog for years and years, I was tired, yes. I was sick and tired of being sick and tired, but I was never ready to quit. There was something that drove me, that was letting my spirit shine through. Something was telling me that there was a hidden truth, and that I could wake up to a different reality, and I did.

You do *not* have to go through a major life-altering crisis to wake up to your own amazingness. By wanting to better yourself, to grow, to be authentic and to be the best version of *you*, I offer you these insights to tap into, to ponder and to play with. Your journey through life is unique, yet together we are stronger.

By reading this book, *you* have been called to step up to your most amazing inner potentials, way beyond physical health. You have been called to action. I hope your beliefs will be challenged, and your eyes will be opened. Let down your guard and shamelessly step into the realm of no-more-lies.

We are all in this together, and you are never alone. Your spirit, your soul, who you *really* are, is always healthy and strong. The real you, is never in despair or pain, only our bodies are. Know that the body is a self-healing mechanism, and that *you* deserve to feel and live amazingly strong! You are capable of conquering anything that comes your way. With your eyes wide open, dressed in truth and dignity, you are unstoppable. Let the shit hit the fan!

Thank you for being a part of my tribe and my life.
Thank you for blessing me by reading this book.
Thank you.
Shine on!

MEDICAL ADVICE/DISCLAIMER

This book, with its opinions, suggestions and references, are based on the author's personal experience and is for personal study and research purposes only. This book is about health and vitality, not disease. The author makes no medical claims. Information in this book is not meant to treat or diagnose any disease. This is not medical advice, but a sharing of personal experiences.

The information, ideas, and suggestions in this book are not intended as a substitute for professional medical advice. Before following any suggestions contained in this book, consult your physician. Neither the author nor the publisher shall be liable or responsible for any loss or damage allegedly arising as a consequence of your use or application of any information or suggestions in this book.

Taking responsibility for oneself is a great message to take from reading this book. This is for educational and inspirational use only. Self-empowering is a great asset to any health regime, and it is of great value for every aspect of life. Seek freedom from disease, seek healing.

PART ONE

YOU ARE THE ONLY ONE YOU HAVE BEEN WAITING FOR

Chapter 1

The same old story.

What if your whole life is based on a big fat lie? What if nothing you have believed in is the whole truth and nothing but? I bet you would not only be puzzled and curious, but angry and pissed off as well.

What if your whole life story was based on a myriad of false beliefs, and that you were held prisoner by your own conditionings? Then what? Would you keep doing what you are doing? Is your life the most amazing experience you could ever imagine? It might be, and it might not be, that is the answer that will reveal what you believe you are. Your story tells us everything.

"Good morning, same old shit. Another day trying to chase the day. Up at dawn, off to work. Some of us are not meant to do greater things. I mean, it is not like a prince charming or a truck full of money is knocking on my door. I've got to remember to pick up the dry cleaning, it's Thursday. Same, same. I'd better pick up my vitamins at the same time, and call my mum. Life is like a replay really, and sometimes I feel

like a robot. Well actually, most of the time. Had I only jumped at the possibility when it presented itself. It still bothers me. Look at my sister, she did it. Lucky her. Here I am, same old shit."

This is how our mind works. It keeps on going, non-stop. Blabbering away, using the same words, the same sentences, day in and day out. Until something changes. Take a minute and observe your own thoughts. Did you know that most of the time we are telling ourselves the same old story? We're actually saying the same things over and over again, playing life as a broken record. Now that is scary powerful! We are not different from the crowd, you and me, even our friends are telling the same old tale. The same complaints are often expressed, over and over again, together with the same wishes and attitude. The story might wear a different dress or suit, but the core message is the same.

The same way we are eating the same breakfast every single day, we are thinking the same thoughts. This is what we call programming. The behind-the-scene patterns that keep us in the same loop. Willing and able to stay on the same track, day in and day out. We are programmed to behave in a certain way, to follow a religious movement, to have a certain attitude towards different people, and to look at ourselves as winners or losers. Whatever you think and believe, you grew up learning it.

Our attitude towards our life, and life in general is a result of our life programming, and is now living in our subconscious mind. It's a reflection of our beliefs, our clutter and how deeply we are sleeping. We can walk through life, sleeping like a baby. Not being aware at all. Cruising along within our every-day, like a zombie.

Sigmund Freud used the metaphor of an iceberg to describe the two major aspects of human personality and behavior patterns. He looked at the conscious mind as "the tip of the iceberg," the small part that extends above the water. The subconscious mind represents the much larger bulk of the iceberg, beneath the water. [1]

The subconscious mind is like a storage room. It holds all your beliefs, your previous life experiences, your skills, and every image you have ever seen. It takes care of and holds on to absolutely everything. As we are not consciously aware of what is playing in the subconscious mind, it can control our lives without us even knowing it. It holds every skill that we have learned, like driving a car. When we first learn, we really need to focus on every little thing while driving. It is hard to participate in a conversation, while driving. After a while, we drive like we are on autopilot. In a sense, we are. Useful, but also scary. As long as we don`t know which programs are controlling our lives, we are not fully free.

The conscious mind is what we see as our awakened mind. It holds our current thoughts, that we can override and change as we go along. It is everything that we are aware of. All our dreams and sensations, our feelings and fantasies that are in our current awareness, is part of our conscious mind.

Freud also describes a third mind, the preconscious mind. He looked at it as being the bridge between the conscious and the subconscious. It is where we retrieve our memories when needed, where we can go to remember important information. It is like a gatekeeper for the subconscious, like a go-between. I keep it as a part of our conscious mind. As long as we can access the information, we can change how we use it. It is when we cannot know what is hidden, we get into trouble.

Observe your current situation:

Think about your life from an observer`s perspective. Look at it from the outside and be mindful about what you do and say in a daily basis. Most likely your days are filled with the same tasks, you go

---

[1] *Freud, S. (1915).* The unconscious. *Standard Edition, Volume 14.*

to the same job, and you hang around the same crowd of people. Look further. Look at the simple things. What are you eating? What are you thinking? When do you get up in the morning, and when do you go to bed? You brush your teeth and you take a shower. How do you dress? Do you work out? A whole series of rituals and repetitions. Most often this is our lives, and that is what is locking us in, holding us back. The sleepiness and the unknowingness of the fact that we are living this life hooked to an autopilot. Unknowingly living the same old story that we were brought up to believe we chose. Most of what we do and say in a day was never chosen, not consciously. It was programmed. Fed to us through television, radio, and society in general. Like in a feeding tube. Bombarding our whole being with signals of the "proper" life. Not all bad of course. Most of us have learned and experienced some beautiful things, great values and have met some wonderful people. Life is good, although the lies will have to go.

The good *and* bad news is; it is not your fault. The subconscious mind is simply a programmed chip, if you will, that is acting like your pilot. It is keeping you locked into the false belief that you are free and in charge, when in reality you're not.

By going to school, the structure of your life was put into a system. Through a controlled education on topics and written "truths", our whole picture of the world, who we are and who we need to be has been molded. Brick by brick, our house and the whole city of reality has been formed and built. Leaving little or no room for creative or free interpretation. The stage has been set. We will be told the same old story, over and over until it sticks. It becomes a truth for all our cells. It does not matter if it is the real truth, it will become *ours*. We will own it and honor it.

Be aware of how you speak to your friends, what stories you tell. Are they the same complaints about work, your husband, the children? Maybe you are talking about how you are not feeling good, your health or other topics that interest you. It can be anything, but as long as it's not uplifting your spirit, and as long as it is not reflecting who you are and your inner most pure emotions, it is holding you back. It's keeping you locked in the grip of the autopilot, and life becomes a different day with the same old story.

If you have children, I am sure you have told yourself *"I sounded just like my mother/father"*. That is not necessarily a bad thing, but it tells us a little something about the programming at hand. We adopt everything that is shown to us, like behavior and thought patterns. We learn through ear, mouth and eyes. As children, we are like sponges, literally soaking everything in. We watch and learn, listen and record. The hard drive is filled up little by little. We have no filter or manual to go by. Save all and delete nothing. That is the only rule. We don't have the ability to believe or not believe at this point. We save everything as our truth. Simple. We hold onto it like it is our connection to ourselves, and add it to our past-life cell-memories. Yes, our cells have memories, and most likely, you are not here for the first time. The story is much older than your current life. No wonder your story is a powerful one, and that it is a hard one to give up. Now wonder we let it run its course, on autopilot, until it really hurts.

I know all about not changing my ways until I was almost dead. I made my story my own, and I believed every word of it. I was carrying so many false beliefs that I no longer felt connected to anything but my big head, my stubbornness and my stressful life. Completely disconnected from myself. There was no inner feeling of belonging or self-worth. Sadly, my story is not unique, in the sense of suffering. My story is different in the sense that I decided I was done. I was done believing in that nonsense, that falsehood and that old programming. I was done believing I would never get healthy again, and that I was somehow not worthy of health and happiness. I was done believing that I was broken or not whole. My life was worth it. I was worth it.

> **"The difference between a belief and the truth
> will reveal itself once the bullshit is gone. What
> is left is always the truth." – Hilde Larsen**

It is easy to believe what everyone else believes. We have children`s stories that are telling us this. It is easy to be a sheep in the masses. The Emperor`s New Clothes is a great example:

Once upon a time, there was an Emperor who was extremely interested in having the best quality clothes. His whole world evolved around it, and he did not care much of anything else. One day several conmen came to see him, and told him they were the World's best weavers. They would make him the most beautiful fabric for his outfits. The Emperor was thrilled. They told him they made fabrics from a very special thread. The garments would appear invisible to anyone who was stupid or not doing their jobs.

The conmen ordered some of the finest materials, and secretly they sold them to get the money. They fooled the Emperor and his servants, by pretending to weave with nothing. The Emperor fired all his staff that couldn`t see this imaginary fabric, as he believed they were liars and not doing their jobs. It became easy for them to lie to keep their jobs. Now they all said they saw the beautiful threads turn to this fantastic textile.

The Emperor ends up getting dressed in nothing at all, believing that his garments were invisible only to cheaters. He started a procession where his servants walked behind him with their hands raised to hold the cape. The whole town admired him and his new clothes until one young boy yelled that the Emperor had no clothes on, that he was in fact naked.

In this story, great wisdom is revealed. The Emperor wanted to keep his position and did not hesitate to get rid of anyone who threatened his position. The conmen were getting rich by fooling, scamming and playing mind games, and the masses were prone to follow the crowd and accept the untruth of the authority. The servants were afraid of losing their jobs, and only the child had no agenda. The young boy is the voice of consciousness in this story. In his naivety and a life deprived of long standing programming and fear, he speaks his truth. I want us all to be this boy, to be able to speak our truths, and to not be held back by the old ongoing story.[2]

> Only when we break free from the old patterns, and awaken to the fact that our power does not emerge from our brain, will we feel and act up to our full potentials. You see, the brain is simply an organ, a tool, to be used or not. Our true power comes from our spirit, our heart and the God force.

The brain can be manipulated, our hearts cannot.

Many of these stories hurt us on a daily basis by holding us back from evolving, healing and growing. They are the roadblocks from hell, and the obstructions of our true essence.

What are the stories we are telling ourselves?

- I am limited
- I can never get healthy
- I am typically not good at anything
- I do not have the right resources
- I am too young/old
- I am not good enough
- I don't have enough money and never will
- I am not beautiful
- I am not smart enough
- I cannot help it, it is my genes
- I was abused, so it is not that easy for me

---

[2] https://en.wikipedia.org/wiki/The_Emperor's_New_Clothes

- I am all alone, and life is tough
- I am sick and will never get better
- Nobody loves me
- I need to be perfect
- It is not about me. I am not that important
- I cannot do this
- My family will not allow it
- Nothing good ever happens to me
- I am weak!

The list is endless. It's a reflection of our bullshit, and in fact, none of this is true. Not ever. Did you find something on this list that you believe is for you? If you did, this book is going to take you back to where you belong. Free of the story of deceit and lies. Free of the old programming. Hopefully you will discover your eagerness to find the truth that is hidden within you.

> "It doesn't matter how many times it has been told, and how many people that believe in the lie, it will never be the truth!" – Hilde Larsen

Let this be the time that you step up and take back your power. Let this be the time that you have been waiting for your whole life. Open your mind and heart, and let everything you have ever learned and known as your truth be questioned, and let all the invisible walls and fences come down. To be able to reach the subconscious mind, the conscious mind has got to be up for the task. You've got to be willing to see with your eyes open and to look at some less than flattering patterns in your life. This is not a competition or a race towards being perfect. Forget perfect. Life is so much larger than that.

A heart felt decision has got to be made to be able to follow in your own new footsteps. You are not only *the one* you

have been waiting for, you are the *only one* you have been waiting for.

You are the teller of your stories, the creator of your thoughts, the master of your actions, and the head of your life operations. You are the BOSS, and right now, it is time to act like it.

Chapter 2

You are the only one.

" *od, I am so tired of this shit! I knew it! I knew this would happen, so why even bother. No way I will ever get that promotion while she is still working here. She will always step in front of me. Look at her, all bright and driven. I wish I could just quit, but I can`t, not now. Never now. This is all you know, remember? Get over it, you are not promotion material, you know that. They would have promoted your ass years ago if you were any good. You suck. When are you going to stop thinking you could ever reach your goal? Forget it, not good enough, never will be."*

The self-talk has no politeness. It has no discernments or a good or bad time for telling it`s stories. Timing is out, all the time is in. It is telling it`s truth as it is, as it has been told, believed and accepted. Not told consciously for the most part, more like intravenously. One drop at the time, year by year. How dandy, and now it is biting your behind. Now it is the little thorn that keeps stinging, and never lets you off the hook. The guard of your illusory fence and shortcomings. Our beliefs told as little lies, from very early age, all there to keep us walking down that same old road, until we wake up. Like from a dream, we can simply wake up and smell the truth. We can choose to open our eyes little by little.

Your life is about realizing that not only do we deserve the best life ever, *we* are the only ones able to make it happen. Not those around us, not the mom, the boss, the husband or wife, the child, the neighbor or the friend. Only *us*, you and me, and everyone who takes back their power. Like from a dream, we can simply wake up and smell the truth. You are absolutely one of them. You are the *only* one you have been waiting for. Get ready and say "Hi" to your true self. I know it will be nice to meet you.

You are on the hook!

There really aren't anyone that can change anything for us, or want to do better for us. Even though we know this at a deeper level, we walk around waiting for someone to step in and take charge. We are waiting for a time in our life when everything will be perfectly lined up for us, all ready for the big change. It is not very likely going to happen that way. We have got to step up all by our very selves, and do what we know we need to do. We do know you see, we always know. Just listen, or dare to listen, you will know right away.

Are you waiting for a particular event in your life to take place, a green light maybe? A sign from above, something that will make you confident this is your time? Are you not sick enough, poor enough, depressed enough, sad enough or just on the hold until next time? Stop it. It is time. It is always time to let go and show up.

I know that intellectually you know that you are the one having to do what needs to be done. You know perfectly well that no one can do it for you. You know perfectly well that no one can decide for you, make you do anything you don't want to do, and not even treat you in a way that is not acceptable for you. Right? Wrong! If it was that simple, this would end right here, and you would not be held back by anything. Nothing would be able to stop you. Keeping you from acting is what the mind-game and programming or conditioning will do. This is what the subconscious mind will keep you trapped in, because it is what it does. Not because it is working against you in any way, but because it believes anything that *you* have ever accepted as your truth. It is simply a hard drive, remember? Programmed by your life. The subconscious is a part of *you*, and as long as *you* and the rest of *you* are not in alignment or agreement, there will be obstruction and frustration. There will be suffering and emotional upheaval. A constant battle is going on within, between the truth that comes from the heart, and the beliefs that comes from the mind. When there is conflict, there is suffering.

> **You are the master of your universe, the healer of your past and the crop master of your field.**

What if your entire life, your health, your emotional state, your relationships, your career and your level of happiness and joy were all linked to the same thing? All of it linked to the inner hard drive, this little chip, the untrue crap, bullshit and false beliefs. What if your whole world were controlled by something that isn't even true? A false positive, a true negative, a complete miss-guidance of your beliefs? The only thing to do would be to set the record straight, to delete all the falsehood and to reprogram the disc with the truth that is your own. As simple as that sounds, it is one of the hardest things a human can do, to change his beliefs. The subconscious is like a wire that holds us connected with everything we have ever lived, spoken, eaten, seen, felt and heard. It has a complete record of it all, and it doesn't have ability to evaluate anything. It does not see anything as no longer valid, or replace old beliefs with new beliefs. It is simply a receiver and a record player. It has no consciousness of its own, so the term is a bit confusing. We confuse it with conscious thinking that we can control and choose, but the sub, meaning beneath or under, is not up for grabs for the awakened state. Not all crap and unworthy thought form or bullshit is hidden there, but I would say up to 80% of it. The rest we are *very* well aware of.

Being aware of our own inner dialog is a more obvious way of changing how we act and feel. Changing and observing what we do not even know is there, is another ballgame. It calls for some true willpower and sincere interest in growing free, and it calls for some fearless and sexy living. It calls for opening the door that will let out the real shit, and it might not be pretty. Every shade of grey and color will surface as you open the gate to your inner hidden programming.

You will have to *feel* the responsibility that you hold for your life and your experiences. The complete freedom that lies in being the one in charge. No doubt are we all a part of the grand creation, and the illusion of not being powerful and sovereign must be left behind. Any power given to someone else is a loss of energy. The truth is all about you. Looking toward others for fixing and healing will only lead to a loss of creativity and enthusiasm.

You, the lead:

The realization that life is happening right now, that the part of your life that you are living right now is not a waiting room, is an awakening to the now moment. Our lives have been colored by the notion that later is when things will change or complete, resolve or unfold. From very early childhood we have been taught to hold on, until we get older, always looking forward to the next step, the next grade in school, to be able to ride a bike, drive a car, get married, drink alcohol and get a real job. Then we want a perfect partner, children and a career. The list is endless like pearls on a string, always keeping our focus forward, putting events and life experiences as our outside ourselves guidance and keepers. We are taught to hold our tongue, to wait our turn, and to stand in line.

The society is built on everyone following leaders and authorities, doing less of the thinking and more of the following. Not every family is the same, but in general it is safe to say that children are told to listen to the grownups, no matter what they are capable of teaching or setting an example as, and we take that program with us. We keep waiting for someone else to tell us what to do, what to believe, when, how and how many times. Think about it; How often do you look to others for validation, or a second opinion? How often do you call a friend to discuss any decisions *you* have to make, and need the agreement from at least that one friend? It is what we were told and taught to do, and it is keeping us from being the freedom of expression that we are. Most of all, it's keeping us from listening to our inner guidance. We are so used to looking outwards, that we have lost the ability to listen to where the real answer is, inside every single one of us.

You are the one living your life, the glory and the pain, every single part of it. That is the core of what this whole book is about, the realization that there are no one to blame, to turn to, or to hide behind when life seems to be stuck or imbalanced. This is your own play, start, middle and finish, even though you are not fully aware that you are actually directing the show. We will dig into the how's and the dirty hidden truth, but first of all, this is the ultimate key, *the* single most important inspirational simple fact. *You* are the storyteller and the writer of your play.

The leading role was yours from the very beginning, even though most of us like to look at it differently. Giving away our power is easy, and at times very comfortable. That way we can point at others' shit, and call it. Look at your life as a stage, and the plot as your life story. All the drama, the action and the hurts, the joy the happy times and the successes, all part of your amazing life story. All casted, directed and played so well. You, the leading role, casting director, movie director and writer, living out your dream, literally. Everyone beside yourself are leads in their own movie. Sure, there are other leading roles, significant people that definitively have strong influence on the story, but you were the one casting them. You are the hire and fire unit.

You are the one on-call 24/7, with sole authority. The responsibility connected with this role is magnificent, and we don't even know it is ours. You might think that one of your parents holds the lead role in your life, or your spouse, or even your children. Anyone but you, and that is "normal". Welcome to the club. The club of bullshit.

Like a soap opera, our lives revolve around family drama, sex, material growth, success in business, health and sickness, fear of ageing and ultimately dying. Everything that we have been programmed to see as our life. From looking at other movies, getting pointers and tips, we are creating the best movie we know how, with the hard drive and chip that is in place. Completely stripped of the ability to see ourselves and our position, we keep acting out this role called life, on autopilot. If that is what you are satisfied doing, read no further, as it will make it impossible for you to keep living without purpose. It will make you want to wake up and realize that what you have been fed, is not serving your purpose, and is by no means letting you spread your wings and fly like you were supposed to.

Question yourself:

- What if what I believe and was taught is not all true?
- What if there is more to life than what I am seeing?
- What if my programming is running my life?
- What if my fears are limiting my expression?
- What if I am the only one responsible for my experiences?
- What if I am re-living an old story?
- What if I am powerful beyond belief?
- What if I am the real authority?
- What if all I have got to do is choose?

- What if I can change anything?
- What if happiness is a choice?
- What if?

When we start to wonder, to think outside our invisible box, to ask questions, we are at the same time asking for guidance to see the truth. We are tapping into the divine, our wisdom and inner power. Simply by asking ourselves to change, a seed has been planted. You need no Guru or leader. You need no one to follow or to copy and look towards. This doesn't mean that you will be alone, or never get any support, it simply means that *you* choose who you listen to. It means that you do so from a true and honest de-cluttered standpoint, with the ability to acknowledge what is in your own, your loved ones, and the world's best interest. You see, once you get rid of the non-truths spinning around in the control room, everything becomes clear. Throw in some courage and passion for life, and unstoppable is the outcome.

I remember going to school, where we were standing in line before class. Being told when to sit, when to stand, and when use the restroom. I remember the fear of being reprimanded, the fear of having to give a note from my teacher to my parents. I remember being fearful towards anything that was related to an authority. This is the programming that will follow you as *the fear of not-being-good-enough, or doing well enough*. It will lead to blindly following a doctor, a minister, or any State official's opinion. As a result, we end up as a follower and a non-thinker.

What we have lived up until this point is the true reflection of our beliefs. If you are wondering what your subconscious mind is telling you, look at your life. If you are wondering what you really believe, look at your life. If you are wondering what you think or feel about anything, look at your life. It never lies, it tells it like it is. Own that, and you own your life, your entire story. Own that, and you are on your way to the reprogramming and deleting of false beliefs.

The subconscious sponge is about to be squeezed and filled with something that will encourage growth and joy. It is to be filled with your own life purpose and music. Playing an old record is so outdated. We know better, so we can do better. Step one is knowing it is there, step two is knowing who can change the record, delete any old songs, and record some new ones.

"As you walk towards the awakening of your inner guidance, all you need is your own true voice and power." Hilde Larsen

There is true empowerment in knowing that nothing but yourself is needed to step out and up to living your optimal life experience. There is true freedom in knowing there is nothing outside yourself that can have real control over any part of your life. To come to this realization will set the stage for the rest of your life, as every evolvement and growth starts with the acknowledgement of self-responsibility.

Freedom ahead:

Where you are right now, is a perfect starting point for growth and freedom. You are with your most valuable asset - yourself. You are breathing, you are willing to step up, and you are in the best of company. The world that we live in is filled with illusions. The rabbit-hole is deep, and our challenges are many. By each doing our part to break free from these conditionings and programs, we are raising the vibration on this earth. We are, by lifting ourselves, lifting others. We are, by walking our truths, showing truth to others. By walking our talks, we are teaching the younger ones how to set themselves free also. By being aware we create awareness and by living our lives free and happy we create more happiness. It all starts with you knowing that you are the *only* one you have been waiting for, to untangle the knots and false beliefs in your life. Still, we are all in this together. Together we stand, but alone as one.

The pitfalls of truly feeling that you are the Boss of your from-now-on experience is feeling lack of support and inner strength in this moment. Never mind, and don`t worry. Your power will come forth so strongly, it will leave you breathless. It will blow your conscious mind and open the floodgate of joy that you hold within. It will show you how beautiful life is, and how numbed down and astray you have wandered from your truth.

It does not matter, any past-experience, what you have lived, dreamed or seen in front of you. It does not matter what you have tried or not tried, witnessed or been a subject too. It does not even matter if you feel lost, out of resources, sick, tired and hopeless. It all starts with you and your willingness to pause and say; I am going to take back my power.

I am going to own my life like a Boss, and I am going to get to the bottom of what it is that is holding me back.

> **"My life is my own and I am the one, the
> only one I have been waiting for!"**

Chapter 3

False beliefs.

" *A* woman walks towards me. Dressed like a doctor, she is calling my name. I feel dizzy. I never did like hospitals. We are walking past a large display of metal joints. What a cheerful way to decorate, *is my thought, as I follow this woman to her office. What would one accomplish by using joint replacements as decorations? Maybe it is the interior architect speaking, but seriously. That cannot be a good thing. I am still freezing. It is hard to walk, and I am happy to see a chair.*

"Please sit," she says. She does not have to tell me twice. She examines me, my fingers, my toes, my knees, reads some of the forms and looks at me; "You will have a meeting with the special aids department tomorrow. They will provide you with what you need." *She is not taking her eyes off my paperwork while she speaks. I cannot think of any special aids that I will need, but that's the least of my worries at this point. What can this woman tell me about getting well and back to work?* "What are the prognosis?" *I stutter.* "When will I be able to get back to my life?" *This is what I have come here to find out. No one has*

been able to help me figure out what is going on in my body, and now I am relying on this woman to help me. Maybe she is the one that can get me back to my life. She now has a diagnosis, so what is the plan?

"You have a serious autoimmune condition and will never get well again". *She says.*

Unaffected, she looks at me and tells me; "You will have to be medicated for the rest of your life, and will need more aids to take care of yourself as the years go by," *she continues …"*[3]

This is a snippet from my own journey, from my life, about living through what I perceived as hell. My own hell, created by my belief system, my physical pain and my emotional suffering and despair. My programming about health and illness was a common one, and not that special. What makes the story stand out in the crowd is that I, by choosing *me* and life, broke free from the chain of disease. I tore down my own walls of lies and false information, and I walked towards the truth. I found my own inner power, and my own sovereignty, and I'm able to see beyond the veil of fear and helplessness.

I believed in the story above for years, and had been conditioned my whole life to do so. This is what I was told, and what I was shown. When you get sick, you go to a doctor, you take a pill and you get better. If you don't, you are in trouble, or worse. You can end up chronically ill, and maybe die. If there is nothing they can do for you, you are fucked. This is a typical Western belief system, the very short version of it. It takes a lot to break out of a strong deep rooted pattern, but we can do it. If I can do it, *you* can do it.

We all have these false beliefs, all based on our history and our lives. Our past lives, the present one, and maybe even the fear of a future one. This is a lot of fear. Ultimately it is all based on fear, more on that later.

---

[3] Hilde Larsen - *From Hell To Inspired*, 2016

Fear becomes us:

Off the top of your head, you might say that you fear nothing. Take a minute to reconsider. Fear is lingering behind everything that you are not happy about in your life. Let's look at some of the most typical life-altering, game-changing fears that are running our behaviors and beliefs. Fears are the same as lies. When we live our truth, we become fearless.

I can never get healthy.

Why do we fear taking charge of our own health? In the Western world of medicine, the medical doctor is perceived as the authority on health, and the person to go to when a symptom arises. The doctor is in-charge of our health, through medications and surgery. The language and the medical terms used are not presented to be understood by the layman. This separation in communication has kept us feeling inferior, and the doctor the absolute educated one. By giving away our power so completely, we have separated ourselves from the fact that we are our own authority. We forgot, or were never told that our body talks to *us*, and that the listening part is the key to any great relationship. From the standpoint of living a life being completely stripped of any authority towards one's own health and healing, we carry this deep belief that the answer and the solution is found in a pill or at a doctor's office or hospital.

You might have watched relatives and family members suffer for years with chronic diseases, or you have heard your parents go on about how the medications are helping them. Remember, everything you have ever heard, seen or experienced has downloaded to your subconscious, forming your belief. You become a believer in chronic, genetic illnesses, suffering and the easy fix-it-all pill.

You have been taught that you are not the authority on your own health, and that your body is not going to fix itself without someone

23

who knows what they are doing. You are left with the belief that you are not your own master, you are not the boss of your health, and you are most definitively not the one to look towards when in need of any form of healing.

Personally, I have experienced many examples of how humans cling to their beliefs and fears, and how they ultimately suffer from it. I have seen people who suffer from stage 4 cancer, after they have been told they are going to die within a few months, still not wanting to change anything. They will rather die than do something different. Their doctor tells them they have a few months to live, and they accept it rather than rebel and search for other possibilities. The spouse of someone in this situation told me they did not want any "false hope". That tells me it is easier to accept anything, as long as it is a sure thing - even death and pain. The doctor is ultimately right. The message is that leaving everything in the hands of others, leaves you powerless.

> "Because there is no glory in illness. There is no meaning to it. There is no honor in dying of it." – John Green

The belief system that tells us health is not ours to have, comes from the feeling that something is wrong with us. We fear not being OK, not being enough. The more we are presented with the term disease or sickness, and the more we have been introduced to the medical establishment, the more we will believe is wrong. The truth is, there is nothing wrong with us at all. We are experiencing a health that is a product of our lives and our handed down weaknesses. That simple.

If you have lived in an environment where you were being constantly critiqued, you will also believe something is wrong with you. You see, the subconscious mind does not analyze anything, it just accepts what you accept. You train it, so to speak. If you don't want it to be your reality, don't believe it. By living, you practice your beliefs.

Believing that you can never get healthy is an old false programming stemming from what you have seen, experienced, but also what you feel about yourself through perception. How can you get healthy if the doctor tells you otherwise? Are you smarter than him/her? Do you know better? Who do you think you are? Why would you be worth a true healing, when others don't experience it? What makes you special? Together with the feeling of not being worthy and loved, you have a cocktail of pain and suffering, BAM!

I am stuck, and cannot do better.

When we are stuck, we are obstructed, constipated and feel helpless. We are not in the flow of life, and we are holding ourselves back. We might be overwhelmed by situations or people, not feeling in charge or in control. Feeling stuck is a sign that you are seeing yourself as a victim of your experience. You have been programmed to see yourself as someone who has no influence on their own life. Maybe you grew up in a large family, where you had to follow everybody else's wishes. Maybe you were told that you didn't know anything, and that someone had to make the decisions for you. No matter the situation, you have been falsely programmed to believe that you are helpless and not capable of moving forward on your own. You believe that you've got to stay where you are, and wait for someone else to make a move for you.

The typical scenario that will make you a perfect candidate for the I-cannot-do-better award is when you drop your diet, drop out of school and skip the art course, all in the name of not being able to make it anyway. What is the point? What is the point in doing this, when I never make it anyway? Can you hear someone speaking these words to you? Can you hear a bird whispering in your ear? Maybe someone indicated, however so loosely that you were not the brightest one, or that you would never be able to make it.

25

Sure, you are stuck, and sure you cannot do better. WRONG!
All false, all bullshit!
You can, you will and you are!

Believing that you are stuck and cannot do better is a grand lie, and has nothing on your new reality. It is nothing but a lie that comes from the fear of failure. The fear of not being enough. Who cares? You are as good as anyone. Amazing, in fact.

I am always going to be poor, poor me.

Another lie, and such an easy one to buy into. Obviously, we will all have a conception of what money is and holds, from what we have experienced early on. The interesting thing is that people can have very different feelings and beliefs towards money. They can have the same background, even be siblings. One might see money as something out of reach, something he or she longs for. Another will see money as evil, as something that gangsters have access to through crime and bullying. A third person looks at money as something that can be used to help others, to create healing and build hope. Then, having a lot of money, can be perceived as being able to live effortlessly, enjoying the life one sees as optimal, with less worries and more play and service towards others.

The potential is endless, and the way you look at money, is only a part of your belief system. The poverty consciousness is derived from the belief that there is purity in being poor, and sainthood in giving up everything you own. The sense that there is glory in being poor, leaves having money the result of greed and ego. That is another topic entirely. When you believe that you can never get rich, or have enough money, this is the story you are telling yourself. The poverty story. This pattern of believing money is evil is one of the most common reasons people shy away from financial abundance. It doesn't matter where we come from, we all have an understanding about money.

Money is also a subject to greed and envy. It can be used as a threat, a collateral, a bait, motivation, help, aid and fun. Being poor can be a way out of having to deal with any of it. Choosing to stay out of the money game can be an escape from responsibility. With money *comes* responsibility *and* work. Fear of money can be fear of responsibility. Fear of money can be fear of appearing to be better than someone else.

This pattern also has deep roots in not feeling worthy. You might simply believe that you are not worth being abundant. You don`t see yourself as being good enough, smart enough, kind enough or lucky enough. No matter what you have been conditioned to believe around money; as long as it is not presenting you with the life you desire - it is false, plain and simple.

I am never good enough.

"Nothing I do is ever good enough. People are constantly putting me down, criticizing me. Always showing me how dumb I am, how stupid I must be. I am never validated for what I do, always ignored. No matter what I do, it is never enough. I feel so inferior, it is not fair, life is not fair."

When we have been led to believe that we are not good enough, it is always an imprint from very early childhood. It is one of the core beliefs that so many of us has had to carry.

A true freedom-sucker.

For you as an adult to actually *believe* that you are not good enough, you would have had to been brainwashed, right? And you were. The smallest of comments and episodes will imprint this belief in a child. A parent, a teacher, a friend even. Even a five-year old friend holds the power to program your subconscious. Every time someone says something that validated an already present little seed, it grows and magnifies. It becomes more true every time it is revisited.

Never being good enough will also keep you from being successful, and that can be a curse or a blessing, whatever fits you the best. You can wallow in the poor-me energy, or you can relax in the; success is not my business, I can just rest over here and not have to take charge or show up in my life. One false belief can have several core roots, so to speak.

"I am never good enough" is also a reflection of disempowerment. The spoken words of a victim and a sufferer. It tells you that you also believe that it is not your fault, and that others are not treating you right. Your subconscious is tricking you to believe that anything but your own inner power and standard is what sets the stage for what is good enough. You are always good enough, and that is a fact.

Life is hard.

All you need to do is to look around, and you will find proof that it is true. People are struggling, working hard and facing devastating obstacles. We are constantly bombarded with news and stories of tragedy and heartache. We are faced with fear based propaganda everywhere we turn. We have been told how hard it is to succeed, and how we'll have to work hard for anything in life. This is very easy to believe, and another victimizing lie.

First and foremost, working hard is not the same as having a hard life. Looking at life as hard is perceiving it as a struggle. The opposite of joyful, free flowing and educational. We can look at a glass half full or half empty. Life is hard or not, according to our belief system, our inner terrain and our awareness. The hard life is a chosen one, and to break free from that chain of beliefs takes a lot of guts, bravery and persistence. Why? Because you need to break free from the perceptions of the masses, and being different is challenging for most.

From living this life on this Earth, most people have bought into the belief that living *can* be hard. We have all had our ups and downs in life, and that is simply called life. Having an hour of frustration, or experiencing a minute of anger is simply life flowing through you. Staying there is something else. Believing life is hard is a false belief that also brings up fears. No one *wants* to struggle. We all want to be happy, both for*ever* and *after*. The struggling-is-normal belief is a common acknowledged truth, therefore deeply rooted in the whole society that we live in. The more validations we find for our beliefs, the harder they are to let go of. Bravery is needed.

Life is what it is. You define it. That "life is easy" can be an equally strong illusion, dictating that there will be no challenges. The label you put on anything will lock in the path that you pave. The moment you realize that life was never hard, it just is, you have your ultimate freedom of creating. The illusion of hardship is shattered. You are a creator, not a victim.

I cannot make it on my own.

The fear of being alone or feeling lonely keeps growing in our society. We live closer together than ever, in larger cities, yet we feel lonelier. Large companies are hosting teambuilding events, we have meet-ups, PTA, and anything from boy's clubs to family camping trips. We are more social, almost to the point of hysteria at times, and still we feel less connected to each other.

What belief system that is run by the subconscious mind would trigger such a longing for connection, yet leave you feeling lonely in the middle of a crowd? This is our disconnection from our inner being talking. This is how far we have strayed from who we really are. It is a symptom of not being connected to the God force and the trust in life itself. We are introduced to religion and the belief that we are separate from God, and that life is something happening outside ourselves. False.

Now to the topic at hand, the not being able to make it or stand alone, to not be the only one you need to succeed. Here we have an obvious tale that has been imprinted. How easy it is to pick up on not being enough on your own. I mean, who doesn't need help? Who doesn't need support? No man is an island, right? Well, the truth is that we all stand alone, yet together as one. We are all the perfect manifestation of creation, with the power to change, create and to choose. Making it on your own does *not* mean being alone, or being lonely. It simply means you are taking charge and stepping up, like the boss that you are.

Any belief that tells you there is something you cannot do is false, period. There is nothing you cannot achieve with time, persistence, enthusiasm, inspiration, work and dedication, nothing. Believe it, you are enough.

I am too young or too old.

I remember when being past 30 was considered old. I was a child, and my grandmother was dressed like an old lady. She sat in a chair, knitting, and always wore a dress and a hat. The concept of ageing has changed, and I am feeling younger every day. Society molds our concept of age. How to dress, what illness to get, how to look and what to do. Even a young child can tell you how life will progress as we age. We are young, healthy and vibrant, beautiful, then successful, going for youthful, maybe some cosmetic surgery, a chronic illness, retirement with as little discomfort and movement as possible, then death. Ultimately from an illness, in a nursing home, on medications.

The assumption that ageing is restrictive leads us to the idea that it can be used as an excuse or a point of retreat or resistance. This conclusion reflects nothing but low self-esteem issues and ignorance. It shows the symptoms of not feeling good enough, not being self-confident and secure. Age can be used as an excuse for why we are experiencing a set-back, or lack or success. Depending on the individual, on his or her background, age, gender and education, something will fit. Too old, too young, too tall, too small.

That being said, the subconscious is not a single component device, rather a complex soup kitchen, where every single drop of information, truths and non-truths have been boiling for a lifetime. What shows up in our expression from fear and uncertainty is a mixture of our entire soup recipe. It can get very messy, and can amount to quite the cleaning job.

You are never too young, and you are never too old. The time is always right, when you are ready.

Age is an honor, and youth is fresh and enthusiastic.

Wisdom does not have a direct link to age, inspired and youthful living. There is more to it, than the number of years traveled around the sun. This false belief is keeping us in the chains of restriction, spoken over us from ignorance and insecurity.

Such bullshit.

The world is against me.

When the broken record in the brain is playing this tune, pain and suffering is the only dance happening on the floor. Nothing will fall into place with this severely distorted illusion present. The world can never be against us. Not in any way, shape or form. Not possible, not ever. The world is a part of us, as everything is connected. If anything, we are supported beyond our imagination, and nothing happens *against* or *to* us, life is always happening *for* us.

From a child's perspective, the experience that has set this train into motion has been very hurtful, and most likely on a continuous basis. This does not have to be abuse as an adult would label it. A child has its own perception and world view. When we feel abandoned, not loved or heard, it is detrimental. The child believes that truth instantaneously. The experience of the world being a place that is cold and going against ones needs and desires becomes an expectation.

Do you ever think that it is typical that good things do *not* happen to you? Your world view is to blame. You have some beliefs that need to be put straight. The world is reflecting how your subconscious and conscious mind are wired at all times, not leaving any room for chance. When your mother or father told you that you couldn't go to the dance when everyone else were going, they were taking on the role of playing out your world view. Your belief could now grow stronger and bigger, easily inviting in more truths to join the party.

Our world view has some absolutes that we cling to for our dear lives. They are challenged when we are told that the world works *for* us.

- *Bad things don't happen to good people.*
- *Life should be fair.*
- *Young people don't get sick.*
- *Work is always hard.*

Not until the false beliefs are deleted, and the void is filled with the essence of truth, will you feel how the world is at your service. How the whole Universe is at your feet, offering co-creation and constant evolving teachings, and a place for growth and inspiration.

Never believe anything that you think. It is most likely not true. The mind is playing a game, and the trick is on you.

I cannot trust people.

When you have been lied to, let down, left and abused, of course trusting people is an issue. Not that it is a valid truth, but it is easily traceable. The origin is naked to the eye, and not only that, it is a sympathetic one, meaning you will get support to keep the viewpoint.

The trust issue is a deeper one, and most likely it was already there when the untrustworthy people showed up in your life. It was already a part of your belief system subconsciously. Hard to believe that a little child would be included in my statement, but children pick up patterns from the womb, and if you are digging for gold, past lives have a tendency to cling to our genetics in a way that easily transfers some deep rooted false beliefs.

Not trusting others, is a self-trust issue, a lack of self-worth and self-love. When you point to others, thinking *they* are capable of hurting you, you are giving away your own power, one hundred percent! It was never about them. It was always about you. Once you realize that no one can do anything *against* you, but rather act and behave as a reflection of their own state, you will no longer feel the need to hold on to this belief.

To be able to trust is to be able to flow. To be able to flow, is to be able to receive. To be able to receive, is to be able to give. Giving is the flow of living.

I will never find true love.

We are all seeking to be loved, validated and to fit in. It is natural to want to feel like you are part of a community. We are a tribal species, and do very well in support, trust and love for each other. Most importantly we *are* love. We are the expression of God, the love for all and ourselves. We often say that we do not love ourselves, and I have also mentioned lack of self-love. It is a perceived lack.

33

The true love is obstructed by the false beliefs. The brain is nothing but a device, an organ. It is not a truth keeper, very far from it.

If you are experiencing not being loved by friends or family, or that you are seeking a partner, and not finding one. If you have been in relationships that reflects to you that you are not loved, you are mirroring your inner beliefs. They always want to be proven right.

How could someone love you?

- You are not lovable.
- You are not pretty enough
- You are not smart enough
- You are not sexy enough
- You are not kind enough
- You are simply not enough

No wonder nobody loves you, right? Wrong! Someone told you this nonsense a long time ago. Once you believed them, you started to tell yourself this. Nothing beats telling ourselves the lies. It makes it even more powerful. No one we would trust more than ourselves, right? Right!

Not being worthy is a deep-rooted core belief. Our whole being feels separate from God, and from separation comes the fear or not being enough. Not worthy is a term that covers anything that touches upon lack in any shape or form. Abundance flows to the worthy. Prosperity and glory to the one who is complete. Not so, we are all complete, only we cannot see it from behind the vail of untruths.

The programming of false beliefs is always a complex cocktail of little hints and expressions, coming through as a truth, all saved and presented stronger and firmer every time it is revisited.

At the core of any false belief of programming is the lack of self-love. The curse and the blessing. A true blessing, as we are in-charge of loving ourselves, and once we realize this, we can start nurturing ourselves and build a solid foundation for a life of strong and healthy beliefs and creative forces.

We have gone through some basic lies that keep us from achieving our ultimate goals and happiness. That is our objective, to be happy. Despite how good or bad we feel about our life, we want the same thing, happiness. What we want is the same, could our fears be the same also? Here are the topics that we looked at:

1. *I can never get healthy*
2. *I am stuck, I cannot do better*
3. *I am never good enough*
4. *Life is hard*
5. *I cannot make it on my own*
6. *I am too young or too old*
7. *The world is against me*
8. *I cannot trust people*
9. *I will never find true love*

The interesting thing is that all the topics lead to the same core-fear, to not be good enough, to simply not be enough. Who told us this? We are so fearful of not being enough, we have lost our power completely. Not being enough also means not loving ourselves. How sad is that? We need to get over it and love ourselves unconditionally. Period.

Identify your false beliefs!

We are here to heal, so here is the deal: Search for your old wounds. Let them reveal themselves to you. Let your current patterns lead the way. Our old hurts and traumas can then be understood and changed. Let's look at an example of how an old false belief is playing itself out in the daily life. A woman that I know, had been married several times. She was now in her 4th serious relationship with a man, and he was bullying her. After having left two ex-husbands, both abusive, she was devastated that this man, which she had fallen head over heels in love with, was showing patterns of the same behavior. He was threatening and unstable and was leaving my friend fearful and anxious. Her health was strongly affected by these relationships. She was suffering *big*time, *again!*

Why is it that every time she thinks she has found the perfect partner, she keeps re-living the same old story? She had to go inward and look for what *in* her was creating this situation. What beliefs was she accepting about herself and her life that was allowing her to keep creating these experiences? The repeat button. Her core belief, her subconscious programming that said; *"I am not worthy of love, I am not worth treating with respect."* No self-love can shine through that fog of misconception. She remembered the first time her mother found her going through her jewelry, shouting at her; *"You will never find anyone who will love someone like you. No nice man would want you. Why would he?"* Message received, saved and accepted. I am sure many similar messages would fly her way later-on, all being confirmative to her early experiences of rejection. Now, she was simply living what she had mapped out, a life where no man would love and treat her well.

Once she stepped out of that emotional prison, and realized that she in fact was worthy, and that she in truth was lovable, amazing, and perfect, she met the most wonderful loving man. He saw what she saw, and she no longer had the need to prove any old program right. She was free.

Take a good look at your life. A long good look at your behavior patterns, how you feel most of the time. Look at repetitive behavior and replays. Search inward for what is not joyful for you to experience, and get ready for some serious work. Polish your enthusiasm towards freedom, and get a hold of a beautiful journal. Writing on your computer is fine, but there is something about pen and paper. The words written are handcrafted, and I find it even more real and personal.

Keep track of your internal dialogue.

Start by putting your journal by your bed. Write in it every morning. Write a page every single day, and read everything you have written, once a week. Take some time to look back, and see the trends that are showing up. Write about anything. Work, family, friends, plans for the future. Try to step out of thinking mode, and write without analyzing or editing. Let whatever is on your mind hit the paper. Then leave it.

Had my friend been doing this, she would have seen the pattern of what she was living. There would have been a red flag, and she would have known where to start pointing the spotlight.

What story are you telling?

You might be surprised at what you are actually saying. We might think we tell a certain story, but in reality, most often we are not. You see, we tell what we live. The words are automated to fit our beliefs. Adopted, imported, borrowed and copied. It doesn't matter if they serve us or not, we speak them as our own. The story is not only told *from* us, but *to us*. What are you judging, and what are the beliefs behind your spoken words? Being aware of the words will reveal your most inner beliefs about yourself, others, and the world as a whole.

Look for the subjective labels and feelings that are attached to your words. For example; "This weather is driving me crazy." A typical statement that is showing us we are blaming an outside source for our emotional state. How could the weather, that has nothing to do with us, and that simply is what it is, drive *us* anything? We are telling a story of judgment, of discomfort, and we are creating more scenarios and hooks to hang our shit on.

Be observant of the patterns that run through your story. Watch your tongue throughout the day, and observe how you paint your picture, so to speak. How you paint and color it, is how it will look. Write the patterns down if you will, to get a look at them from a distance. Often, revisiting written material will open our perception and gift us with some "aha"-moments.

Here are a few examples of what to look for:

- *"Did you hear the news/read the headlines/watch the show last night?"* Followed by a tragedy or crime story.
- *"He/she makes me feel so sad/angry/upset, etc."* Constantly referring to others making you feel.
- *"I wish I could handle that/I wish he would learn how to".* Speaking of the current life as something that needs to be changed. Wishing someone or oneself to change.
- *"When I get a better job, I will plan my traveling. When the kids grow up/when I graduate,/when I have lost the weight I will go out more."* The story is telling a tale of a person that uses excuses for not living in the now. Procrastination at its best.

Every reaction that you have towards people, situations, and your own self-image, is a reflection of those same old lies, the false beliefs. By monitoring how you speak out loud, together with journaling your inner thoughts, you can expose yourself and look deeply at what it is that you are really telling yourself. Emotions will be present when you speak of how you feel, what you sow and so on. The emotion is the largest clue, as it reveals your attachment to the words. They are also the lead to the underlying belief. Don't assume anything. Go after the truth, write, monitor and have fun with it. After all, it is only an illusion, remember?

Be ready for some serious resistance, as any old pattern will want to fight for its position. A new Boss is in town, you! If the belief is not serving you, and is free from falsehood, it better be ready to dissolve. Love, uplifting and positive healing vibes are welcoming replacements. Happy journaling!

How do we change our false beliefs and replace them with supporting ones?

After we have identified what has never been true, and what has been holding us back, we need to fill the void. Life always wants to fill a void. Sit down and look at what is the opposite of the belief that you have identified. Let us go with it being; *"I am not worthy of real health, there is something wrong with me. My body is not working for me, it is working against me."* This belief needs to be replaced with; *"I am worthy of perfect health, and my body is my best friend. It is always working for me, and is always on my team. I love my body, and I love me."*

To lock in a new belief, put yourself in a comfortable state of mind. Sit quietly and relax your whole body. Still the mind and tap into a peaceful place. Repeat the statement while you connect with a positive feeling. Work on one belief system at the time, and be diligent. It takes time to turn around an old record set on repeat. Inspire yourself by celebrating your path of truth and freedom, and be kind to yourself, always be kind.

Nothing you say, do or feel can change the true you. It is always ready to shine through, and will continue to send you signals and hints until you take them. Any rejection to listen is rewarded with some form of suffering.

Chapter 4

The power of ignorance.

"*My stomach is acting up again. Another ulcer is brewing. I can feel it. Every time I walk into my office, I feel my whole body go into stress mode. I know, too much coffee. Don't think my stomach hasn't been telling me that for a while. Where are my medications? I always seem to have to take a larger dose during the week than on my days off. The rare days off that is. I swallow another pill and chase it with a sip of coffee. Ouch that hurts.*

I almost swallow my pill twice, while trying to breathe through my nose. The boss is here, in the flesh, and it is like the uneasy feeling of being here, magnifies and resides in my abdomen. I know, I hate this job, really hate it. If I could only sleep and not have this terrible pain. I cannot afford another hospital stay with a full-blown ulcer. Oh, reminding me I need to return that health magazine to my sister. Interesting enough to read about diet and ulcers, but if it had any truth attached to it, my doctor would tell me. If all those health and healing freaks were onto something good, it would be in the news, right?"

How we love to indulge in the shadow of truth. Not knowing is one thing, not wanting to know is another. "When we know better we can do better" is a phrase I have used a lot. It is such a simple statement, and you would expect it to be a no-brainer to live by. Well, actually, that's exactly what it is, a no- brain achievement for the brave. The highly sought after brain power, through intelligence and mental ability, is obstructing the truth from speaking clearly. I am referring to simple intellectual knowing, not the inner *knowing* that comes from the source itself. Once you tap into *that* pure energy of truth, goodbye ignorance. They cannot exist side by side.

First and foremost, what is it that we so proudly believe that we know? *Know* to the point of defending it with our lives, so to speak. We are certainly defending our truth with our health and happiness, agreeing to let someone else be the authority in our lives. You might not think about this, but everything that you hold as true, as a belief, is what has built the framework of your whole life. Everything that you agree to adopt into your space, is your chosen building blocks. Just like food is the building blocks for your cells, your beliefs, your thoughts and your emotions are the building blocks of your mental and emotional body. Everything that you take in, be it physical food, a belief, a visual picture, a sound or a trauma, will serve you well. Anything that you experience as real will affect you. It will stick like glue and become a part of how you live your life and how it unfolds.

Everything we do, say and practice will keep us accountable in one way or another.

Every word that comes out of your mouth, every thought and emotion that you hold, becomes the net sum of your ability account. The power of ignorance is strong, and the price you've got to pay for the continuing investments in non-truths, might be more than you are willing to cash out. It might even be more than you are able to pay off. It will certainly be more than you bargained for, once you

41

see the truth. Although it might piss you off, it *will* set you free! The rabbit hole is deep, and your responsibility is huge. From being a sovereign being, capable of choosing, acting, creating, dreaming, thinking and praying, you have been hired to step into your own power. You have always *been* that power, you now need to power it up and own it.

Constant confirmative information.

We are surrounded with confirmative information everywhere we turn, until we change our belief system and look elsewhere. What you put your attention towards will grow. What you look for, you will find. What you believe, you will find to be even more true. The key is always your own inner hard drive. Turn on the TV and you will receive a large dose of confirmative information. Terror is everywhere, the world is a dangerous place, people are criminals and you need to go see your doctor. Watch a reality show and be fed more drama, heartaches, frustration and anger. The sense that this life is but a game, mostly for the fittest, is confirmative. Over and out.

Fear based information for control: Any information that is based on fear will suck you in deeper. It is designed to keep you from thinking your own independent thoughts. Being afraid is a debilitating emotion, and it makes you seek shelter and support, comfort and security. The more fear that is created, the more we will look to the authorities. Put out a fear of a flu epidemic, and the masses run to get vaccinated or to see their doctor. There has got to be a massive amount of fear present to willingly have a child vaccinated with more than 20 shots before the age of one. Complete brainwashing. CDC's recommended vaccination schedule in the US is 49 doses of 14 vaccines by the time he/she is six years of age. Put out information of a terror attack, and you might reconsider buying a gun, building a fence, not allowing your children to ride their bikes to school, and to wish for more police. Put out the information that there is a storm raging, a flood or a tsunami, and we are kept in fear of Mother Nature's unpredictability. Fear will throw you off center and make you an easy follower.[4]

Anything taught from fear is control based. The agenda is to keep you from being a free thinker, but staying a consumer and a dependent persona. A pill-popping, sleeping zombie that will stay in line and not stray towards truth and freedom.

Love-based information for freedom: A growth in love-based information and sharing is blowing like a cool wind on a hot summers day. The information of hope and growth. People are growing fruit trees and nurturing Mother Earth. There are countries sending out signals that they are supporting organic farming only. Circuses are banned, and zoos are being shut down. Pay it forward has become a movement, and eating raw living food for health is showing the way in a world of poisoned foods. People are throwing out their television sets, doing their own research. Grounding has become a trend, and if you are aware that your body can heal naturally, you are on the winning and upcoming team. Love-based information will make you feel safe and supported, and will inspire you to believe in your own ability to make good choices.

Ultimately, we are all on the same team. We all want the same, to live in peace, to be healthy, feel loved and to be able to give.

We live in the age of the internet. It has allowed communion and human connections. It has provided knowledge and useful information, as well as fear-based propaganda and untruths. It is a magnificent tool, a blessing and a curse, and only by the people who use it can it be valued or not. A tool is never better than the ability of its user.

---

[4] NAIC: National Vaccine Information Center.www.nvic.org

A life without a television is a life with less programming. The news will keep you programmed for mind control. It is time to "shoot" the messenger. Simply turn it off. Stop taking in what is not nurturing your ability to see the truth of who you are. Let your capabilities shine through, by setting yourself free from any form of mind control. Notice the billboards, the television ads and the sponsored sporting events. All of them are selling a story of belief, all emphasizing something that you already buy into. Be it the belief that milk from a cow is good for you, that you need it for calcium, or that the solution to sleepless nights is sleeping pills from the drug store. You see, the belief that is already there is so easy to feed. We are always looking for validation. It is the "I knew it" validation. The subconscious mind has a feast every time we feed it. It becomes stronger. Have you noticed that when you are looking to buy a certain car, they pop up everywhere? A pregnant woman will start seeing pregnant women everywhere, or so it seems.

Ignorance is a bitch!

By ignoring the truths that are presented to us, simply because it is easier than to change, we are digging a whole lot deeper than we realize. Every day that you keep on doing what you know in your heart is not good for you, you are playing out the zombie act. You are allowing the subconscious repeat to keep on playing. Every day that you keep speaking those hurtful words, or telling that same old sad and negative story, you are ordering more for your future. You are not being true to yourself, and by turning away from what needs your attention, you are turning your back on life.

We are also turning our back on ourselves, our children and our planet. They are the real sufferers. The children, *our* children and grandchildren, are counting on us to step up and take back our power. What will we tell them when they are sick like everybody else, disconnected from God and nature, and are feeling depressed and anxious. "Sorry, it is not my fault, I knew but did nothing about it. I was too busy to notice?" What are *you* going to tell your grandchildren? The blowback is potentially there for all of us, and it *will* hit us. Bigtime! You might call it karma, cause and effect, one of the true laws of nature.

Ignorance is a form of resistance, the well-known and so very strong resistance to change. We face a catch 22, as it is the subconscious false beliefs that are holding us locked in, and at the same time it is the very reason we *need* to change. It is a double challenge. The reason we feel resistance is the reason we need to change, delete, reprogram and let go. The symptom might not be an obvious one, but if you have ever met a sceptic, are one yourself, you know how strong the force of holding on to present beliefs are. The only one standing in the way of your wisdom is your education, or; *"the only way of interfering with your learning is your education"* – Albert Einstein.

Another way of putting it is; the only thing stopping you from living your dreams and doing what you really want, is your bullshit false belief that you for some reason cannot.

There is a phenomenon called the **Stockholm syndrome**, or capture-bonding. The definition is; *the psychological tendency of a hostage to bond with, identify with, or sympathize with his or her captor or abuser.* Most people know the phrase Stockholm syndrome from the numerous high-profile kidnapping- and hostage cases. It got its name after a 1972 bank robbery in Stockholm, Sweden, where bank employees who were held hostage for six days, bonded with their captors. The hostages resisted rescue, refused to testify against the robbers and even raised money for their legal defense. For an outsider, this seems completely insane! What had happened to all these people? Had they lost their minds? Another famous case is that of Patty Hearst, a rich heiress who was kidnapped in 1974 by the Symbionese Liberation Army, an American terrorist group.

Patty, at the age of 19, seemed to sympathize with the group and even participated in a bank robbery with them. [5]

The phenomena shows us that our feelings and behaviors are largely governed by how we are mentally and emotionally prepared, aka brainwashed. Rational or not, it doesn't matter. We are triggered by fear, and feel sympathetic even towards those who hurt us and rob us of our freedom. We are clinging to authority and leadership, and it is why we are so skeptical to anyone questioning our beliefs. When they do so, we are ready to defend our teacher, even if the teaching is hurting us, or keeping us *"hostage"*. Keep this in mind the next time someone is defending the use of hurtful medications, which hasn't been serving them, over learning and exploring nature's way of self-healing. Remember this when you see ignorance and even hostility and anger towards new ideas and different approaches. Fear, anger, hurtful remarks, even threatening behavior can surface when the programmed belief is being challenged. In the Western world today, there are some basic "truths" that are accepted by the masses, and anyone challenging it, will often be ridiculed, shown the door and laughed at, at best. Anger and hostility are not far behind.

Accepted truths/beliefs of the masses:

- Without control and surveillance, humans are criminals and not trustworthy.
- The human body needs animal protein for health.
- There is such a thing as incurable sickness.
- Cancer is cured by chemotherapy.
- The doctor is the authority on your health.
- We need to eat three meals a day.
- School is important for all.
- You need to work hard for your money.
- Life is hard.

---

[5] http://medical-dictionary.thefreedictionary.com/Stockholm+syndrome

- Always listen to your teacher.
- Vaccines are for protection.
- GMO food is not hurting you.
- Fruit has too much sugar.
- Crying is a sign of weakness.
- We need the military for our own protection.
- Being different than the horde is not acceptable.
- Questioning authority is rebellious.
- Chemtrails are not real.

This is the short list containing a selection of imprinted beliefs that are typically holding back our full life expression. These beliefs are inhibiting free creativity and dumbing our inspiration for life. Exploring and experiencing, like a child, is our true nature. Anything *but* that is not truth. Anything taking you away from your passions, your health and your emotional balance is not truth. Be it what you believe, eat, think or act. Truth will always feel good, it will set you free of all boundaries and it will show you the best version of *you*.

> Nothing is more freeing than recognizing the power you hold within. It is stronger than any old belief. Why do you think it is important to keep the bullshit up and running? Your power is unlimited, and if you only knew, well, imagine that!

Ignorance might be bliss, but not for long. By looking the other way, you are not keeping your eyes on the ball, the truth.

Chapter 5

Fear, the ultimate challenge

" *I am running down the stairs, I cannot believe this is happening again! Oversleeping, having to skip breakfast is one thing, but seriously, elevator malfunction again? What are the odds of that happening twice in two weeks? Me and my luck, so typical. The story of my life, having shit like this happening to me. All I need is that the investors are already there, observing my unprofessionalism. My mom was right- she was always right. It is only a matter of time until I blow the only good thing I have going for me. It is always a matter of time until good things evaporate from my life.*

I will survive though, I always do. Life is hard, I know that, believe me. Ok, focus, step on the pedal, and watch that crazy maniac. Frustrating ignorant people, in their nice cars living their fab lives. The office is packed already. It irritates me to watch those laughing, smiling people, acting like there is not a care in this world. People are suffering, don't they know this? I need to sneak to the restroom before anyone sees me. I am sweaty already, stressed, I need a coffee, or a drink rather. Headache is coming, I need an aspirin. At least it won't make me fat like

48

food does. Everything makes me fat, story of my life. I hate my body. I've always hated my body. I need to tell my brother he is getting too skinny. I mean, have you seen how he looks? Sick is what I call it. Always running around, going to the gym multiple times every week I am sure. Every day even. It cannot be a good thing to be so focused on health. And what about his girlfriend? Always so well dressed and beautiful, smiling and being positive all the time. Who does that? Not natural and it makes me sick. They are here, I knew it. I just love investors that have been kept waiting. Another shitty day."

The most interesting part of the above scenario is that it is typical. What is going through our mind, is reflecting and explaining what we are living. For some, more non-stop than for others, and if you really pay attention, you will hear that your inner dialogue is the storyteller of your play. You are simply the actor. We are here presented with the expectation of bad luck, of screwing up anything good. Life is believed to be hard, and so it is. Happy, successful people therefore represent an annoyance. They are making you feel less than. This shows a pattern of falling for the old lie of not feeling good enough. Criticizing people becomes so easy when we hurt. It turns into a defense mechanism. By making "them" not normal, *you* will be. You feel less fat if skinny is unhealthy. You feel in better shape if going to the gym is hysterical, or at least that is what you are telling yourself. You don't actually *believe* it. None of it. *You* know the truth. Your heart always knows.

The story you accept, is the one you live. Until you stop. Until you stop believing the bullshit that you tell yourself. The story that *you* were told. Truth is not a story, and it is certainly not the one told by others. The common belief of the masses has nothing to do with *your* truth.

You get the point, and you know that you need to stop it. You see that what you are telling yourself, and what you believe is not serving you. You get it, now what? Now it's time for action, for taking charge and for stopping what you are doing. When you are ready to stop, the fear of change will knock on your door. Invite it in. Facing the true fear of change, requires taking full responsibility for not only the obvious feeling of not wanting to change what is, but all its family and relatives. It has many; The fear of failure, of ridicule, of being alone, standing alone, and the fear of rejection. The fear of not having a community, and the ultimate fear of them all, of dying. *That* is the real bullshit, as you cannot die, not really. It is the ultimate deception, another untruth.

> The ultimate challenge is always fear. In some shape or form, it has you wrapped in your own invisible prison.

What is stopping you from stopping YOU?

Let's take a look at the fears that seem like heavy bolts on your door. They represent the gateway to truth. Behind any fear is a truth. It is like a locking mechanism that has been put in place to secure the truth to stay hidden. Elegantly guarding your false beliefs. What is real is never fear-based, only the perceived fear of change. We have looked at the different types of false beliefs, and their origin. Now let's look at the different fears that change represents. They might give you a few ideas as to what your inner locks are hiding. The subconscious mind is heavily protected, and fear has many faces.

- **Fear of change:** Familiarity gives comfort, and we perceive comfort as safe. It's got to do with security and protection. The misconception lies in that we somehow need to be protected from this world, from our lives. Which of course is not so. It seems true, as we look around and soak-in everything presented to us. The fear of change will keep us from growing, evolving and thriving. It will keep us enslaved by all our fears and old programming. It is the mothership of all fears, and that is why it is so hard to let go of. Most of the time we know what is good for us, but we resist to do it. Blame the fear of change. You might feel that your job is hurting your health or not being aligned with your passion, but you still stay put. Had you known how to keep going on your own, what tomorrow would bring, you might have left that dysfunctional relationship years ago.

- **Fear of being alone**: As a victim, you will see this as a disempowering state, aloneness. It brings up the feeling of not being good enough, the belief that being alone is not enough. Fearing this means you believe that by being *you* only, you are less. You might doubt yourself, and your ability to make your own decisions. You were programmed to rely on others, a parent, or an older sibling. You are not truly fearing aloneness, as it is natural to be alone at times. You are fearing your insecurity. It is natural to feel good in one's own company, secure and safe. A healthy community is created for support, from the place of self-confidence. Never from the place of fear. Sharing and working together is not the same as relying on someone from the fear of being alone. When you change this false belief, you will find that you are being surrounded with more people that feel like family. Old friends might leave, and that is okay. Everything is okay when you cut to the chase and set yourself free.

- **Fear of standing alone:** This is the energy that comes from the belief that you need others to validate your opinions. That you are afraid of speaking your own naked truth. What if no one agrees with me? What if they think I am crazy or strange? This programming will keep anyone terrified of going against any common belief. "Who do you think you are?" I know many people who feel this energy. Who are we to speak up and question anything? Being an outsider is the ultimate rejection, and on top of that, it indicates that you are stupid. Questioning your own life, your relationship with appointed truths and beliefs might bring up this fear as a gift. Once you detect it, you *know* you need to break free. By revealing your own truth, you will never be alone, on the contrary, you will be drawn to likeminded souls that share your freedom.

- **Fear of ridicule:** Sadly, as children we might be bullied by classmates or ridiculed by our parents or other family members. A child has a completely different perspective than an adult, and will put up a wall of defense towards anything that feels uncomfortable. Against anything that does not resonate with the soul. The mask is born, one of many, and as it is worn, our true self shrinks a little. One can later hide behind a mask of more fear.

- **Fear of separation:** I believe that from birth we need to feel connected to our mother. Anything that has disturbed that natural connection will leave us vulnerable to the fear of separation. Not being breast fed, having a distant mother, or being a part of a larger group of siblings, might leave you feeling disconnected. Separation from family, not feeling a part of a group of friends, or simply not feeling part of society itself, will later enhance this type of underlying fear. Not feeling that you fit in will bring up that old wound. Separate is not a good word, it tells a story of being outside, when the fun and security is on the inside. As I've already pointed out - the truth is we are all separated from each other, yet we stand together as one.

- **Fear of failure:** Who told you there was such a thing? Failure is a misused word, often thrown at us when things do not turn out as we would have liked them to. The concept of failing comes from being the opposite of winning, or not being able to accomplish a particular task. Our society has molded this win-or-lose mentality, which is hurting every soul that buys into it. To not succeed, as in things turning out differently than desired is simply a lesson we can learn from. Without them there would be no growth, no evolvement and no eagerness to expand. No master has ever gotten around the lesson of so called failure. Not only that, they are highly valued. Have you ever heard someone say: *"If the seemingly tragic situation had not happened, I would not know what I know today. I would not change a thing. It has made me who I am today."* You have been led to believe that hitting the right spot is what makes you a winner, when it is the direct opposite. Being able to adjust, to redirect and to learn is where success is. Being fearless of the outcome is the key.

- **Fear of rejection:** There is no rejection, only redirection. This is an easy bullshit to call. When you feel secure in your own place, and when you clear the old conditioning of rejection, you see the magical direction that the Universe is showing you. *When one door closes, another one opens*, or; *when a door closes, two windows open.* I love those old sayings. They tell us that no matter if it seems that we are being rejected, it only means that another path is open to us, and it is always a better one. We have been led to believe that being rejected is another tint of failure. The same old not-being-good-enough topic. When a boyfriend/girlfriend turns his/her back on you, it is easy to feel that you are the one not being good enough. It is what you were taught. What if in reality - it means that there is a better way for you? What if it means you have something to learn by choosing another path? Once you trust the path of life, the flow and directions presented to you, the fear of rejection will fade. Being under its spell will trap you into believing that you've got to change something about yourself and keep on knocking on that same door, until it opens.

- **Fear of success:** Yes, there is such a thing! Hard to imagine for many, I am sure. This is connected to self-sabotage and what we will do to keep ourselves from succeeding. The fear of change shows itself again. Together with the fear of being alone, being rejected, feeling different and every other fear you can think of. Why is this, you might think? It simply boils down to the fact that succeeding will bring with it some major shifts. You might have to move if you get the new job. If you get healthy, you will no longer want to stay with your mother. Your boyfriend might leave you if you finally do what you always wanted to do and are good at. You might feel you are not valuated for who you are and *you* might leave some of your old friendships.

- **Fear of pain:** We hate pain. Physical, emotional, mental and spiritual pain. One of the purest things there is, all about truth, the compass of our inner terrain, and we hate it. We have been conditioned to believe that it needs to be numbed down, shut off and that we need to look the other way. It is even looked at as a weakness.

  Being in pain is not considered to be a cool thing, and certainly not showing it. Big boys don't cry, remember? Most people will do anything to get out of pain. This is what we have been told through the marketing of the magic pill. Big Pharma`s flag ship. The pride of the tribe. *"Pop a pill and feel better. Make it an easy fix. Let us show you the way out of misery."* A whole gigantic industry keeping us numbed down by our fear of pain, that and death. When we realize that pain is inevitable, but suffering is not, a whole new trust in God and creation opens. It is natural to be happy, healthy and spiritually connected. It is natural to feel pain when the body is speaking to us, and it is natural to feel sadness after a loss. We *should* feel fear when a tiger comes towards us. We *should* get upset about a wrong doing. It's called LIFE!

To even for a nanosecond believe that we are supposed to artificially numb our pain is a lie. A big fat lie. Listen to it, it comes with valuable information. It is trying to get our attention for a reason. It needs to heal. Pain is simply a sign of acids and toxins, traumas and nerve signals. A healthy body does not signal pain. So, if you are being poked by your dear body, listen and *take action*. There is always a cause to every effect. For us to be able to live in a pain free body, we need to let it heal and restore.

- **Fear of dying:** Just reading this word can trigger fear and anxiety. I will be bold and say that the majority of people on the earth today have some kind of fear associated with dying. If not for death itself, then for the loss and grief that comes with it. To grieve the loss of our dear ones is a natural and a healthy emotion. It shows we have compassion and humility. Fearing death itself, and making it control the life that is here and now, is holding us back from exploring it fully. So much joy is lost. I see this as the largest sign of our disconnection from God, and the biggest sign that we have been bullied into thinking we are not a part of a magnificent creation. Our body will die in the sense that it will change form, but our soul never will. We are merely spiritual beings having a human experience in a physical body. Everything is energy, and energy does not die, it changes form. By believing that death is horrible, that it is dark and scary, you are kept brainwashed to be the perfect candidate for fear propaganda. As long as we, the masses, fear on a large scale, anything can be implemented into our reality that will save us from dying. We will stand in line for a shot of anything if we are told it will save our lives. I am not saying you should not do anything to stay alive. That is natural, an instinct, and a healthy one. To blindly let any bullshit alter your state of mind, is not as healthy, and not at all to be considered freedom.

> The fear of fear itself is a product of our society telling us feeling good is a must to be a success. A strong and successful person cannot walk around feeling fearful. Not acceptable. Shy away from anything that resembles uneasiness or fear. Walk the other way, take a pill, get over it. Numb it down or run for the covers. Bam, mission completed. We stay put.

Did God make a mistake? Do we even think about that? Were we not supposed to be able to think, live in joy, health and take care of ourselves? Are we simply a weak, fearful and lost species? I don't believe so. Quite the opposite. There is never anything to fear but fear itself. It is part of an old programming and can be reprogrammed as anything else. Calling the bullshit takes time, and digging into all aspects of it takes persistence. Roll up your sleeves, allow the mess to unfold, and get ready to look it straight in the eye. We need to cut the crap. No change comes from holding on to what is.

Once you become fearless, life becomes limitless.

PART TWO

POWER UP AND GROW FREE

Chapter 6

The true story

" *P*lease, just leave me alone. All I want is some peace and quiet.
*I cannot pop any more of their pills, not a single one. My
stomach is turning, I feel nauseated. I always feel nauseated.
How is it that all these synthetic drugs are going to make my body want
to balance again? I cannot remember the last time I felt good. I cannot
even remember the last time I felt OK. Why do we do this shit? I mean,
since my body started to give me so much trouble all I have done is to
try and fix it. My savings are gone, heck, my parent`s savings are almost
gone. My wife works her ass off trying to keep everything together,
while I know how devastated she is. Who wouldn`t be? A husband that
keeps ending up at the hospital for treatments, and a son that needs
his asthma meds and his diabetic shots. How is this natural? How is this
anywhere near what life is supposed to be?*

*The nurse can talk to me all that she wants, I am so done with this.
There has got to be another way. There has to be a way out of this
hellhole. Excuse me, but I really don't like the smell of this place. Give
me a forest trail any day of the week. Oh, those were the days. Tracking*

with the whole family. How I wish. I would give anything to get healthy. I hate my genes. Bad luck they call it. Is it? Is that what it is? Sometimes I wonder. What if there is another way? What if I can be healthy again, we all can? Wow, that would keep this nurse off my back."

Do you like your truth? Do you love yourself and your life? Is this it? Is it true? Can you feel the bliss and the love from just being alive right now? What is the truth anyway, you might wonder? What is the truth about anything? To be honest, it doesn`t matter. What matters is what you feel and perceive. What makes *you* happy, and what makes *you* thrive. That is your truth, and that is the path you should follow, always. Every symptom of despair, anxiety, uneasiness and frustration is telling you you are not living your true story.

There is something about awakening to even the smallest of possibilities that what you see is not all there is. That there might in fact be another way. What has been presented to you might not be the only truth, or not a truth at all. The thought of there being another story to be told, will bring enthusiasm and eagerness to your cells. It manifests as a feeling of anticipation. You will feel drawn towards research and reading. You will feel the hunger for more knowledge. You have triggered something inside you that knows better. You are inspired. Your soul is doing the happy dance.

Finally, you are getting it! Finally, you are tearing down the wall, lifting the veil and decoding your brainwashing. The old programming is not being fed, and the old false beliefs are being challenged. You will feel this happy dance coming from the real you, the part that wants to grow free!

When you start to wonder about new solutions, something you haven't done before, you know you are on to something magical. You have cut some crap. Once you realize that you know how to call a lie from the very beginning, you will feel empowered. You will feel eager to find your own way. You always knew, you just didn't know you knew. Your soul, the real you, *knows*. It always did. No bullshit could ever enter your divine space, the part of you that is connected to all that is. The God force.

Referring to our lives as a story is a perfect way of looking at it. It makes it easy to see how it can be rewritten. We can write another chapter, turn the page, and use our imagination. It can be sad or happy, it is all in the power of the holder of the pen. Conditioning oneself to not only be a writer but a rewriter takes guts and a dose of warrior material. It takes the boldness and the fearlessness of someone like you. Yes, you got it, we all have that ability. No one is excluded. False beliefs are clouding the vision, but the veil is lifting.

**Nothing can ever change the fact that you
are the storyteller of your life.**

There is nothing that you can't do. No one can ever tell you that you cannot do something, and be telling the truth. Not *your* truth. Don't buy into the lies that come from fear and ignorance. They are deceiving. False beliefs set into motion. Imagine for a minute that everything you wished for was true. That all people were good, that no one needed medications, that there was free food and medicine for everyone. Imagine there being no wars, no suffering, no violence and no greed. In this imaginary world, people were naturally happy, the air was clean, the ocean pure, and the food was poison free. Everyone were living their dream, and people took care of each other. Animals were free, no killing or captivity. No disease, vaccinations, and no pollution. Sounds too far out? Almost like a fairytale? It isn't. It is bullshit-free living.

What we are told leads to suffering, while the truth brings us home. The false beliefs show us limitation and restriction, while the truth will set us free.

The truths that will change your story:

We all hold on to some general beliefs that has a profound impact on our lives. We are not that different. We have different backgrounds, yes, but still we believe in a lot of the same basic ideas. We are presented a general world view that tells us what is true and what is false. Through our culture and day-to-day living, we each have our specific beliefs, but they have all taken us to this same place. Searching for something more. Knowing what we have been told might not be all that.

Being healthy is natural.

Our body is a living organism. Made of more than a trillion cells, it is constantly healing, repairing, decaying and growing. It is a constant life and death of cells. Some die, while new ones are born. A sick cell is eaten, and waste is transported out. New cells take over, and hurts and injuries are repaired. In the perfect world, that is. Being healthy is what the body was designed to be. Like any other species, we were meant to thrive and to function at optimal capacity well into old age. We were meant to live a healthy life until death.

"Our true path has been lost to us, in so many different ways, and we are now living the sum of our actions and ignorance. We are experiencing cause and effect, pure and simple. The cause being not honoring creation, and the effects being illness, stress, pain and depression. Violence, anxiety, fear and frustration, are all part of the same manifestation. The one we as humans created, and we as individuals can change one step, one bite, one thought and emotion at a time.

From once living barefoot in nature, we are now living in high-rises, surrounded by wireless electromagnetic radiation. This is a huge deal for our cells. The electromagnetic noise is hitting us from many different sources. Our wireless communication devices, including wireless power meters, cell phones, cell towers, wireless routers and cordless phones, expose us to both electric and magnetic fields (EMF). Anything that has a cord or a plug emanates an electric field. That includes all appliances, electric wiring, power outlets and extension cords. On top of this we are also exposed to power lines. Some are above the ground where you can see them, but many are below.

From being a tropical species, born without any clothes or shoes, we are walking on rubber soles, covered from head to toe to keep warm and fashionable. We even need the shoes to be comfortable, for support. Our body was not made for walking without shoes, so we need support and padding, really? We are now disconnected from the vibrations of the Earth, from the negative ions that nurture our cells. All this EMF disturbance, the electromagnetic smog, is subjecting us to positive ions, disturbing our cells in their natural healing and regeneration. We are experiencing decay and cell mutation, instead of natural vitality and strength.

We are really just scratching the surface of understanding what altering and tampering with our foods are doing to us. We are accepting the most dangerous paths of them all, the road of starvation and self-poisoning. Yes, starvation. Unless we are eating fresh produce, we are not serving the body the nutrients that it needs. Instead, we are eating what will keep us malnourished by clogging up our system. We are consuming nutrient-lacking food that has been altered to the point of complete unrecognition, and the body will react to it as poison. It makes us constipated, as the body is trying to hold on to it, to store it away. Also, the lack of fiber and natural enzymes will leave the body unable to get rid of the waste created. Mostly we are not aware that the intestines are where most of the absorption happens, through the villi of the small intestines. Foods like pizza, bread, hotdogs, and hamburgers, processed, powdered, canned, fried and baked products are all a burden to our perfect machinery. Our bodies are not meant to be hit with such massive amounts of poisons."[6]

The body is a self-healing mechanism, and will always seek to be healthy. Regeneration is the golden key, and in nature it is an ongoing process.

Even weak genes from birth can be regenerated. The beauty of truth is that it gives you the freedom of creation. Nothing is too small or too big. We can rewrite our entire blueprint, by simply returning to the basics of life. Look to the animal kingdom. They do not suffer from any so-called chronic diseases. They do not get cancer or diabetes. It is natural to be healthy at any age. It is natural to be pain free and happy at any age. Live it, feel it and *know* it!

Having money is not a sin.

Who doesn't care about money? Not many. Unless you are living on a remote island or in nature somewhere else, completely self-sufficient when it comes to food and other needs, you will need money. Or you will need someone to provide for you. This evil, cursed, still sought after asset brings out some kind of feeling in all of us. It can represent everything from the devil himself to being the savior of your life. Your relationship with money is your business.

This energy of worth, of opportunity and growth, can also be a crime in the making, and a motive for terror and greed. You might have heard; - *The love for money is the root of all evil.* I see this as a truth. The love for money itself *will* get you into trouble. Fame, status and power *will* alter your path of love and compassion.

Money itself is nothing but energy, but how we feel, think and act around it is everything.

---

[6] Hilde Larsen – *Know the Truth and Get Healthy, 2016*

Even coming from the same background can leave us with different connotations to what money represents. Two people that have grown up being poor might have two very different feelings around money. One person might have lived in compassion and gratitude for what they had, while the other one in blame and envy. Depending on the past-experience, location, and stories told, we live our lives expecting, and seeing, the world we believe in. What we expect to see, is most often what we actually see. No matter your story, let go of the negative connotations to money. Set yourself free from the bondage to any negative implications surrounding the topic. Don't set yourself back due to the false belief that the money itself is a negative, and don't allow other people's opinions color your life.

- **People can do good with their wealth**: The movie industry is showing us how money is involved in a lot of terrifying plots. Real life will show us the same. *Follow the money*; meaning, behind everything lies the motive of greed and control. While this is for the most part true, a lot of amazing souls are here doing a fantastic job with what money can buy. Some of the most successful people are contributing to other people's growth and joy, by helping and sharing. Money is nothing itself, it's only what you put into it. It is an exchange of energy. It is what you make it up to be. Use it for good, and it becomes a riches. Those who invest in Mother Earth, will receive the largest return of investment.

- **Money does not have to own you**: Once you get attached to anything, you lose. Anything, be it people, assets, food or situations. Once you give away your power, you give away your true balance. You don't need money, in the sense that you don't need what it represents to the ego. What you need is food, shelter, love, community and self-worth. That's it. Money is merely a means to some of this for most of us. In a perfect world, food would be free for everyone, and the land would be shared in peace. Until you can live under the roof of nature, money is a part of your world. As long as your intent is pure, the energy will be also.

- **It is ok to be abundant:** You might see being poor is being pure, but there is nothing romantic about starving, or not being able to provide for your children. There is nothing noble about not being able to live your dreams and your desires. Money itself can never be good or bad. You are the only one that is holding your energy, not the money. It is okay to surround yourself with beautiful things, and it is okay to travel the world. It is okay to want to make sure that your family is provided for, and it is more than okay to reap what you sow.

Money is nothing but energy. What you put into it is up to you. It is okay to enjoy the finer things, the best of food and to travel. Money is not evil; the act of people is. Being poor is not glorifying, it is neglecting the fact that abundance is natural. In nature, everything is abundant. No money needed. Stay true to the abundance of love, health and faith, and money itself will never be your focus. Use money to do good. Pay it forward!

> Be fair, be humble, be generous and be compassionate. Money can contribute to amazing life-saving help for many people, and it is okay to be the carrier of abundance.

Getting old is not the same as getting sick.

Ageing does not have to be related to sickness or pain. Getting old is not the same as needing care or medications. These are all lies and misconceptions. What we see is what we believe. We are programmed to believe that we live longer, and that we live healthier. Not so. We live a short life in pain, and are kept alive longer than the past hundred years, in terrible health. We are building nursing homes and producing special aids. Surgery, drugs and therapies are only slowing down the death process. Some might be as bold as to say we are all killing ourselves with our lifestyles and drugs.

In the Bible, the Old Testament tells us that humans can live for an exceeding number of years. Adam is told to have lived to the age of 930, while his son Seth to the age of 912. Seth's son Lamech lived for 777 years, his son Noah lived to be 950, and so on. They are told to have lived in great health their whole lives. Are we all supposed to live this long? Do we have any idea how long the human body can live and thrive? No, we don't. We keep telling ourselves these little lies, until we believe them. Is our body showing nothing but the sign of abuse and weakened genes? I believe so. I see evidence of this, every day. A healthy body doesn't show decay and degeneration, not at any age. Through my own experience, I see what we perceive as signs of ageing disappear in both myself and in people I have crossed paths with (who also are on a journey of regenerating their true selves). The cleaner and healthier we get, the less signs of living we show. The constant regeneration and duplications of cells show us that the human body is able to sustain a high level of health for a very long time. I am looking and feeling younger, or what I perceive as such, and am getting healthier every single day.

When you buy into the ageing game, you are accepting your own suffering to come. The accepting becomes an expectation. The world you live in, including the experience of ageing, is dictated by how you were conditioned to perceive it. By changing your perception, you change your world *and* your body.

Who you are depends on what world you see yourself living in. Everything you experience must pass through a mental filter before it registers as real. We are constantly engaged in creating our own reality. Our worldview has a lot of absolutes. We get old, we get sick. Delete it, it is not a truth. It is Bullshit![7]

---

[7] Deepak Chopra - *Ageless Body, Timeless Mind: The Quantum Alternative to Growing Old*

Simply put; if you want it, live it, if not, don't.

You can work and play at the same time.

Absolutely you can! Although there are as many variables of a belief as there are people, most of us has been told to work hard. There is nothing wrong with working hard, but this belief often includes leaving out the fun, the passion, the play and the enthusiasm. Working hard is most often associated with doing something out of commitment. Out of not having a choice. We won't have to go that far back, to see where this pattern might come from. From the practice of slavery, the energy of confinement and abuse is connected to hard labor. Even the word "hard" has stuck. "Working hard for the money" follows us, and tells us that money comes as a reward after long and tiresome hours. Work and play are therefore considered opposite poles, completely different. In our modern World, this is complete nonsense.

First and foremost, it is all about your belief system. *You* are in-charge of how you feel about anything. It does not matter if it is driving a truck, sorting marbles or playing golf. How you feel about it is all up to you.

The most successful people would never take a vacation, as they are doing what they love every single day. Do they work hard? Heck yes, but not in the way that most people see as hard. Their life is a vacation, and their work is how they play. Their work is their play. Loving what you do will do that. To believe that working is something that we have to do, and that we have no choice, is like accepting an invisible prison wall. Life is not supposed to be hard. Life is supposed to be whatever you want it to be. You are the creating pilot, the one that makes up your experiences. Never the victim, and never the sufferer.

Once you free yourself from the programming of having to do anything, it will be easier to recognize your true passion and mission. We all have one, or several. Once you realize what you love to do, it will never feel like work, and even if it does at times, that is okay too. To stay focused and determined is a key ingredient when you are driven, but it must not be confused with hardship. Once you buy into the "work is hard" lie, you are easy to manipulate. Your own inner guidance and intuition is shut down, and you become a machine that cannot tell truth from a lie.

If right now you do not do what you love, love what you do.

You can love yourself first.

How many lives have been completely messed up by the crazy belief that one's got to love everybody else more than oneself? What a hoax. "Love thy neighbor as yourself". There we have it, right there. All love emanates from self-love and the love of God. You cannot love God and not yourself, as you are part of that same love. Before you love yourself, you cannot love another.

The taboo that we are looking at, runs deep within our genetic imprints. Self-love has been confused with self-righteousness, with wanting to be better than and more than. We have been controlled by the lie that loving ourselves is the same as being egotistic. Think of others first, and be a saint. Put yourself on the back burner, and forget your worth.

Loving yourself is honoring yourself. A hater hates him or herself first. A lover loves him or herself first. Focusing on *you*, to gain acknowledgement or status has nothing to do with self-love. We call that arrogance. We all have an ego, and when it takes up too much room, we get lost in our head. Love lives elsewhere. The beauty of true love is that it already *is*, all we've got to do is to let it come forth. How can you control someone who really loves themselves? Not an easy task.

You will find that ones you love yourself unconditionally, you will no longer need to do anything that is not right for you. You will not need to be bullied, lied to, treated badly in any way or live your life in a manner that makes you feel depressed or fearful. Once you feel that love, you will crave serving and helping others, as you realize that we are all one. All here together to do our very best. You are lovable, worthy, amazing and loved. Honor it, and love everything about yourself, and let it grow. It will set you free.

> **When you truly love yourself, you become impossible to manipulate and control. You will protect yourself, as you would anyone else.**

Fruits do not have too much sugar.

What? Can this be true? Yes, indeed! One of the most profound lies out there, is that fruits have too much sugar. It might seem like a small little false belief, but it is not. It is absolutely detrimental to our health, and completely misleading and misguiding. I cannot even begin to count the number of times I have been presented with this lie. Fruits, the perfect food for man, not suited for consumption? Really? Leading to sickness, diabetes and candida? How far from the truth we have strayed, and how far from our inner knowing we have all been lured. It is like saying that creation failed, and that something went wrong. Nature must be all upside down, and man must be so much smarter. Seriously, think about it. How could every other primate thrive on fruits, but for humans it is not a good idea? Don't buy it. Fruits are the elixir of health, the food for man, the food from the Gods.

We are frugivores. We heal when we eat our specie specific diet. We are vegans, we don't need to consume any animal proteins to thrive. We do not need much protein at all! Such a false belief and a wrong teaching. Most people will never kill the animal they eat. Someone else will kill for them. They refrain from watching the torture and the suffering, the grief and the agony. The animal is then cooked and seasoned to taste. Think about it. How would that even be interesting if we were created to eat in such a way? If you walked by a monkey eating a banana, would you look at the monkey or the banana as food? We were not meant to eat animals. They are our friends. In a natural world, would we need weapons, torture and captivity to gather food? Never. Nature is perfect and we screwed up. Now, we are living the consequences. You will never see an elephant eat a cat, or a lion eat a banana, not unless something was very, very off balance. We represent the complete imbalance.

The natural diet of a primate is primarily fruits with some tender leafy greens, seeds, blossoms, some bark, pith and an occasional insect. This is an important realization to us, because by eating what we are designed to eat, our body will be able to heal and restore.

We are designed to eat our food raw, like all living beings. There were no mistakes. We love animals. We naturally have compassion for all of them, and if you leave a baby with a rabbit and a carrot, I will assure you, the rabbit will not be looked at as food. We are drawn to the produce market by the smell and the colors. These are the living foods, the source of our sustenance. When we see road-kill, or even a slaughter house, we are easily revolted. Our mouths do not water from seeing a cow walk by. There is nothing about a living animal that makes us hungry. We are simply not designed to look at them as food.

What most humans are consuming today is very far from being foods from nature. We were not made to consume pesticides, fungicides, additives, carcinogens etc. We were made to eat *food*. All this poison is making us acidic. It is creating so many imbalances within our system that we think we are different from each other. We think we need chemical medicine to function. An animal will only get a human disease when it starts eating human foods. Think about that for a minute. The food and health connection is huge! No matter how spiritual we get, it is all energy, and foods are energy also.

Breast milk from a cow? No thank you. Need the calcium? Think again. Everything we will ever need is right there in our raw living fruits and vegetables. The dairy industry is horrific in so many ways. The meat industry as well. Our food is poisoned, and non-foods are sold as edible. A crime and a big fat lie. Pull back and think. What seems natural to you? Fruits do NOT have too much sugars, or anything else. It is our perfect food. Eat more fruits and less of anything else, and feel for yourself. Do your own research. Be your own expert. Careful who you listen to.

> Don't be fooled. By eating what you were designed to eat, you can find your way back to your natural healthy state. That is the truth!

Only the body can heal, medications cannot.

Technology has helped us do some amazing things, like emergency lifesaving surgeries. Anyone who has broken a leg, been in an accident or have watched a family member be saved by an emergency team knows the gratitude we share for this. I have tremendous respect for them, and I honor everyone who stands by to help others in need. Thank God for the ER. Nevertheless, we have been told the lie that we need medications to heal, and that the body cannot heal itself. Another one of nature's big blunders.

In all boldness, there are no chronic illnesses. Not by definition. There are most certainly symptoms defined as such, but chronic simply means longstanding, or incurable. It stands for no-can-heal, and that is not true. That is a way of fearing anyone to stand in the chronic line at the doctor's office, waiting for the meds that will make life livable. The pills that will keep you coming back for more. The truth lies in taking care of the cause of any illness or imbalance if you may, never in the industry of addiction to pills. This is a great example of how we can follow the money. If the entire World's population became healthy, the world economy would collapse. Interesting?

I have seen this false belief play out first hand. I have lived through severe, debilitating, so-called chronic and incurable illness. I have walked my own way and saved my life. I have seen what we are doing to our bodies by feeding them pills containing toxic chemicals. How the medical industry is focused on suppressing the symptoms, not on true healing. How we are sucked in and addicted to drugs that keep tearing us apart, from the inside out. How we are presented with lie after lie about our body. We are the ones that need to step aside. The body knows what it is doing. We have been given the gift of life, and are disrespecting it by accepting the Western medicine's galore for money.

The body is a self-healing mechanism. God made no mistake. What we do to ourselves takes a toll, and we need to take responsibility for that. When man tries to outsmart nature, he loses. We lose.

Happiness is a choice.

Imagine that. Even our happiness is up to us. There really is no end to this self-sufficient existence. Is happiness not a product of what happens to us? Is it not a feeling that comes with success in one form or another? If it was, it would leave you a slave to the outcome, and that is what your subconscious has been programmed to believe. The so-called search for happiness. The endless drive towards some form of fulfillment and accomplishment. Even the notion that someone else makes us happy is not true. It comes from dependency. It is part of an imprisonment, a lie that keeps us believing we are not all that we need. The less powerful we feel in ourselves, the more dependent on others we will be. The easier we will be to control, and the less we will be able to decide for ourselves. Disempowerment is loss of self-control. An unhappy person is a dependent person.

The power of choice is endless, so endless that we are tricked to believe otherwise. If you only knew how powerful you were, it would blow the lid of your whole perception of the life you are living. First and foremost, any feeling of not being truly happy and free is just that, a feeling. Happy you see, is not really a feeling, it is a state of being. It is your true state that never leaves. All we can do is suppress it, cloud our vision, dumb it down and turn away from it.

Being happy does not mean you never feel emotions. They are your compass and friends. Like the healthy child, we should always return to happy. Look at a toddler. He might cry if he's hurting, and then, just like that, back to happy. There is no holding on to what was, or dragging old wounds along. Living in the moment will erase everything but the now, which is the clue to letting the happiness flow freely. As we grow older and are conditioned by what we experience, we adopt to letting our subconscious mind play out its repeating old story.

> Be your own cheerleader and coach. Inspire yourself every day and choose to be happy. Don't let anyone lead you to believe that an outside circumstance is controlling your inner magic. Rich or poor, young or old, happiness is yours to have, if you so choose.

You are in-charge of your entire life.

I can think of a thousand situations when this would be annoying to even hear. That, or it would be absolutely freeing. Not everyone wants to be in-charge, it takes work, and it leaves no room for blame. Being in-charge of your life, means being in-charge of everything. Your emotions and your whole perception of what you are experiencing. If you want something to change, *you* are the one who holds the power to do just that. You are powerful beyond your imagination. Your little hard drive on the top floor is trying to run the show, but even *it* cannot really be in full charge. By realizing this, you can override anything. With work and persistence, goals and a dose of fearlessness, you can rewrite your entire story. Start to finish. Your power is so much stronger than your mind, and your inner light and ability to heal and restore is grander than you can ever imagine. No person, no event or circumstance can stand in the way of your ability to choose life. The inner strength that we all hold is released when we allow it to be. This is freedom. This is growth and infinite possibilities.

> **Your life is your responsibility and your business.**
> **Don't let anyone or anything stand in your way.**

By simply changing the way we think, we will change everything that we see as our reality. Imagine if everyone were aware of that power. How would the world change? On a grand scale, I am sure of it. We have been led to believe that we are lucky or not, that intelligence serves as a nominator for success. That money leads to happiness, and that loving ourselves is narcissistic. Let's call the big fat lies, and create truth from the standpoint of being the most powerful person we know. False beliefs be gone. Truth is in the house.

> **Change your thought, change your**
> **story, and change your life.**

Chapter 7

The truth will set you free

❝ *still can`t believe this. My mom is actually telling me that what I have been studying is not correct? As if the textbooks at the University holds untruths, I mean come on. Who does she think I am? I know right from wrong, and respectable literature from propaganda, thank you very much. I look up to all my professors, and would never doubt that they are teaching truth and nothing but. What is she up to? Some conspiracy theory stuff again?*

She did have a few good points though. I will give her that, going on about how vaccines were not really made for protection. How they cause autism. If that were true, why in the world would anyone subject their children to such a thing? I am sure it would be all over the news, and we would learn about it at the University. First of all, my education is where my knowing comes from, right? Second, third and fourth of all, at least our information comes from reliable sources.

She is my mom and I love her and all her organic, save-the-planet, anti-Monsanto stories. They sure keep her enthusiastic. I know she only means well, and after hearing about genetically modified food and the dairy industry, I will watch the movie she sent me. I will, I promise, when there is time. I can't even imagine if what I have believed is not true. I can't even go there. Frustrating.com. What would I do? Who would I believe?"

The truth will set you free, but first it will piss you off. It can be challenging to realize that most of what you have believed is false. It can feel like a betrayal and deceit. You might feel dumb or ignorant. You are not, it's just another lie.

Every time you feel that you are not reaching your potential, or feel discouraged about where you are at this moment, it is the inner knowing of what you *really* deserve that knocks on your door. The inner place beyond any subconscious programming that knows that you are worthy of everything you desire. The space between where you are and where you want to be can be experienced as frustration, anger and depression. Your inner guidance is telling you it's time to step up and live like you mean it. Freedom is knocking, invite it in.

What is freedom?

When we talk about freedom, there are many different associations to the word that arises. The obvious freedom of speech, and not being physically restrained is often the first connotation to the word. Depending on where we live, our culture and our life experience, we will have different expectations to what freedom is and will provide. You can live in prison, in poverty and material lack, and still feel free. You can live in material abundance, surrounded by family, in great health and physical freedom, and still feel imprisoned. True freedom is not a physical thing. It is a feeling, a state of being. It is a perception, a result of the same old programming and the same old hurts and wants. No one can tell you what you need to do to feel free, but the closer you get to your truth, to letting go of all the bullshit that you have been telling yourself and believing, the less burdened you will feel.

Walking in your own truth is walking lighter.
Walking lightly is walking freer.

Often, recognizing lies and deceptions will piss us off big time. How could it not? It is challenging our beliefs and our investment in them. They have formed our reality, claimed our souls and molded our expression. Think about it. If you just came out of medical school, and found that a large portion of what you have been taught is simply not true, then what? Pissed off? What if you realized that what you have been feeding your children, after being told it is good for them is actually hurting them, bigtime, more pissed? It is easy to turn the other way, to bury your head in the sand. The truth simply rocks the boat too much. There will be consequences. There will be changes, big changes. It does not matter if you realize your medications are what's killing you, or you find out that your old wound from being bullied as a child is holding you back, something has got to change. After any new realization, change will happen. The first and most amazing part of freedom is the power we have, to choose change.

Ignorance is a bitch, the worst kind there is. The face of true betrayal. Turning the head, looking the other way is never the solution to anything. You are not only turning away from the obvious challenge, but from yourself. Living truthfully, and always seeking authenticity is what opens the door to your own freedom. It does not matter what lies or false beliefs or even bullshit we are referring to. Be it your inner self talk, what is looking at you from the newspaper, or what is whispered into your ear by your friend. You are the gatekeeper of all your gates. No exceptions.

As we walk through life carrying with us a fraction of everything we have ever experienced, the weight can get unbearable. It can be too heavy to carry. The backpack is filled with subconscious beliefs of shortcomings and criticism. Every trauma, hurtful episode and belief is tucked in tight. Extra pockets are added for unforgiven events, rejections and longings. Not the most fun bag to carry around 24/7. Imagine how this is weighing you down and holding you back. Now, add some chains to your hands and legs, and the picture is not only sad, but completely unacceptable. The accumulation of everything that you believe, is with you. Carried around like a friend. No one *has* to live like that, yet we do. So burdened by our own baggage, like a collector, we save it all, no matter where it came from, good or bad. As long as *you* are the one carrying the load, *you* are the one responsible of setting yourself free. As long as *you* are the one believing you need to bring it with you, the only one who can lighten your load is *you*.

Not everything you believe and know is false or untrue. The real you, the one that has direct contact with the source, with God, knows the difference. The real and true you are not even carrying any load or burden. There is no questioning or blame. There is only true freedom. What we react to and are frustrated with, is everything *not* in alignment with our true selves. When what we are living, believing, doing, and accepting is not in direct truth with our highest good, we suffer. We literally hurt in every way possible. Our health is facing degeneration, we experience depression, anxiety, emotional imbalances and even what can seem like a spiritual shut down.

The freedom that comes with realizing you have the power to change your life, can feel like a burden at first, and why I said it can piss you off. Living in a world of authorities and systems, giving someone else the responsibility seems easy and safe. So, you are medicated, you are suffering and you are not happy with the situation. Now you learn that you *can*, in fact, by changing how you eat, think and live, *take back* your health. Still, you will not. Instead, the new information of health and vitality feels like a burden, like a turn off. It might even aggravate you and make you feel irritated. This is interesting. Why would you not jump at the opportunity to take charge and change your life for the better? Because it feels like a burden to have to take on such a large responsibility. Because it means you will have to change how you look at the world. Because it means you have not been doing what is best for you. Because you are afraid of what others might think. Because you might not know where to start, and because it is not what you have defined as truth.

You are used to sabotaging yourself, and you are used to being a follower. Now, what happens when what you are experiencing, hearing and learning rings true, deep down within your cells and your soul? Everything that you are taking in is added to your carry-on. A whole new compartment of information is added, and until you realize what you have been clinging to is all imaginary, like in the story of the Emperor with the invisible clothes, the extra load will piss you off. It will irritate you like an itch, like something that is annoying and obstructing your peace. And it is. The truth is annoying. It is making your old beliefs feel awkward and sometimes even embarrassing. If you are an intellectual, it will feel extra challenging. Have you been stupid? Are you not as smart as you thought you were?

This is the core reason to why we react to hearing the truth. Not because *it* itself is pissing us off, but because what we believe in does. The itch, the heavy load of shit, is what is weighing us down, truth never will. The more truth we are subjected to, the stronger the smell, so to speak.

> **Truth always brings freedom to those**
> **who are ready to experience it.**

"We do not see the world as it is. We see the world as we are." This quote has been attributed to several people, although no citation can be found. It summarizes the idea that truth is subjective, and a product of one's own way of perceiving it. It paints a perfect picture of how the way we live is a direct product of our inner making. Our beliefs, our wounds, victories, experiences, programming and conditioning.

The freedom that arises:

The word *freedom* has many connotations. It means different things to different people. If you have been locked up physically, the meaning becomes obvious. If you have been abused and tortured, locked up in your own false beliefs, or if you have restricted your own expression in any way, you will feel trapped. If you are physically ill and cannot move, you will experience another variety of being held back. The emotion of not being able to live fully is the same as being un-free. Most prisons are invisible. Most gatekeepers are lies. Most sentences are self-appointed, and most escapes are voluntary.

> When you are ready to question *what* you believe in, no matter what it is, you are knocking on the door of expansion. Growth is inevitable when you let the air and sunlight in. When we lose the shades, everything is seen in a new and truer light. Burdens turn to choices, which represents our free will. No chain or lock can ever change that, not even our own. The choice is always there, representing the power you have been given.

You have the freedom to choose: Being able to choose is part of our free will as human beings. We always have a choice. Even when seemingly limited, it is there. Choosing anything requires action of some sort. It requires that we get our butts off the couch and our heads out of the sand. It might not seem like much, but with a cluttered mind and a broken record, be patient. The fact that you are free is not going anywhere. You can choose to act and to step up at any time.

You can set the bar as high as you wish. You can set your own standard. This goes for any area of your life. When you realize that you can choose to *see* the freedom that truth is bringing, it will knock your socks off. It does not challenge your already true beliefs. On the contrary, it will able them to come forth. Not every standard and belief you live by is hurting your expression and life. Not if you are one of the so-called lucky ones. Is there such a thing as luck? Not in the world of cause and effect. What we live is a reflection of our choices, conscious or subconscious. Nothing is random, even though it can absolutely seem that way at times. Your participation is not insignificant. It is everything. When you truly realize that holding on to what *is*, is nothing more than clinging to your baggage, you will have to face it. You will have to look at either the pissed off; *I-do-not-believe-in-this-crap* energy, or the enthusiasm from learning about freeing yourself. Either way, it is a choice. Although not necessary a conscious one, nevertheless a choice.

Not only do you have the choice to change and grow, you also have the freedom to stay where you are. If you want to stay in a job that you hate, you can. If you want to keep listening to others, and not yourself, that is your choice. The magic is in the realization and the acknowledgement, as from that comes the ownership of the choices made. Bottom line is this: No matter what you choose, you live with it.

You can choose who you listen too, which is a choice that should not be taken lightly. What you read, what you watch, what you listen to, and who, is all up to you. When you were a child you had to listen to your guardians and your teachers. Not anymore. It is time to break those chains, and to realize that your life is between you and God, and no one else. Who and what you listen to, is your own decision to make. The challenge today is not only walking away from the media and sources that keeps spreading untrue information, it is also knowing how to maneuver through the crazy amount of information found on the internet. You can research any topic, and find a confusing amount of conflicting information. Careful who you listen to. Spend time finding reliable sources, and remember, nothing is as reliable as your inner voice and intuition.

If something doesn't resonate with you, walk away. If someone is telling you anything that does not reflect your greatness, walk away. If anyone is trying to tell you that you cannot do, be, have or believe, walk away! Freedom!

You can choose how you respond and react to every situation that arises. Will you use *it*, or will you let *it* use *you*? Will you let someone else be the boss of how you feel, or will you step up to that job yourself? Will you let the bus driver, the cashier or your father dictate how your day evolves? Most often we do. We let their actions and reactions step all over our old beliefs. Bringing forth the emotional baggage and untruths. We can simply say no and stop it. Nothing that anyone says or does should bring you off balance. We tend to get triggered by the ones that shows us we are not good enough, and now we let life happen *to* us.

Believing that there is good luck and bad luck, good days and bad days. All dependent on something outside of us. Not so. All a choice, every single day. Every action has an equal reaction. Cause and effect, again. Two different people can experience the exact same scenario, reacting completely different? Why? They react according to their beliefs, their old garbage, and their chosen response. Some live on the positive side of life, some on the more negative. To see the glass as half full or half empty is a choice. The less we hang on to our pride and our ego, we will be able to untangle ourselves from the need to react to every little thing that comes our way. For some, even a dog barking will throw off the morning. For others, slow traffic will do the same. For others, none of it matters, they have a life to live, and are noticing how great their life really is. How will you choose to respond to what you are experiencing?

Even when you shop, you are reflecting your freedom. Every time you spend money on anything, you are choosing what you want to experience. You are voting, so to speak. Whether you are spending money on food, a drug, a household item or a service, you are inviting it into your life. You are accepting its quality and usage. If we want something to be taken off the shelves, we need to stop buying it. If no one paid for it, it would no longer be offered. Simple. A true freedom of choice. We can change the world just by changing how we spend our money. We need to be respectful when we spend our money. It is an energy exchange. We are sending out the signal that we honor the product or service. If you cannot honestly say this about your purchases, don't make them. Be truthful when you vote.

Imagine not feeding anything that came from cruelty and harmful behavior. Imagine supporting sustainable, organic farming and positive-growth based companies. We would change the world, literally.

You can choose what you eat. Within a few limits, like your place of residence and income, you are free to swallow what you like. Unless you are in a prison, or anywhere where certain food is restricted, on a feeding tube, or in another type of extreme situation, it is up to you. Even then, most likely your influence is greater than you might think. The point is, that for most of us, no one is forcing us to eat anything we don't want to.

By choosing our food, we are choosing our health, pretty much. We are allowing into our temple, either nutrition and life, or toxins and death. We are allowing into our being, either vitality or degeneration. On top of this, we are promoting sustainable organic farming, or cruelty based torture and pain. We are choosing toxic or non-toxic. We are teaching our children to follow what we do, with every single bite, and at the same time loving our body- or not so much. What we eat is a choice that should not be taken lightly. Without this body, there is no human life.

You are free to change. A simple, seemingly small and insignificant change will have a massive impact on your life. Just by changing a simple thought-form there will be ripple effects beyond your imagination. Change may be hard, and it is for most people, but the benefits are enormous. For a professional golfer, changing the pitch, the angle of how the club hits the ball by only a millimeter, will determine a winning game from a losing one. Change can be subtle or radical, forced or planned. Lucky for all of us, we can change at any time. We do not have to wait for any particular moment. We have no obligations to stay the same, as if that was even possible.

Using change as a freedom of choice is truly empowering. Even though we change over time, just by living and experiencing, we can use this force as a game changer on all levels. Everything that is holding us back, or cluttering our vision so to speak, is there to show us that we need to change something. One of those things that requires *us*, ourselves and our very own determination. To want to change has got to come from the willingness to do the work that is required. A freedom that no one can take from you.

If you want something to change, change something NOW!

You have the freedom to live. To simply be. To experience without having to do anything. It is your life to live. No one else can live it for you. When you realize that no matter what you have been told, or what you have believed to be true, the freedom to live as you please will always be there. Your life is a gift, a blessing. It is a manifestation of creation, and anything that does not resonate with that, is not true. Anything that does not reflect the power of your own being is simply not a truth.

Being alive is not the same as living. Being alive technically requires that you breathe, and that's it. Living is expansion. It is an expression of all that is. Being alive is a gift, how we live is a choice. From my own experience, I can report that awakening to the fact that I am able to live as I choose, saved my life. Seeing this gift that had been given to me, by me being alive, changed everything. I could not be anything but grateful. I had the freedom to live! It changed what entered my being, what I ate, thought and believed. I was free to live! I upped my self-protection towards negativity and bullshit in general, and I welcomed every truth that was revealed to me. I was ready to want it all, my life. I was ready to let death and clutter leave my space. When the bullshit leaves the house, the party can begin!

> To claim one's own life is also about being humble to the responsibility that comes with the claim. The ownership as well as the freedom. We need to be ready to show the creation that we are up for the task. We need to live like we mean it by leaving simply being alive behind.

The freedom to let go will free your soul. Holding on is the opposite of freedom. It is the darkness entering the light, the clouds in the sky. *The truth shall set you free, but first it will piss you off,* and this is the pissing off part. The reason we get upset, have resistance or at all react to truth in a negative way, is because it is showing us what we are holding on to. Constipation is never a good thing, and obstruction of flow *will* hurt. The mind is a great analyzer and a great gatekeeper. So, don't you try to get in there with those ideas that will stir the entire pot. All the false beliefs have got to be let go of, and there will be hesitance for sure.

The term "letting go" is widely used when it comes to forgiveness, and when working through any type of trauma or anger issues. It means to leave it behind. To stop carrying it. It means to choose something different, and it does not have to be complicated or a long process at all. It will take some practice, but you can leave something from one second to the next. Here today, gone tomorrow, or here at this moment, gone *now*! No cleaning job will keep you from getting your hands dirty though, so dig in, and use your freedom to let it all go.

You are free to think and perceive. I choose to see this as a freedom, although it is more of a conditioning. I want to bring in the thought, as one of the strongest cards we have for breaking some old chains. As long as we are able to change our thoughts, we are able to change our perception. The old conditioning cannot override a strong will and a determination to set oneself free through changing the way we think. One thought at the time, what you live changes. While looking at this from a perspective of subjective perception, the freedom lies in the ability to choose it. As long as it is subjective it is changeable.

You are not your thoughts, so don't believe any single one of them. Question everything, and feel more than you think. Our brain is nothing but a tool and a storage device. I believe it is a highly overrated one as such. From silence comes true knowledge. Once you stop your thinking, truth will come forth. Every thought is an obstruction of flow, but when we use them intentionally, they can help form a whole new reality. Everything starts with a thought. Everything you ever created has a thought attached to it. The freedom of thought is always your own. You don't have to earn it or deserve it. All you have to do is to claim it. As long as you choose your thoughts, you can use that freedom to change your life.

Taking responsibility is true freedom. This might not seem like a freedom at all. How can this set you free, to take on a responsibility? Are responsibilities not extra work? Do they not require more attention and time? Well, the good news is yes! It will absolutely require you, not only to step up, show up and grow up, it will also require you to break free from your baggage filled with lies. You will then be able to harvest the fruits of your own life design, and you will be able to live stronger and lighter every day.

You are only responsible for *you*, no one else. Except for being caretakers and mentors for our children, we are not in-charge of changing anyone else's life. It seems this job is easier for people to partake than being their own manager. Fixing or assuming responsibility for someone else's actions, feelings and life seems to have such a high priority for many. Wishing to change ourselves is hard, wanting to change someone else is easy. When you become aware that your life is your responsibility, and that it comes with the freedom to make every change, enjoy every result, and claim every success, you will want and need to step up to the job. Being the responsible creator is a job you were born to have. You are the only one suitable for the job, and the only one eligible for the harvest. You have all the skills, the knowledge, the experience and the motive. After all, it is *your* life.

You are born free. All you need to do is to claim it.

> The freedom that comes from realizing that you are the most powerful life-force there is, and the most amazing, creative, blame free being you know, whatever you have been told to believe can go. It can take a hike down the same road as the rest of the lies.

As you see, no matter what you are experiencing or believing today, the freedom is yours. You even have the freedom to let go of everything you have believed you are responsible for. Like your friends or family's happiness. Your adult children's choices. You are not the one who is responsible for changing anyone's life. You don't have to stay at a job you hate, you can either quit or love it. You don't have to stay in a bad relationship. You can either leave or change how you live in it.

The truth that will set you free:

Any feeling of freedom comes with the realization that the burden of crap is no longer yours to carry. The consequences are amazing. There is an endless list of empowering benefits. Here are a few:

- You don't have to wear any masks
- You don't have to pretend anymore.
- There is no more trying
- No more looking to others for validation
- No more hiding from the truth.
- There are no more excuses,
- No reasons to hide or to keep your voice down.
- You are free to live authentically.
- You are free to make your own choices
- You are free to choose happy
- No more lies
- No more false beliefs
- No more blame or shame

The realization that your life is not all based on truth, is going to show more than your own beliefs. It will show you how deep your illusionary roots go. How hard are you clinging to your knowledge? How much of your reality is based on that same knowledge?

An academic, an intellectual and a theorist, will struggle more than someone who lives by their heart and their craftsmanship. How we define ourselves will show up as resistance and struggles towards change. Not only the change itself, but the ability to acknowledge the need for it, and the willingness to own it. A scientist for example, will have an extremely hard time admitting that his truths have been lies, or that his education has been based on some rocky information at times. A teacher, that has been relying on the text books her whole career, will find it hard to face that some of what she has been teaching has been false information. A doctor, and any authority will struggle to admit they did not know what they have claimed to be in complete control of. It is human.

The academics of our Western culture has put a bondage on the free thinkers, and that is a part of the ongoing programming. The massive control and power of the financial market, the big pharma, the food industry, the weapon industry, religion and media, will keep you locked in if you let it. Luckily you can choose otherwise. You can set yourself free. You can turn away from anything that does not resonate with your joy and enthusiasm. You have the power, use it.

By changing you, you are changing the world. By no longer allowing yourself to be kept a prisoner of your thoughts and your programming, you are freeing your energy. By setting your spirit free, you are allowing the creation to flow. By realizing that the truth will set you free, you are raising the vibration of your whole field and the one of those around you. By living your truth, you are changing the world.

"For as he thinks within himself, so he is." Proverb 23:7

The truth will set you free, even of blame and resistance.
There is no freedom in holding grudges towards anyone.
Holding on to un-forgiveness and hatred
is a prison of another name.
Every such emotion is a lie.
It is not from who you are.
Not the free true you.
Not the one you are meant to be.
Not if you were free.

Your true power = Truth = Freedom

Chapter 8

No more resistance

should start exercising. I should renew my membership at the gym. I think the office has a special employee deal even. I don't like the way I feel not being able to walk up the stairs without losing my breath. The pounds just keep piling on me, and I don't really eat that much. Must be hormonal. I read about that somewhere, about people gaining weight and it was not their fault. I never feel good, but you know what they say; we all have our struggles.

After all it's not that bad. Even if I smoke, and even though I do have that cough, I do pretty well. I didn't miss one single day of work last month. Not one. So, I am fine, I am my own master. I don't need all that propaganda telling me that I should to get healthy. Have you seen all those skinny people? As if they are any healthier, no way. I know where the problem is, it is them not leaving people like us alone. That is the real issue. I am enjoying the finer things in life. No one will ever be able to take away my cigarettes and my beer. What a sad world that would be. I would rather be a little chubby, and not in the best of shape, at least I have my sofa, my beer and my Marlboro's. Life is supposed to be fun, right?

Get ready to dig deep within your belief system, and get ready to feel confused at times. Let the shit come to the surface and let it all out. It is yours to claim, and there are no more excuses to be made. Every excuse you've got to not move forward is a sign of resistance. Your old beliefs are trying to pull you back into a comfortable position. We love comfort, familiarity and the feeling of mastery. When life clearly hurts, or is falling apart, we might not feel as such a master after all. Even though we are.

Resisting change is the same as making excuses to why you can't. We have all done this. You know what you've got to do, you have seen the truth, now just get going in the right direction and … nothing. You stop, procrastinate. Something happens between realization, planning and doing. Or the whole project stops before the plan is even born. Or there was never a project, only the moaning and acknowledgement that something had to change. The inner knowing that the path you were on was going to drive you into a pit, or it was going to suck the life out of you. I am a strong believer that we all sense when this is going to happen. One can be pretty dumbed down, and out of sync with one's own body and inner voice, but this much we know. When the shit is about to hit the fan, we "know".

Again, the difference between knowing and doing can be miles apart, decades even. How is that possible? Resistance, the old fear of change. Another great way to break free is to notice resistance. All the excuses in the world is not going to change the fact that something is going to have to give. It will only pull you into more pain and unhappiness, feeling inadequate and unable to handle your own life. Feeling like a victim hurts. Feeling helpless and powerless is depressing. No wonder we need excuses. It is a survival mechanism of our ego.

Making excuses that sound legitimate is an art, and we call it self-sabotage. Once you get the hang of it, you won't even know you are doing it. Your subconscious mind has come up with a very clever way of keeping you locked in your old ways. You might look at it as a defense mechanism that is very subtle and clever. Like a whisper, it shows you how to stay on point, and not rock the familiar boat. It wants to hold on to what is, it is comfortable, even though you are hurting.

You might recognize some of these patterns of self-sabotage:

The not-being-worthy identity: A very common subconscious belief that I have seen surfacing for many, is the "I do not deserve to get well, or I don't deserve to succeed."-pattern. It emanates from the lack of self-love. While deep down, you do not believe that you deserve to live the life you desire, you will keep doing things that will make that manifest as a truth. That way, you were right. Even though this is a subconscious belief pattern, it might be so strong, that it shows up in your conscious thinking as well. The feeling of unworthiness comes from holding on to old hurts. As a child, you might have been scolded and abused, physically or mentally. A child will believe that it does not deserve any better than what is, and this will be imprinted as a truth until the spell is broken. As the child grows, every time the same pattern of abuse or critique appears, it validates the already known inner truth.

A very typical way for this self-sabotage to manifest is as a self-created, very valid-looking obstacle. You will not reach your goal because you found that this was not the right time for you. Your husband lost his job, your children are too young, and they need you to do what is expected for them. This really is not the best time to take care of *you* – *"It did not work out, because I did not have a car at the time, and could not get what I needed for my juicing"*. Or: *"My business would never grow anyway, so money spent on the course would have been wasted"*. The stories are endless, and all valid. They make sense as something the conscious mind can sort of believe, as the subconscious mind keeps playing the story of your life. The truth is though, that nothing, and I mean nothing will stand in your way once you are ready. No-thing. Once that tape is turned off and replaced, none of these reasons will feel valid anymore.

What you know, and what you are programmed to believe, is not in balance, and inner chaos will arise. Even though your inner belief system is telling you that you are not worthy of this amazing life that you so long for, you consciously might want it more than anything.

The fear of the new identity: Another aspect to have in mind when we are dealing with self-sabotage is the "fear of losing what we know"-pattern. It is the flip side to change, so to speak. It is the direct opposite of inviting in the change that is needed, this fear of losing what we already have.

Once we have made the decision that we are ready to go, to move forward, and to walk towards health, we know that change will be ahead. We know that we will have to change something. That is logical. The intellect knows that the protocol of eating and living will be different, and the conscious mind is ready.

Then, even if what we have been experiencing is not good for us, it's hurting us even, it is still what we know. Even if we are in an abusive relationship, and we *know* that we are, it is what we are familiar with. Breaking free means uncertainty, and insecurity. The obvious scenario is that we would rather stay in pain, in fear of the unknown. I know, it really does not make sense, but for those that are living by their inner-beliefs of not being strong enough, or smart enough to be on their own, this is very real. This pattern arises from the understanding of not being able to take care of ourselves.

A typical scenario might be that you decide you are fine as you are. There was no need for any major change after all. You are fine. Your health is so much better now, it was all just a false alarm. Nothing to worry about, you are fine. No change needed.

The attention identity: Being sick, abused, sad or poor, might have given you more attention that has led to the feeling of being loved. This pattern is most likely imprinted in our early childhood. The experience of getting more attention and love, will stay with us, and we will continue to use the same patterns into our adult lives. A child will do what it feels it needs to do, to feel loved and accepted, and if a need was fulfilled when health was impaired, the pattern will stick for life. This does not mean that to get attention you are making yourself sick, or willingly staying unemployed, not at all, but not being healthy or lacking money will be associated with something that feels familiar and safe. That way, once you change your life for the better, you might feel unsafe, and fall back to the old comfort zone. Some relationships are built on this energy. The pattern of one being the needy and one being the servant, the caregiver. The partner, in need of care, might feel extra important or seen, while the caregiver feels there is need for them.

The fear of loss is also present in this pattern and belief-system. *"If I get well, he will no longer need to be here, and he will leave me."* The fear of not being loved for who you are, has made you, through your experience as a child, holding on to pain and disease, so that someone will care for you, and therefore love you. The self-sabotage might sound like this: *"Nothing works for me. I have tried everything, and nothing works"*. This will draw in even more of the compassionate attention that you believe that you need. The truth is that you do not need any bodily dis-function, or anything else for that matter, to get the attention that you need.

The disease identity: Without even knowing it, you might be holding on to a disease as an identity. For example, that you feel like your chronic diagnosis is serving you in some way. How in the world would being sick serve anybody, you might ask? *"All I want is* *to get well, and there is no way being sick would serve me or anyone."* Well, I am afraid there could be. Any number of things might be lingering as a subconscious belief and understanding. These are beliefs that will keep you locked in your current situation, clinging to what is, even if it is suffering and pain. Remember, these are most often unconscious patterns, not something you are choosing in awakened state. Unconscious meaning hidden to us, but often we can still feel the pattern when awareness is brought to the situation.

This programming comes from the need to belong. We all need to feel that we belong, and when we have not had that feeling growing up, we will search for it in any community or situation. Once we find it, as it is one of the basic humans needs, it is very hard to let it go. We tend to want to stand by our tribe no matter what. They are the ones that have stuck by us, and have taken us in. We've felt welcomed and loved. The disease might even be our livelihood now, our business. A very good and sane reason to hold on to it, now that it is "working" for us. Our perceived identity is worth holding onto for our dear lives, and the true and devastating story is that that is exactly what we do

The "loser" identity: This might sound very strange, but it is absolutely a pattern for many that are not living up to their potentials. The identity of not succeeding creates a space where self-pity will go a long way. How would it benefit anyone to wallow in self-pity and to be seen as a so-called loser? Holding oneself locked into this particular pattern, emanates from the fear of failing. It is safer to stay a loser than to fail and face the shame and ridicule even. Past experiences of being laughed at and bullied for not succeeding will feed the pattern of self-sabotage. Just the smell of stepping out of the comfort zone and stretching towards something better could bring up too much fear.

The result is excuses and more excuses of why this and that cannot happen. Even though you might have to stay overweight, at least you won't have to live with the ridicule if you fail. Even though you cannot stand not speaking up at work, and telling them what you feel, at least you don't have to show them all that you turn red just opening your mouth in front of more than one person.

All self-sabotage is born from the misbelief that we are less-than, not good enough, do not deserve and are not worthy of love and abundance. We carry with us the pattern that reflects back to us what we believe. All depending on which types of situations we have experienced from the early part of our lives, those same patterns are still ruling.

Resistance towards building a better life, healing the body, growing and thriving, always comes from resistance towards change. It is never truth, it is always a sign of old hurt and programming. It is never the real truth. It is always a lie. Call the bullshit and let it know you are on to it.

Once you're able to identify that you are in fact resisting to do what is best for your life and growth, the real work can begin. Now you can work the muscle of perseverance and persistence. Two strong and key attributes of breaking free from anything that is weighing you down and messing with your true potentials. You have to condition yourself to break free. The magic is in the realization and the determination. Knowing the truth is one thing, being a determined go-getter is something else. It is the top league of self-mastery and authentic living.

It is easy to stay semi-comfortable. By that I mean: We tend to resist change if where we are doesn`t hurt too much. If it is still livable, we stay put. This is the reason we see so many stating that what was perceived as a tragedy at first, turned out to be a blessing. It became a life altering event that even though painful and devastating at the time, looking back, it changed the person and their life in a positive way. Old believes where shattered and old habits had to go.

> Your life is yours to live. Hold no prisoners and
> hold no lies hostage. Set them all free, and
> reap the fruits of prosperous living!

Chapter 9

What is your excuse?

"*Being ready to change is never easy. I have too much to do, and I know that is no excuse, but it is the truth. I will get started next week, I promise. I know I should do better, and I know what I need to do. I am so sick of not being able to take the first step! Geez, how weak am I? Why do I always seem to find a reason to procrastinate?*

You can call me anything but lazy. I really did want to start working out this week. I even looked for my running shoes last night. I know they are around here somewhere. Got myself this bright new expensive outfit. This is it, I am going for it this time. I need to get my gear together, I know, and I will, soon."

We are all humans, not perfect, yet part of perfection. We are all a reflection of our conditioning. That is ok, as long as we get it. The self-sabotage runs deep, and as long as we are within the range of reasonable comfort, it seems stories told as excuses will feed the ego and pride that we carry.

Being comfortable is a relative term. It is natural to want to seek safety and painless existence. When you build your life on what feels familiar, when anything outside that norm feels unsecure, fearful and scary, you are setting yourself up for some challenges down the road. The comfort zone is defined by how comfortable you feel within it. Is it making you ignorant, lazy and careless? Are you using it as a hiding place and a shelter? There is nothing wrong with being comfortable. *But*, when it is keeping you from exploring, changing and taking charge, it is no longer a zone worth keeping. We might like things the way they are until they hurt, or until they simply do not work for us anymore. Even then, we run for tools, therapy, support and cheering on, to stretch and reach. Some zones seem to be harder to move than mountains. Completely carved in stone, almost unmovable, but not quite. This invisible line that we don't feel comfortable crossing, is built as a protection from pain. Any type of pain. Emotional pain is most often a more feared pain than the physical. It's not tangible, and it is invisible and private. The privacy that we have been taught in the Western world is that of separation and exclusion. Another great building block for keeping a close and strong comfort zone.

Magic and growth happens outside the comfort zone.

The saying; "Magic happens outside the comfort zone", refers to how you, by stretching outside what is common and comfortable, will be able to see the opportunities and truths that are invisible to you at this moment. How will you know what good feels like if you are not willing to change what is keeping you in pain and lack? How will you ever know or experience health, if you keep doing what is making you sick? As long as we believe that our lives are based on truths, on reality and what is, we are kept in the bubble created by our past and current perceptions. A whole chapter is dedicated to this powerful comfort zone.

You might find an excuse to keep working where you are not appreciated, treated right or given any opportunity to grow the way you would like. You might even believe in it. It might even sound reasonable to others when you keep it for the sake of having an income to support your mother, your husband or your children. It is still just an excuse, a fear and resistance to change. It is still a sign you are not taking charge of your life, and that you are believing and playing out a false belief.

> **"Only by going where you have not yet been, can you see things you have not yet seen." - Hilde Larsen**

The level of pain that we are willing and capable of enduring is individual. You can see people running from particular situations after one single day of discomfort, while others have endured the same scenario for years. We all have a limit. At one point we have had enough. Depending on our pain threshold, our endurance skill, our subconscious beliefs and our patience, we all have a point of; *I-am-done*. Some, sooner than later. Have you noticed that some will absolutely not stand for any bullshit, while others allow themselves to be walked all over? Some will choose to stay in an abusive relationship for years, while others will take a hike after the first sign of disrespect. While those who love themselves will shy away from anything that feels less than comforting, uplifting, compassionate and loving, someone who lacks self-love will allow the opposite. This is a catch 22 if you will, or force of confirmation.

As you subject yourself to abuse, your self-worth will diminish. As you surround yourself with love, your self-love will grow even stronger. Hence more abuse is welcomed.

Look at this from the perspective that we all want the same thing. We all want to be happy, healthy and feel loved and appreciated. The only reason we seem different is the color and the weight of the load we are carrying. The more we carry, the more we accumulate.

The more we accumulate, the further away from our true self-expression we strive. The longer we have walked with a heavy burden, the more accustomed to it we've grown, the harder it gets to even recognize that it is there. The ignorance, the excuses, are all a sign of endurance really. You are acknowledging that you are not living your truth, while at the same time agreeing to keep on keeping on. You are signing up for another term of *not* changing what you know you *need to.*

You would rather repeat a tough day, than make an effort to change it. The day wasn´t that bad after all. Not painful enough, not quite, not yet.

Excuses and procrastination towards self-growth, are all symptoms showing us we lack trust and confidence in ourselves. We know that everything changes, it is the law of nature. Everything evolves and expands. Either we grow, or we die. Either we strive to do better, for us, for the children, for the planet, - or we slowly die. Being a sufferer and a victim is a slow death. Being a creator, an enthusiast and an empowered being is life. We all have the same potentials to be both. Divided by our shit, our thoughts and our determination, we walk through our lives very differently. Yes, some are born into money, while some are born down right poor. Yes, some are born into a poor health, while some seem to be able to abuse theirs for a lifetime, and still live somewhat healthy lives. We did not all get here with the same starting point in life, but we sure do have the same basic ability to choose. We can all live authentically, excuse free, positive, compassionate lives. We can all walk our talk, empower others, serve, grow and do our very best. That alone will turn stone into gold. It will reveal diamonds and pearls.

Keeping yourself from moving forward is only keeping you from achieving what you want. You know that what you have believed and adopted as truths, are not really true, and you know it is up to you to take charge. Now it is time to look at why you are still holding

No More Bullshit

on to your old patterns, why you are still clinging to the notion of being stuck, and being a victim. It is nothing but an act. You are never a victim, always empowered. Seeing oneself as a victim of time, of circumstance, of events and of how others treat you is like hitting the break on any growth, and at the same time feeding your own current situation. Making sure *it* keeps you locked in. Everything will reflect how you condition yourself. The input equals the output. Your effort reveals itself in your results. Cause and effect. The blessing and the curse is that we all have to live with the results of the choices that we make.

> "It is better to offer no excuse than a
> bad one." – George Washington

There is no right or wrong:

When it comes to how you choose to live your life, you can never get it wrong. It is ok to "fail". The word itself indicates lack of success, but as long as you are doing something to move forward, it can never be failure. Every step of the way has value. Learning by experience is the most treasured kind of learning there is. What you live is what will teach you the most valuable lessons.

We can see how much the subconscious mind has absorbed from our experiences. More than anything read from a book, it is what has been felt within us that is filling the space on our hard disc. From your firsthand experiences comes the beliefs that will form your whole system and perception of truth. It doesn't matter if it is beneficial or not. By learning through trial and error, you are imprinting your brain with valuable knowledge.

Leaving wrong out of the equation, makes it easier to step into the unknown. One less fear to worry about, and one less reason to create excuses for ourselves. The fear of failure is deeply rooted in the majority of people. I believe it is the main reason why so many never even reach for their goals. The fear of failure is debilitating. It is associated with ridicule, rejection and lack of respect. It is also associated with any type of lack, from being poor to being alone. We have been taught to measure our whole life in how we succeed within the appointed rules and norms already set for us. If you succeed, you have been doing it right, if not, you screwed up. Failure equals less value. Excuse me, but *that* is true bullshit! All we can do is walk towards a true and authentic life, and all we can do is try our very best. No matter the outcome, the lesson is valuable. No matter how many times you fall off the horse, you get back on.

Sure, there is deceit, lies and crappy deals. There are moral and legal rights and wrongs. Killing, stealing, raping etc. will never be anything but terribly wrong. Doing the right thing is part of a compassionate and truthful way of living.

No more excuses:

Shift your mindset, and change your game plan. This is an important point in any walk of life. No matter what you are looking to improve, be it your health, your relationships, your self-love or your work situation. You need to step out of the victim mode that keeps you from moving forward. No more excuses, and no more telling yourself the lies that you have believed for too long; *I am not good enough, I am a failure, I will never make it, I will be alone, nobody loves me. I cannot get healthy.* There are more, I am sure.

Make a list of your own excuses. Write them down. It will tell you a lot about yourself, and why you are not in complete sync and flow. What you focus on, grows, and what you put your attention towards, you will attract more of. The law of attraction is undisputable. Analyze your life. Look at what is not working for you. Why are you not changing? What are you telling yourself? Remember, the answers might sound very valid. They are cluttered by years of reasoning and false beliefs. There are no reasons good enough not to move forward, or to take better care of yourself. The time is always now. Not for everything, but for something. Not for every step, but for some of them. For the first one, always. For moving forward, always.

> "He that is good for making excuses is seldom good for anything else."- Benjamin Franklin

Upgrade your powers:

Give yourself a reason to bloom and prosper through recognizing where you are and why.

Gift yourself with the space you need, to do what you have to do, to get the life that you deserve. The past is what it is, the now is in your hands, and the future is a result of this very moment. Of every moment. Start by conditioning yourself for success through realizing that you hold the power. Don't look back unless you are going that way, and realize that every person you meet is your teacher. Like every experience is, every encounter is also. Use it to grow, not to blame. Instead of looking for faults and shortcomings, look for opportunities and growth. Look for smiles, and you will recognize them everywhere.

- **Everything is a muscle:** How you think, feel and act is a result of your hard work. You have been training towards everything that you see in front of you. Your health is a direct result of your lifestyle, paired with a genetic starting point, but still a reflection of life. Weak organs and glands can be regenerated. So-called chronic diseases can be turned around. With hard work and dedication, you can build a strong and vital health from any starting point. All of your patterns are mirrors of what you have been working on. In the same way you build a muscle in the gym, you build your mental and emotional strength through hard and focused repetitive work. Through meditation you exercise stillness. Through showing up to your appointments you are building ability to follow through. Through writing a gratitude journal, you are connecting with your compassion and ability to forgive. You will find me mentioning the connection between a muscle and our growth several times throughout this book - as a key understanding to true freedom, and the fact that action is the driving force in creation.

- **Think for success**: Start by conditioning your whole being for success. Talk, think and feel like the winner that you are. Your cells are listening to absolutely everything. To every thought and emotion, you have an audience, your life. When you think about your health, think about being healthy. When you talk about your health, be positive and enthusiastic. As your old programming dissolves and a new mindset is in place, what you are sending out will also change. This might result in some change in friends and associates, but that is ok. When friends leave, you know you are moving ahead. You will naturally be drawn towards those that have the same creative, positive, solution-based, loving mindset as yourself. New like-minded friends will eventually knock on your door, so don't worry. Only those that were of no support to you will leave. The old programming will show up as your need to speak about the disease, the broken relationship, or the terrible job and boss.

Every time you feel the urge to tell a story about something that you would rather change, you know that you are in the mind-game-mode. As long as you keep telling that same old story of what you do *not* want, you are heading down that same old road. When we have the need to talk about what is not serving us, we know that we need to change. What we resist, persists, and what we talk about the most, we will keep creating more of.

- **Take a stand:** Choose *you* by standing up for yourself. This goes hand in hand with living authentically, and taking a stand can be scary and hard. You might have to stand alone in a decision. We love to hide in the crowd. So much safer. Not only that; it's "normal." Be clear on what you want, and stand by it, stand by *you*. Many of us grew up never having anyone take a stand with us. Supporting our decisions or choices. This is one of the reasons it is hard to step up and be that authority. It represents feeling alone and neglected all over again. Once you are clear on your objective, be it your health goal or your career move, be firm, and make a deal with yourself. Be ready to stand your ground, and to let your voice be heard. Nothing is more detrimental to your feeling of self-worth than not having a clear and firm opinion about your own life. It is yours, for heaven's sake, who else would have an opinion on it? It is nobody's business but yours. It is empowering and freeing and crucial that you find out what it is that you want and need.

- **Set a goal:** Once you have taken a stand, and are clear on what it is you want, get ready to act on it. Once you have spoken your truth out loud, set a goal. A real tangible goal. "This is what I want, and this is how I am going to work towards it." Not a detailed plan of action, as that could be a big mistake. But a directional plan with steps that are constantly moving you towards the goal. The reason I say a detailed plan is a mistake is that there is no way of knowing the whole path unless you are actually walking it. Situations, people and events will constantly come into your reality, shaping your twists and turns. As long as your focus stays on the ball, the path is always the right one.

Remember, there is no failure, only learning and experimenting. The goal can be small or positively huge. There is nothing wrong with thinking big, although smaller steps will be more rewarding. That way, success is easier to achieve, and the motivation to move forward is ensured. Ensuring motivation and confidence is a big deal. Slow and steady wins the race. When I went from HELL to Inspired, which I chronicle in my book by the same name, I had *one* superior objective. It didn't matter how sick I was, or how many doctors told me it could not be done. I was going to do it, and I was going to show them all. And I did. Why was I able to achieve what was supposedly impossible? Because I stopped believing in their bullshit, and I conditioned myself for success, for true health. I sat a goal, a very clear one. No mumbo jumbo. No excuses, and no more listening to any of my false beliefs. Let me tell you, the reward for breaking free is indescribable.

I had a goal, not a mapped-out plan. It had not yet revealed itself to me. All I held on to was that one *end goal, and I found my path as I worked and studied towards it.*

- **Work on it every single day:** Yes, every single day. When you have taken a stand, set your goal, mapped out some steps to start with, you start working. What makes it or brakes it is your own willingness to give it your all. If you want to see those pounds gone, or that build muscle, you need to show up at the gym or in the woods. You need to invest in that rebounder, or set aside an hour a day for other types of movement. You've got to educate yourself on diet, and get smart about what you eat. If you want to become a successful entrepreneur, you need to get yourself a mentor, study hard, call yourself to action and condition yourself to breathe and live in the mode of success every single day.

If you want to heal from a chronic and serious so called disease you need to read books, talk to experienced health practitioners. You need to study, think, and breathe health.

It will take a super focused individual that is ready to do what it takes. We never know how long anything takes, it is a process. It takes so long as it takes. Everything I did was to get better. Every waking hour I was either studying health or practicing a health promoting activity. It does not matter where you are or what your focus is, so long as you keep working on it. You might want to leave a dysfunctional relationship, or you might want to stay and work on it. Either way, you will be taking action towards the outcome that you are seeing as optimal. Action is underrated.

- **Be your own critic:** Often we find a whole bunch of people applying for that position. Self-appointing themselves even. Such a popular position, to be someone's critic. We all go there from time to time. Putting our nose where it doesn't belong. Giving away free advice when it is not asked for. Pushing our opinions on others like it is our mission. Telling someone they need to change, or that they are doing something wrong. By being your own critic I mean you need to be the one you are accountable to. No matter how many well-meaning little comments flow your way, stand your ground. Be firm on your own behalf, and be your own worst critic. Take the blame, and move on. Learn from it and do better.

It is quite ok to have support, and to have someone with who you can measure progress with. It is quite empowering to connect with a community of likeminded. They are not your choir of criticism, but your cheerleaders. Constructive feedback is also quite valuable, when asked for, and when given in a way that will build and challenge. Sometimes we need a push, or a friendly reminder. A mentor is invaluable. Haters are better lost. Criticism, enough of that. Just say; no thank you, been there, done that.

> Be in-charge of your thinking, and watch how
> everything changes. Time is on your side, as
> the journey is the real destination.

As you realize there is nothing holding you back except yourself and your inner dialog, subconscious *and* conscious, you wake up to a whole new reality. One that smells like freedom and looks like happy. You no longer believe everything being served. Only plates of real true food are allowed at your table. Excuses be gone.

Have fun with this simple exercise:

This simple exercise might give you some insight on your beliefs and patterns that you are not fully aware of. Bring out your brand new journal. Find a pen that feels wonderful in your hand. This pen is only to be used for writing in your Success Journal.

1. Keep the journal by your bed and grab it first think when you awake. Before you even brush your teeth or get into the shower, open the book and write.
2. I want you to start by writing out your life as you see it today. Don't hold back on anything. Put the pen to the paper and let I flow. For one week, write about 1 page each day, about anything. Anything that comes to mind, or to the paper. About life, work, people, health, money, sorrow, joy, anything. The more you step out of the mind, the better. This way the subconscious can come forth to play. Be authentic, be bold, and be truthful. No-one but you will read this, so don't hold back on the ammunition.
3. When the week is done, you should have seven pages, packed with what has been on your mind. That will give you valuable leads as to what you truthfully believe about the life that you are living. You will see patterns of complaint, irritants, fears and drama. Spend some time every day for another week to thoroughly go through every page.

4. Read through everything, and look for the top three people that you are referring to in your writing. The top three events, the top three complaints, pains etc. Make a top three list that will summarize what you focus on. Look for hidden emotional triggers. What is setting you off, and what beliefs are you clinging to?

5. The pattern might not be what you were expecting at all. You might realize that some people have a much larger influence on your emotions than you thought. You might see that you do not feel as good about your vacation that you thought you did. You might awaken to the fact that you keep doing the same thing over and over even though you know you need to change it up.

6. Make a list of areas where your life needs adjustment, and convert it into a list of goals. Start with the smallest things first. You might find that you are not happy with how you keep your home, or the way a friend treats you. Perhaps your car needs to be sold, and a vacation is in place. Maybe the children need to learn how to do some chores around the house, or you need to tell a friend to stop criticizing you.

"Your life experiences make you eligible for an amazing fulfilling life. Truth revealed." Hilde Larsen

No matter what this exercise shows you, it is all about you and your self-talk. Nothing really exists outside of you, in the sense that it is all your perception and how you act and react to it. So, take from this some awareness, and *know* that what you see, feel and think you know, is changeable at any minute. If you don't like what you see, change something. If you don't like what you feel, change something.

Your life does not happen to you. It happens through you. It happens because of you, excuse free.

Chapter 10

De-clutter and Grow FREE

If only I had the time to do everything that I know I should have. I don't get how some people seem to be able to keep everything together. I mean, with the family, work, my social calendar, there is no way I will ever get some me-time in there. I need a break from my life, that's for sure. It feels like my brain will explode from having so much to deal with.

The house looks like a mess, never like I want it, and I am always behind on my tasks. The to-do list is longer than there are days in a year, I am sure, and if someone asks me to help them I will freak. I mean, let's get real, I've got to take care of absolutely freaking everything. Like today: The dog needs to be groomed, I need to go shopping for the dinner party tomorrow. Two of the kids needs to be taken to practice, my period is killing me, and I need to go through the paperwork for the meeting in the morning. I feel like my whole life is cluttered just from being me for heaven's sake! Enough already!"

Once we realize that life has a hold on us, and not the other way around, it will feel like we are literally cluttered from the inside out. The wind of change is whispering in our ear. We see the madness, and we feel its rage. The time has come to stop pretending to be something but our authentic selves. It is time to strip naked that facade that is falling apart day by day. There really is nothing you need to do, have or accomplish, not for all the wrong reasons. What I call clutter, is everything that is standing in your way of your true inner potential. Keeping you on hold from an optimal happy life free of bullshit, obstacles that you are tripping on, and most of all, the general clutter surrounding us, inside out. So much clutter. Everywhere. In our house, office, car, relationships, mind and emotions. Something has got to give. Cleaning and organizing to the rescue. You won't believe how much better life looks when the mess is out of the house.

Everything we draw into our lives, be it a physical thing, a thought or a person, we are storing it, carrying it and being affected by the meaning we have given it. Our old beliefs might tell us that giving something away when we no longer need it, is not a good thing. We might need it later. There might be famine, we might end up in lack, therefor holding on, storing and cluttering our space is natural. It is needed. It is safety. It is our burden to carry. We are owned, by things.

Whenever you are battling between your emotions and your mind, your schedule and your time, you are held hostage by your own clutter.

Let's look at some signs that you are full of shit, or that your spaces are. Clutter is a sign of congestion, obstruction and stress. External chaos is a reflection of the internal status. The perfect motivator for action, and a great tool for stepping up to the true freedom.

The key to de-cluttering is to simplify and organize.

113

How to start releasing the clutter:

Start by acknowledging which part of your life, if not all, needs examining. Start small, and be diligent. A little each day goes a long way. If you are facing a lot of what you perceive as obstacles in a specific area of your life, dive right in. Get your hands dirty, your feet wet, and get ready to pull up some roots. One thing is realizing the mess that has filled up your inner and outer space, another is having the will and the spunk to actually do something about it. You need to activate the release button, and let go of the patterns that keep you piling up and holding on. Where in your life do you need to improve? What are you not happy about?

We all do this by the way, collect unneeded and unwanted crap. We all need a spring cleaning now and then. A detoxification from day to day waste and un-serving habits. Every area of our life has potential to improve by de-cluttering its space, be it physically or mentally. No one wants to trip over a box or a piece of furniture, and the same goes for unwanted thoughts and debilitating emotions. Our focus and our ability to create is greatly impaired by the unnecessary burdens we carry. It is like driving a car in pouring rain with no wipers. Like walking in heavy fog, not seeing clearly where you are heading.

Once you realize that a lot of what you have been told, and have been telling yourself, are lies, the clutter will be more visible. It will be easy to stumble upon, and get annoyed by. Who wants a mind that keeps reminding you how you can't do this and that, or an office that looks and feels like chaos? That is not a successful office. It reflects stress and chaos.

How is a relationship going to move forwards, when it is cluttered by old hurts and disagreements, constant nagging and replays of the same old stories? Once you realize you are walking around in a dirty shirt, you will want to clean it, or get a new one. Once you get that your business is not moving forward due to lack of structure and organized actions, you will want to learn and do better. Clutter grows where it is welcome and left alone. Like a weed. Invading the space, leaving you feeling helpless, overwhelmed, confused, and unable to focus. As you wake up to your own power, this will be clear. When it is clear, you are ready to start the process. One step at the time, let's get rid of some serious shit. Flush it. Let the sunshine in, and say hello to more freedom.

Like no two physical objects can hold the same space at the same time, no thought or emotion can arise simultaneously.

Your thoughts and emotions:

Everything starts with a thought, so let's start by making space for some new ones. The mind is the root of all clutter. It has helped you create everything you see and live. It has been you best friend in all crimes, the good the bad and the ugly. Now, let's put it to work, to de-clutter your whole life. Step by step, freeing you from unwanted and unneeded life-sucking energy and burdens.

First and foremost, you need to monitor your thoughts. What are you thinking? Look around. Everything is a reflection of your inner terrain, both mentally and emotionally. Be mindful of your thoughts. Be observant of how you respond to situations and your own beliefs. You can only hold one thought at the time, so remember that a negative, or un-serving thought is occupying the space of a serving one. The subconscious mind, constantly bragging away its mostly false beliefs, paired with your mental conscious blabbering, will create a clutter that can drive anybody off balance. Often referred to as the monkey brain, it goes on and one, like a non-stop train. Not leaving room for anything that the ongoing internal dialog. It might feel like a trap, or you might not even be aware that it is occupying your space. Not until you become more mindful, and able to observe your own thoughts and emotions.

1. **Start by minding your thoughts**. Write in the journal. Listen more, and be mindful throughout your day. What is triggering your internal chatter? What are you saying about yourself and your situation? Keep your thoughts under surveillance. Let them know you are watching.

2. **Be quiet.** Spend at least 30 minutes every day in stillness. Let the mind settle, and just observe any thought that might arise or drift by. Practice makes all the difference. It takes time to change any old pattern, so give yourself time. Stillness is making room for grandness, the gems that you want to fill your life with. With too much clutter, the door to the divine wisdom is closed.

3. **Think uplifting and empowering thoughts**. As two thoughts cannot enter the same space at the same time, choose to think more positive, serving thoughts. It might feel awkward at first, but it will change your life like nothing else. *You* are the thinker, and you absolutely hold the power to choose your thoughts. Use that power wisely and start affirming new and better thoughts consciously every single day. Once you observe a negative or un-serving thought sneak in, delete it and replace it with one that is. Write down positive affirmations everywhere. On your computer, on your phone, in your journal and on your bathroom mirror. Constantly be on the lookout for that weed, for that clutter.

4. **Be the observer.** By that I mean; step back and look at your inner and outer life from a perspective. Try to be more objective and less subjective. Observe from a far, without involving your feelings and emotions. Detach from the outcome of your desires. Let go of the need to know, and the need to control. Being an observer simply means that you are stepping back from the situation, without turning your back on it. It is so easy to get lost in the emotional and mental clutter, it can be hard to see the underlying patterns. Internal clutter is hard to see when it is embracing us with its false truths. Step back and think less.

5. **Be grateful.** A game changer in any situation is gratitude. The gate opener for love and peace. A feeling that will dissolve any negativity, and bring calm and ease to our whole lives. So simple, yet forgotten and overlooked by most of us. Stress and gratitude are as different as hate and love. They cannot exist at the same time. Inviting in the grace of appreciation and gratification is a great tool and key to lifting your life to that new level of awareness. Although not of the mind, and not a thought, gratefulness starts with the willingness and the mental conditioning of appreciation. Practice it every day, though meditation and your chosen focus. Be grateful for everything in your life, also the ability to do better. Be grateful for your own free will, and your new path to freedom and a clutter-free, true life.

6. **Do something kind for someone.** Anything. This energy opens your ability to let go of any self-pity and victim pattern. It has a ripple effect beyond belief. The best way to wipe out any dusty and negative pattern is to use a force or something better. Something of a higher vibration. Where there is light, there can be no darkness. Always speak with a kind tongue; *"Is it kind, is it true, is it necessary?"* Pride yourself in your words. They reflect your inner terrain, and therefore your own outer life. Speak uplifting words, help someone carry a heavy load, and assist a stranger. Donate your time or your smile. It does not matter. True kindness comes from the heart, and it will nourish your ability to open up and change.

7. **Let go of the control.** Yeah right! I know, this might sound crazy to anyone who is running a business, trying to keep everything together. It is everything *but* crazy. It is one of the greatest secrets to growing and evolving. Not to be confused with being the authority or the goal-getter. I am not talking about not working systematically and diligently towards what you want. When talking about de-cluttering our minds and lives, letting go of the control means not clinging to an outcome. It means resting in faith and knowledge that

everything will turn out in the best possible way, so long as you keep doing your part. Your best, always.

8. **Be creative, laugh and dance.** Being physically open and playful has a great bearing on our mental state. Open up some space for easy going and flowing energy. Don't take everything so seriously. Life is short, and every day has an opening for some fun.

"Sometimes we just need more zen and less chaos in our lives. Less mind and more stillness."- Hilde Larsen

Your physical body:

You might not think of your physical body, your health and your appearance as a de-cluttering project, but it very often is. Any physical symptom you might experience is a sign of clutter, of obstruction and stagnation. Health and disease cannot coexist, and neither can stiffness and flexibility. When you are overweight, you are constipated, and when you are in pain, you are the same. Any less than optimal health and vitality experience is a product of your level of acidosis through stagnant lymph and weaknesses in organs and glands. From genetic hand-me-downs, to self-inflicted intoxication, the body is simply a by-product of our lives in full.

We are damaging our cells by leaving out real foods, poisoning the body, but also by hindering elimination. Our great grandparents would have had a hard time recognizing 80% of what is today sold in a typical supermarket as food. The health of a cell, therefore the whole body, is mainly about elimination. The cells can't be healthy if they are bathing in waste and acids. The environment, the internal terrain, needs to be supportive of healthy cell formation and regeneration.

Look at it this way; if you leave a diaper on a child without changing it, a very sore little behind will manifest. The acids will burn. Waste is acids, and when left inside the body, it will burn our cells. The waste is created in many ways, and I will get back to that, but the simple explanation is this; The lymphatic system is our sewer system. It is where our metabolic waste and the waste in form of any bacteria, toxins, acids and damaged cells, goes to be eliminated. The kidneys are then filtering out this acidic waste, and this is where we've gotten into big trouble. By our consumption of a high protein diet, our poor genetic composition and stress, our kidneys are getting weaker by the generation. The stress that we put ourselves under has slammed our adrenals to the point of fatigue, and as they sit on top of the kidneys, controlling them, we are heading for a fall. Our precious adrenals, those little glands that have such an impact on our elimination of waste, are such an important key to our lost health. They fire up the kidneys, and by being impaired from stress, it is easy to see where things are heading. When the kidneys become weak, they stop filtering, and we are left holding on to that acidic waste. The acids are burning our cells, and we are living the result. Day by day, meal by meal, hectic day by stressful job, we are living and experiencing the result of our sick lifestyle. [8]

By detoxifying our body, we are inviting in true health and vitality. Shit out, vibrancy in, literally.

1. **Being the authority and taking charge is vital to any success**, and when it comes to our physical body it is very transparent. We are feeding ourselves, and we move by our own accord. If you let anyone else decide what you eat, or authorize your exercise plan, how much you move or not, stop it. Let them go right now. Tell them "bye, bye", and take the wheel. Being head chef can be scary and intimidating, but no-one but *you* will have to live the result of your body's health and strength. Believe me when I say this: Without your health, everything falls apart, and to not be the one

---

[8] Hilde Larsen – *Know the Truth and Get Healthy*

accountable is even more devastating. Take out the garbage, condition yourself to do what you need to do, and show up every single day. Like with everything else, practice is mandatory. Always doing better, working it, changing the input to change the output.

2. **Educate yourself like a boss,** and strive to make it your own business to have the knowledge that you need. You need to know a weed from a rose, good food from bad. You need to know how health is built, how toxicity is avoided, and you need to coach yourself to be your own health-keeper. De-clutter your informational sources. Be wise and critical about what you are reading and listening to health wise, and get focused on what rings true. Spend time listening to those that have lived what you want, and that have first-hand experience. Get a mentor, and learn how to be smart about your body and it's amazing healing abilities. Read more books on the topic, and watch less TV.

3. **De-clutter your body like your house**. Let uninvited guests go. Realize that parasites thrive in a less than optimal inner terrain. They might show up uninvited, but they only stay if they are fed and nourished. Like we would. Detoxify your whole body, through parasite cleansing and alkalization.

4. **Use it or lose it**. Movement and exercise will always keep things flowing in the right direction. If your health is optimal, you know that being active is a great part of that scenario. Sometimes building what we want is what will force out the old and unwanted. A reverse way of cleansing and de-cluttering any space. Once you start exercising and building muscle, as well as building health, extra weight and illness will fade. Look at your ability to move every day. Do you need to de-clutter your garage, let go of old equipment not used? Are you one of those who have exercise videos collecting dust somewhere, and old high school gym shorts hidden in the closet? Re-examine your whole wardrobe and equipment halt, and throw out everything you haven't used

for the last six months. Give it away or sell it. Clear the space for your new routines. Even though you have old stuff sitting that might be perfectly alright, you need the energy of new. If your current situation does not allow you to invest in your own home gym, or a fitness membership. Don't worry. All you need is a new pair of shoes. Put them on and get going. Moving is free. Get creative.

5. **Take a serious look at your refrigerator.** Open all your kitchen cabinets and start throwing out anything that is not serving you or your family as real food. Read my book *"Know the truth and Get Healthy"*, and other books like it, to get educated on what real food is. Bring into your house only that which you are going to eat. Shop smart, and make your food from scratch. When you de-clutter your mind from false beliefs on health and healing, you will automatically start to clean up your diet, your kitchen and shopping habits. The circle of growth. It is showing us how everything is connected. Change your thought, change your habits and change your life.

> **"Keep your temple neat and clean. Your**
> **health depends on it." – Hilde Larsen**

Your home:

Where we live, what we call home, is the most visual part of our environment. Even so, as with every other aspect of your life, physical or mental, you're able to hide and shuffle away some nasty clutter. The appearance might not be a true indicator of neatness. The living room and the front yard can absolutely look bright and shiny, while your closets and attic is very far from it. You might brush any imperfection under the carpet, so to speak. I am sure we have all done that, and some are worse than others.

We tend to wear masks to appear in a certain way. Another stressful part of our programming. Trying to live up to an unrealistic and completely false image. From not feeling good enough, and not feeling loved, we keep trying to appear how we perceive success looks like. Be it our body, our home or our behavior.

The home also reflects our status, and so long as we buy into the strive for that whole concept, we will keep being hungry for stuff and things. Not focusing on the real values, like being the best version of ourselves. There is nothing wrong with having a beautiful home, or owning great things that you love. The trouble becomes double when they own *you*.

No matter how large or small your space is, it needs your respect and your love. Everything is energy, and it will be inviting and structured, or it is congesting and stressful.

De-cluttering a home can be time consuming, but also freeing and necessary to get rid of the old energy and patterns. It will reflect your mental clarity, and inspire positive change in all aspects of your life. It will require action and systematic planning. You might feel challenged by having given up all the stuff that you felt you needed, but you will grow by doing so. The whole process of cleaning out what is no longer serving you, and having to organize and tidy up what you *will* keep, will lift your spirit. Take a load off!

1. **Start by taking a critical look at your home.** Are you a collector, or just a messy person in general? Are you holding on to everything that enters your home, for sentimental reasons, the fear of lack, or because you believe you will need it someday? Maybe you seem to make a mess no matter where you are, no matter how organized you were from the get go. This is about to change. The process of freeing yourself from unneeded items, together with honoring what you have, will feel like a gift once you experience the

difference. Everything you own is for you to treasure. If you don't, get rid of it. Believe it, many will keep things they don't even like, because they don't have the heart to get rid of it.

2. **Focus on one room at the time**. If you take on too much, it can easily get overwhelming. The whole project will suffer if you lose your focus.

3. **Love to make lists, and make many.** List-making is underrated. Trying to keep everything in the memory bank is exhausting. Putting everything onto paper makes it more real, more clear and less overwhelming. Make a list for each room. What does it contain, what do you want to keep and why? What is no longer working or being used, and what has very special value to you and why? Be strict with yourself. You most likely need to get rid of more than you would like to admit. What about the clothes that you are saving for when they come back in style? Really? Most likely you will never wear them again. You can go to someone else's garage sale for that bad-taste party. How about the linen and the old towels you are saving just in case? Be happy to throw them out.

4. **Sentimental value can be tricky.** Sometimes we value something just because it means something very special to us. That is fine. Most of the time this is not an issue, but when it is, let's deal with it. If you inherit an object, and you would love to keep it, let go of the item you are replacing. Don't just add it to your space. Find a suitable place for everything you value and treasure, but never let it sit in a closet as clutter. If it can't fit in a small treasure box, or is replacing another item, let it go. Discern between sentimental value and the it-is-too-valuable-to-get-rid-of items. It doesn't matter that it's pure gold, or silver. You can donate it, give it away or sell it. Many are sitting on items that would be better off sold, freeing the energy while the money could be spent on something more useful. If you don't need the

money, maybe someone else does. Sell the valuables and donate the money.

5. **If you collect, honor it.** Photos and collectables needs to be thoroughly organized and put into a system. Are you going to find the time to enjoy a box of old photos? Make picture books, scan them and get rid of the paper versions, and file everything in your office or library. Let your special collection get a special place. If you don't think it deserves it, get rid of it. Simple as that. Maybe you collected glasses, stamps or dolls, but no longer have the passion. Let it all go. Ask family members if they would like to adopt some of it, and if not, out the door it goes.

6. **Throw away anything that is broken or no longer in use.** There is no appreciation in letting anything sit around half-broken. When something is no longer functioning, fix it or replace it. Period. Stuff not in use, is obviously no longer needed. Be decisive about your storage space. If you have any at all, use it carefully, and keep it neat.

7. **Make a system.** Organize and systemize papers, bills, contracts, anything that is important for your life and work. We've all got bills to pay, and if you are a home owner, you'll have to keep everything from insurance papers to appliance receipts and warranties. Make folders and binders. Throw out anything that you no longer need. We tend to keep old receipts and bills, when we don't even know what they belong to. Travel light in any department, and strive to know everything you possess.

8. **Keep a neat closet.** Organize your clothes, shoes and jewelry. Make sure everything fits you and reflects your style and image. Get rid of anything that is not comfortable to wear. It is not reflecting your authentic self. It is ok to love your clothes, and it is ok to have them in abundance, *if* you have the space for them, and *if* you keep and store them the way the deserve to be kept. Still, do you need all those shoes? Are you collecting dresses or suits like they

would never go out of style? You might collect watches or cufflinks, and if you do, honor them by making the perfect space for them. A cluttered and disrespected closet reveals a lot about its owner. Are you being respectful towards your hard-earned money? Do you have what you believe you need, or trying to fill a void? Do you believe you deserve the best? Is having nice things a sin, an escape, a joy or a belief? Some become shopaholics, using the rush from hunting down more stuff to feel better about themselves. Make some notes while you do this process. I am confident you will learn something new about yourself.

9. **Everything should have its own space.** That way, keeping a clutter-free home is easy. Now, all you've got to do is to put everything you use back in its place. Throw out anything that you are replacing. Fix or throw away everything that breaks, file and organize new paperwork and the likes, and once a year, do a new cleansing, to make sure nothing has been able to sneak up on you. Get a container, or hold a garage sale. Ventilate a little.

10. **A new era of clutter is here.** Nowadays, not all our extra modern type of clutter is physical, some of it is on our electronic devices like our computer and our cellphone. Make a separate list for this, and get an external hard drive if you think you will need it. Move pictures and documents that you want to keep safe, into folders, and then transfer them to your external device. De-clutter your Facebook account, and other social media platforms that you are a part of. Slim down your friend lists, and focus on what matters. Spend less time in the virtual world, and more in the world of face-to-face-contact.

> As your home becomes clutter-free, the air becomes cleaner, and the energy becomes clearer. Take pride in keeping your home clean, fresh smelling and inviting. It is your extended body, where you spend a lot of your time.

You might have heard of Feng Shui. It is a practice based on the idea that our homes are a mirror of what is going on inside of us. It is based on the concept that everything in our environment has a life-force, and energy called chi. When the energy flows, we are believed to be supported in all our wishes for good health, harmonious relationships and general prosperity. When the energy flow is stagnant, from clutter and being unorganized, the chi will be out of balance and lead to concerns for our health, financial situation and relationships. The same goes for the placements of stairs, trees, mirrors and objects. This might be something to look into for more inspiration on keeping a happy and prosperous home that supports your life and harmony.[9]

> **"The clutter doesn't own you, you own it.**
> **You invited it, now dump it. Keep the pearls,**
> **let go of the garbage". - Hilde Larsen**

Your office:

If you have a home office, the challenge is keeping it professional and in its sacred space. Don't let it be a part of your living room or bedroom. Separating your time spent on your business from the time spent with your family can greatly benefit you, and your business. If you work at an external office, make sure that your space is defined, and that your desk is clean. Being organized makes you more efficient and more productive. No matter what line of

---

[9] http://fengshui.about.com/od/glossaryofterms/ss/What-is-Feng-Shui.htm

business you are in, if you have small work space, a shared space or a home office, you need to get organized and structured.

1. **Start by sorting everything that does not belong at work.** Personal stuff. Take home private belongings that only take up space and distract you from focusing on your daily tasks. We want to make the office a cozy and homey place, but in truth, it will clutter our clarity. No more overloading with family pictures, little nips and cute home-made figurines. No vacation magazines and cooking recipes. Let your space reflect your mission, and nothing else.

2. **Clear your desk.** The more papers and the likes that pile up on your desk, the harder it is to stay focused. Get rid of the post-it notes that tend to be sitting way past their lifetime. Use your computer, your phone or an old fashion almanac to stay on top of your tasks. There are many different online calendar programs to make it easy to connect all your devices to your schedule.

3. **Find a place for everything**. Put your paperwork in folders and binders. File everything in cabinets and drawers. Find little boxes for your binders and pens. Make sure you have all the tools that you need, and none that you don't. Clutter is interfering with the flow of productive energy. Be strict with yourself.

4. **Lose as much paper as you can**. Scan and store your documents electronically instead of keeping paper. Devise a plan for the location of electronic files. The last thing you want to happen is to lose an important document because it was misfiled. Also, do not forget to do backups, and do them regularly. Shred or toss the paper documents once a copy resides on your computer and the original is no longer needed.

5. **Organize your computer.** This is an ongoing project. Every now and then, make sure that you delete unnecessary e-mails, files and pictures. Transfer pictures to a separate

hard disc. A computer that is not running up to speed can be irritating and frustrating. Unsubscribe to anything that you don't need. Online or offline. Make sure that you have the most efficient online programs for your particular needs, and don't let social media or personal surfing interfere with your work.

6. **Love your space.** Cherish it, you are a team. Do what you love, by loving what you do. Condition yourself to honor your work space as an extension of you and your creative force. It is your chosen partner in growth and expansion. No reason is ever good enough to clutter your sacred space for inspired work and growth. Every hour spent doing what you have decided to spend hours and hours doing, is worth honoring.

Spend some time at the end of every work day to clear your desk, and to clear your mind. Make it clean and inviting for the next day. Nothing beats coming to work, feeling like someone kick-started your day by organizing everything. The practice of Feng Shui in your work place is believed to have a powerful transformational impact on your success as well.

Not everyone has an office, and not everyone needs one, or want one for that matter. Many do not even distinguish between work time and private time. They simply do not separate work and play. They are living their dream by doing what they love, in a more flowing way. Some are living a great combination of the above, or have many different offices. Some are happy never doing what we call work, which I define as being paid for a service or trait. They might choose to live of their own land and live their dream at the same time. So long as you are living what you desire, it is right for you. So long as you are growing and evolving, feeling inspired and enthusiastic, you are on the right path. The moment you are confined by your own mind, and lack of trust and confidence, you will find yourself in an undesired place. All the bullshit reasons that your false beliefs have served you, will keep playing in your subconscious mind until you replace them with your true power.

"What you do is not who you are, but everything you do reflects on who you think you are." - Hilde Larsen

Relationships:

No man is an island. We all seek companionship and support. We search for love and acceptance. Once we find it, we realize it was never about them, it was always about us. Us and the Creator. We are enough, and we are everything we have been looking for. Still, we are here together, being able to connect, play, strengthen each other and grow, together. Think about that. Strengthen and grow, support and empower. Our relationships with others are gifts of riches, and should be treated as such. The relationships you choose to have in your life, have the ability to lift you up or tear you down if you let them. De-cluttering your relationships is a beautiful opportunity to practice self-care and compassion. Strive to surround yourself with positive and uplifting people that you enjoy being around. Say goodbye to the toxic energy of others that like to throw you their negative comments. The kind that suck all your energy and rains on your parade.

1. **Love yourself first.** There is a difference between loving yourself and being full of yourself. This has nothing to do with narcissism, on the contrary, I am talking about being compassionate and true to yourself and your feelings. It is ok to be kind to yourself, it is necessary for your happiness. Self-love is self-care, and taking full responsibility for one's life. It is also about being authentic and true to one's own needs and desires. Once you know what is serving you, it will also serve those around you. From loving yourself first, you will be able to grow better and deeper connections with those that you love.

2. **Set some limits and boundaries.** Don't let anyone invade your space with anything that is not serving you. You make the rules. Be clear on what your perspective is. We sometimes keep old friends in our lives that do nothing but suck our energy. Constant complaining and negative inputs. No thank you. You are the sum of the 5 people that you surround yourself the most with. Think about that. Careful who you listen to, and careful who you engage your energy with. Once you are clear on what it is that you want from a relationship, let the rest go.

3. **Family can be tricky.** For some, it is the greatest blessing, filled with love and authentic support. For others, family life is a detrimental story of abuse and neglect. Besides the fact that we are all people, trying to do our very best with what we have been given, I believe that our true family is a consciously chosen group. Your tribe is that which you surround yourself with for comfort, community and companionship. It has nothing to do with blood or biology. If your birth family is not giving you what you need, find someone who will. Re-define what family means to you, to set yourself free. So many are carrying old hurts and trauma from early childhood and adult lives. It is time to let it go. Forgiveness and compassion, then realizing that you chose who you want in your life. It is ok to feel good, and to let go of what is not in that category. If there is someone you need to clear the air with, do so. If there is someone you need to forgive, then do. If there are situations that need to be discussed and agreed on, get to it. De-clutter everything that is polluting your inner terrain, the air that you breathe. Take from it only what will make you grow, be a better version of yourself, and give thanks for the experience.

4. **Friends come and go, although some friendships last a lifetime.** Our need for friends are different. Some surround themselves with a large number of friends, while others have a few carefully chosen ones. There is no right or wrong,

only choices. As we go through life we have different needs, although we tend to hang on to the same people. They might not be serving us or themselves, but for old time's sake we stay. De-cluttering friendships is about discerning between the relationships that make you feel good and those that don't. It is that simple. I am sure someone comes into mind when I mention; envy, stress, negativity, criticism, loudness, drama and being untrustworthy. Let them go. Clear the space for new friends to come in.

5. **Learn to say no.** You don't have to go to every party, and you don't have to attend every event. Popularity is a hunger by the ego, and will only keep you in the claw of untruth. Be yourself and do what is right for you. Let go of the needy and toxic people, but also of your own need to do and be everything, everywhere. Who are you trying to impress? All you should care about is living up to your own potential, by being the gift that you are. No one else can define you or make you something that you are not.

6. **Find a mentor, and stretch instead of crumble.** Walk towards the truth, which is always that of growth and expansion. Your friends and your family are supposed to be your support system, your cheerleaders and your knowledge bank. They are supposed to love you and be your greatest fans. Invite them in. Look to people who will act as motivators and inspiration. Look for support, and uplifting people. You deserve to be taken both seriously and to be treated with respect. Open yourself up to meeting new people, in new places.

7. **Be kind and compassionate.** No matter what the situation, you are always the one responsible for your own actions and responses. You can always be loving and compassionate towards another soul. You don't have to follow in anyone else's footsteps. It is your right and your possibility to choose how you interact with anyone. Be kind, and be true. Never hold a grudge, and set yourself free. Forgiveness and

gratitude goes together with almost anything. A smile is a gift, and a friendly comment can change a life.

"Friendship is always a sweet responsibility, never an opportunity." - Khalil Gibran

Money and assets will never outweigh love. All our relationships need to be the extent of our riches. Choose wisely and keep the gems close to your heart. Those that love you are your allies.

Make the list:

Putting your thoughts down on paper is always an eye opener. Make a separate list for each of the above topics, and you will easily see what needs cleaning the most. Write down how you feel about the topic, and why you need to de-clutter it. Write down what you need to get rid of, and start constructing a game plan. Make a timeline, and be accountable. Do you need any help? If so, start planning it. Call on friends and family if needed. Get support.

Make a list of physical things that needs to go, but also of obligations that you have. How about the magazine subscriptions and e-mail lists that you are on? What can you do about all the social events that you really don't want to attend? You will be amazed at how much is filling up your everyday life. Not only the physical time spent dealing with it all, but how it sucks your energy on an ongoing basis.

A great practice is to start throwing out three things every single day. It can be any small item like a pen that is no longer working, or single lost socks. You can find stuff lying around, or go search in an old draw. It will keep you in constant de-cluttering mode, and it will keep things from piling up. Clear your calendar every now and then, and put in "me" days. That way you will keep it from filling to the rind. Clear your desk every day, and make sure everything you own has its own space. Be diligent and persistant. It goes such a long way. All great achievements require that magical combo. Together with pure intent and the right mindset, you are set for success.

"When space is cleared and disturbing noises are stilled, expansion and growth has a place to thrive." - Hilde Larsen

This process will allow you to see just how much you've taken on, and the weight it puts on your shoulders. Cut back and cut it out. Keep what you truly love. This goes for both material things and obligations. This is about getting rid of, and letting go of the extra weight. Stress will diminish, happiness will increase, and your outlook on life in general will change. You are walking towards the authentic freedom with less bullshit and more *you*.

Have a garage sale, a giveaway party, and set yourself free. The less we carry, the lighter we feel. As we walk lighter, we open our hearts to the flow of true happiness. It is never attached to things or people. It is never valued or measured in material riches. Less if often more. Simplicity is the key. Honor and cherish what you have. Love everything, your friends, your work, your family and your space. Have compassion, and don't let anything own you or your energy. Detach and know that there is always enough, because *you* are enough.

The known anecdotal story of a time when Gandhi met the King of Great Britain in London comes to mind. Gandhi wore his simple wrap-around cloth. A journalist asked Gandhi; "Mr Gandhi, did you feel under-dressed when you met the King?" Gandhi then replied; "The King was wearing enough clothes for both of us!"

Gandhi was a true minimalist, a man who died a pauper but who affected the lives of many. He was born into a prosperous family, highly educated, and still he possessed very little. He gave away most of what he was given, freeing himself from the energy that possessions make. Gandhi wore simple clothes that conveyed his message. We can all take something from this story. We can simplify your life by dressing for comfort, not to impress. We can live with the simple focus of love and compassion. [10]

"Out of clutter find simplicity; from discord find harmony; in the middle of difficulty lies opportunity" – Albert Einstein

---

[10] Louis Fisher - *Gandhi, his life and message for the world*

Chapter 11

Authentic investments

"**L**ook at her! I mean, how is it that she looks so much better than the rest of us? Always so rested and cheerful. How does she do that? I bet she never has any fun at all. Always going to bed early. I have seen her jogging by on the weekends. I could never do that, but damn, she looks good. Would be nice though, to even want to get up on a Sunday to go jogging. All I want to do is to stay in bed – so low in energy, and so not happy with how I look and feel. Not that I look any worse than my friends, but seeing my old friend makes me think. I mean, she obviously has a better life for making different choices. I might have to change something. I should say hi next time I see her. I definitively want me some of what she is having. If I can only get my back to agree with me, and my leg. Not that I could jog anyway, not now. I wish it was me. Lucky girl, how does she do it?"*

Everything we do, think and feel is an investment in our future. Good or bad, profitable or not, it is an investment. The same way that we vote with every dollar spent, our future is determined by what we invest in today. What we bring to the table reflects our willingness and determination. What we put our focus to will grow, either it is positive or perceived as negative. When we think, we invest. As we raise the bar on how we want our lives to unfold, we are saying we are ready to invest more consciously. By being aware and mindful, by letting go of all the lies and false teachings and conditionings, we're able to invest with awareness and clarity. Powerful beyond belief. An unstoppable combination, and a sure bet for any good investor.

> **When the clutter is gone and the false beliefs are fewer, the opportunities reveal themselves more clearly.**

There is a return on investment (ROI) on everything. It refers to the ratio of what you've gained or lost.[11] We are talking about so much more than financial or material gain or loss, like spiritual, emotional, health, growth, happiness and fulfillment.

What to invest in:

It is a common belief that our education is an investment in our future, and it *is*, to some extent. On the other hand, Albert Einstein said; *"The only thing standing in the way of my learning is my education."* What did he mean by that? When we accept a school system, with an appointed curriculum, to be our main source of learning, we have restricted our horizon. By giving any institution, be it college, university or a highly respected private school, the power over our learning, we are giving away our own. By appointing an authority, we are again losing our own. We now protect and defend our new knowledge like gold. It is what we were told, it is truth and it is solid. Not only is our formal education something that we put all our faith into, it can directly keep us from learning valuable knowledge. How? By blocking our eagerness to explore, and by keeping us less open to new ideas. When you believe that you know the truth,

---

[11] http://www.investopedia.com/terms/r/returnoninvestment.asp

everything else is opposing it. This is in my belief what Einstein was referring to, our ability to be teachable.

To be able to make any clever and wise investment, we need to be educated. How would anyone know what to put their money, time and efforts into if they didn't know what was going to provide the highest returns? If you were going to invest everything you had into the stock market, what would you look for? Most likely you would look at a portfolio, your timeline and the desired outcome, and explore the market you were investing in. Do some research, and learn from those more educated than you. Learn from those who have walked before you, done their mistakes, learned from them. In every area of our lives, there are people to look towards for knowledge and guidance.

Being teachable is having the humility to say; I don't know everything, so I will open my ears and keep learning. I will keep exploring and I will implement everything that resonates with me. It is all an experiment. Tai Lopez, a very successful entrepreneur, told me that everything we do is an experiment. There is no right or wrong, only trying, learning and using it all as a stepping stone to do better. I like that. I used the same philosophy when I went from HELL to Inspired. When my life and body was dying, when I was so sick and tired of being sick and tired I would rather die than live my life the way it was, I failed constantly. Always doing my best, I still did a myriad of things that did not work for me at the time. I learned from them, kept going, and never stopped until I got it. I never stopped exploring and learning, and I never will. Life is a journey, not a destination. We are always moving forward, even when it doesn't seem like it. Reading is one thing, but until you're able to adopt what you learn and implement it though action, nothing happens. You are not making your investments grow.

We are all responsible for our own learning and growth. It doesn't matter what you think you know. It doesn't matter if you are a college graduate or if you dropped out of high school. You, alone, are in charge of your efforts and enthusiasm. Only you can read that book, study that topic, and find your own answers. Nothing will hold you back more than believing you know it all, or that there is no answer. Anything that stops you from growing is prohibiting your desired outcome. No one has all the answers, but everyone can teach you something.

Nothing is more lucrative than putting your efforts and energy into your own future. Read more, learn more. Simple math. The number of hours put into educational and inspirational work will raise the value of your investment. When you put your time and efforts into your business, structured and determined, it grows. Maybe not right away, but growth is inevitable. The same happens with every aspect of life. When you meditate every single day, you get better at it, and you can harvest the fruits in abundance as time goes by. As you practice, the benefits grow.

> **"By putting serious amount of time into reading and learning, you are not only getting closer to the truth, you are also claiming your authority." - Hilde**

Our relationships require work. Our family needs nourishment. The more we engage in our children's activities and lives, the closer we grow. A relationship, be it with our spouse, our siblings or our children, is built on respect, love, engagement and the willingness to give. What you send out always comes back to you, in tenfold. Both commitment and gratitude are associated with positive relationship outcomes. When there is an agreement of joint efforts, the bar is set even higher, and the outcome is thereafter.

When you interact with people in an authentic way, willing to learn, willing to invest your time and efforts, and willing to give of your own knowledge, the relationship stock will skyrocket. By embracing every opportunity to serve, you are inviting in people who will be willing to serve you back. Who you spend time with, is underrated. Not only for your overall feeling of happiness and appreciation, but also for your career and financial status. Your co-workers are your references and can offer you opportunities in the future. If you have a boss, he can obviously recommend you for your next job, and even your social media tribe and followers are potential business and investment partners. Show up in all your relationships. The currency that will give you the highest ROI is honesty, truthfulness, authenticity and teachability.

To invest in any relationship with the focus on the return is never a good idea. That is not what we are talking about. The return is what it is, and so long as the investments are of a pure heart and intent, the outcome will be a desirable one. Cause and effect. You reap what you sow. It is also about giving, and serving as a human being. No true return will come from stepping away from gratitude and truth. You need to value and respect, and most of all be true to yourself and any partner, college, friend or family. When you are blessed, pay it forward.

Investing in your health is the retirement plan that has one-hundred percent payback, a stock that seems to have an invaluable ROI. And it *is*. What you invest will not only secure the pay-off, it will unfold its value in all areas of your life. Once you realize that your wellbeing is your business, and that you have the power to influence and secure a thriving physical, mental and emotional health, you will most likely invest more. Once the false bullshit belief that chronic and degenerative so-called disease is a sign of bad luck, and bad genes are exposed and eliminated, you won't want to miss out on the opportunity of a lifetime. We are what we eat, think and feel. Simple, yet often both frustrating and overwhelming. Health is easy, change is hard.

Invest in the best real food that you can find. You and your family deserves it. To me, it is on the top of my priority list. Without health, we have nothing. I know, I have been there. Even though the truth has set us free, we need to continuously take action and set our knowledge into motion, into action. Small efforts, small results. Large efforts, large results. This might be the one part of your life that you have complete control over. No-one but you will ripe the benefits of a glowing energetic and healthy body. Not first hand. No partner or coworker is needed, no investor and no-one that needs follow up or convincing. It is all you. Use it and reap. Invest all that you have, and get ready for the return. What you will realize is that even though you are the one reaping the benefits, everything you do, feel, breathe and think, reflects onto others. How? As you change, your actions and attitude changes. You do better when you feel better. When we are more positive, we do more towards others, and as we feel grateful, we have a higher desire to serve and give.

> You always have something to invest, so the
> potential for abundance is always present.

How you spend your time in general will give you a pretty clear picture of what you are willing to invest, and in what. If you are not completely happy with what you see in your life, you are not authentically putting your "money" where it needs to go. Work on loving yourself fully. When we see ourselves as being worthy and lovable, we automatically do more of what is serving us and others. Every aspect of our lives are connected, although they all need separate work, investments. Be decisive how your time and attention is spent, as it is one of your greatest assets.

Spiritual growth might be our absolute mission in life. It might be what we are here to explore. No matter where you are today, I believe you will grow and awaken as you take back our power. Life is fluent, never stagnant. Energy can get obstructed, redirected and transformed, but everything is constantly moving. As life unfolds, we keep changing. By spending quality time invested in meditation and gratitude, the awareness and mindfulness will grow. You cannot *get* spiritual. We *are* spiritual beings. What we can do, is fine-tune the direct connection with source, the all, God if you will. Opening up, by training ourselves to be able to listen more clearly. By doing so we are reaching our own authenticity, the real us, the naked truth. I believe that any recipe for success will have a mixture of all the ingredients we have discussed. Investing in your health will require some alone time and some quiet time. Investing time and money into your business will require more of the same. You cannot stay on top of your game without a clear mind, and a vibrant energetic body. Emotional balance together with physical strength and endurance is needed no matter what you spend your life doing or creating.

What is your goal?

Be aware of the outcome that you are looking for. Ask yourself these simple questions:

Am I willing to invest what is needed to reach my goal?
What am I expecting in return?
What is my timeframe?
Do I trust my ability to succeed?
Am I doing this for the right reasons?
Do I have the support that I need?
Am I teachable?
Am I humble?
Am I worthy?

Let's say that you can have and do anything. That there are no restrictions to what you can achieve. It is all up to you and your willingness to invest. To spend the time, the determination and the efforts needed to reach the goal. How much would you put into it if you knew that the outcome would reflect directly on your invested energy? Most likely a shift in perception would appear rather quickly if we could see the direct correlation between every action that we take. To every action there is an equal reaction. Cause and effect. I call it freedom.

Once you know that you are ready to step up and be real, make a list. Spend time finding out what it is that you want. Do some soul searching. Take your time and analyze your life and your potentials. We all have potentials for growth. Follow the passion. Be still and listen. If you are going to invest in your future, you need to make a game plan, and it starts with knowing what your ultimate goal is. Think big. What is it that you really want to do? I am not talking about the general; *I want to be happy,* or; *I want a great relationship.* We all want that. You are an investor, and you need to know exactly what to invest *in*.

Let us say you are not happy in your current living situation. Your home doesn't have the space that you need, and it does not have a garden that you so highly desire. Why do you feel stuck? What are you willing to do to be able to move? Maybe you can't afford a new home, and you need more money to invest. Maybe your family has inherited the property and you feel you cannot sell it. Maybe you can't find anywhere else that close to work. Your spouse doesn't want to move. The market is down. There can be a myriad of reasons, and often there are more than one thing that keeps us from moving ahead. The goal is set. You want to move. Not a complicated goal in itself. So long as the desire is authentic and aligned with your true desire, start planning your strategies, your invested efforts. So long as finding a new home is at the top of your list, it reflects on every part of your life, and needs to be your number one priority. Move from goal to action, by investing your time, efforts and energy.

If your holdback is money and not finding a new home close enough to work, this would be a list of authentic investments to consider making:

- **Make more money:** Consider taking a second job to be able to make the money that you need. Ask for a raise or other opportunities at your current place of employment. If you are an entrepreneur, spend more effort on growing your business. Invest in seminars and knowledge. Find a partner, or expand your product line. Your time needs to be invested in learning how to bring in more money. Spend time on learning skills, doing research and expanding your horizon.

- **Re-define "close to work":** Sometimes we just need to re-set our mindset. Maybe your definition of being close to work has got to change. Look at how commuting to a community further from your current job could work out. You might find that you are willing to move further away from where you are to find the new home. Realize that your workplace could change at any time. Maybe a new job opening or a home office will be a reality in near future. Another goal to invest in.

- **Create positive energy around finding the perfect home:** Make a wish board by putting up pictures of the perfect house. Feel it, be excited about and *know* it will manifest. Keep looking at prospects that you like, every day. Speak positively about it to yourself and others. You are creating it, by doing what you need to make it happen.

- **Be grateful for what you already have:** Gratitude is the language of the universe. It is love in expression. What we send out always comes back to us, and this investment is a must. Say thank you for everything about your current place that you *do* love. You will attract *more* of it. Your home is not the reason you want to move, so thank it for having served you well.

- **Spend time every day searching:** Commit to a certain amount of time every day, working for your goal to manifest. Drive around and get to know new neighborhoods, look for new jobs, talk to real estate agents. Make a strategic plan. What to do, and when. Stay accountable and focused.

"The only thing stopping you from achieving your goals are your false bullshit beliefs that you cannot." - Hilde

You can categorize your whole life and make an achievement list. Small or big, it doesn't matter. It is your life and your list. This is different than a bucket list, where you map out what you want to experience in this lifetime. This is a list of what you want to live right now, what you realize needs your energy to move forward. This is a list of your upcoming most important investments. Prioritize by number.

It can look something like this:

1. Health issues and goals.
2. My living situation.
3. Manifest more alone time.
4. Relationships that I need to shift.
5. Trips to plan and manifest.
6. Business and workplace growth.
7. People I want to meet.

Lower the stakes, find a mentor:

I spent years reading about health, healing, self-empowerment, truth, false beliefs, spirituality, herbs, nature, and anything that would keep me on track. I would have been lost if it weren't for the different amazing people that offered me their knowledge and wisdom. I was able to learn from their experience, and also to know and feel what was right for *me*. Finding a mentor, no matter what you want to achieve, is valuable beyond imagination. Look towards those that have already done what you want to do. They are ahead of you, and can give you valuable information on how you can reach your goal faster, by sharing their experience. You will also get the opportunity to learn about humility and paying it forward. To give back directly to you mentor, and to someone who needs what you already know.

By being authentic and willing, you are teachable. By being teachable you show humility, and by being humble you become worthy.

Mentors are everywhere. A teacher, a friend, a boss, a celebrity, it does not matter. A mentor is defined as a coach, tutor, facilitator, guide, counselor and trusted advisor. It is someone willing to spend his or her time and experience to guide another person through development and growth. Their degree and status means nothing. What they have achieved, that you are looking to achieve, is what matters.

Investing in the truth:

Hold your dreams and visions alive, and invest what you can to see them flourish. Willingly share what you learn along the way. I am a firm believer that what we send out comes back to us. Investing in the truth is being humble and grateful. Your true essence is love, and anything from it is your truth. By listening to your inner voice spoken through your enthusiasm and passions, you are led to the absolute truth. Your passion is your compass. Walk towards what makes your heart sing, and what makes you enthusiastic about life. It is the clue you are looking for. Bullshit will no longer resonate. Crap is out. Humbleness and willingness to learn and grow, is in.

Not every lead or idea is worth spending a lot of time on, and not every prospect is worth following through. You need to know when to hold them, and know when to fold them. Let go when the time is right, and listen to your inner guidance. Sometimes what we think will be a great way to invest our time, efforts and money, turns out not to be. It becomes an experience, an opportunity to grow. Know when it's time to change something, and head in a slightly different direction.

By being honest, not subjecting ourselves to bullying and falsehood, the truth will always shine through. So long as the focus is kept on the goal, and not on the number of reasons why it "cannot" happen, we will know what rings true and what doesn't. Being inspired is the currency you are looking for. Turn off the TV, take a walk on the wild side, barefoot, outside. Soak in your own amazing being, and know the truth when you feel it. Nothing is more freeing than knowing your investments are true, pure, kind and empowering. Every conscious breath, positive thought, smile and uplifting words will come back to you with interest. You have a purpose, and it is grand. You have a calling, a life of abundance and freedom. Claim it by investing in your true self!

Every experience has real value, although not always obvious at the time.

Chapter 12

Finding your purpose

" I can't believe it. I completely lost track of time. I have so much I should have done. What happened? Once I start painting, it's like everything else disappears. Well, I don't care, not now. My heart sings. I feel happy. I feel at home. I can't wait to have my own exhibition. One day, soon. I can't even imagine the feeling when someone feels happy or inspired by looking at one of my paintings. Now that would be magical. Just to think that by painting, I could uplift someone who needed it. Right now, all I want to do is to capture this. I wish I could spend all my time here. Like this. Me, my canvas, my paint, and unlimited time. Not sure if anybody would understand how it feels. It is like my whole world is complete when I am in my zone. I love it. I feel free and complete. This is the reason I am here on this Earth, to paint. That's it. One day."

We all have a purpose, either we believe it or not. If you have a corporate job that you are okay with, but it was never your dream, and your life feels dull and mediocre, you are not fulfilling your purpose. To find it you've got to let go of what you already believe, and why you are not living it. I remember an old story told to me, about Bruce Lee, where he was asked what he knew about martial arts. He held up two cups, both filled with water. He said; "The first cup represents what *you* know about martial arts, and the second cup represents what *I* know about martial arts." Then he said; "If you want to fill your cup with *my* knowledge, you have to empty your cup of *your* knowledge." This is such an amazing insight that takes us back to the basics of this book. No more bullshit. Not only untrue perceptions and programming needs to go, but everything we ever believed. In order to fill our cup with the valuable lessons of life, and to find our true purpose, we need to empty our cup of what we already believe we know.

"Before I can tell my life what I want to do with it, I need to listen to my life to tell me who I am," - Parker J. Palmer

Mark Manson talks about the *do something* principle[12], leading to the understanding that passion comes from action. "When you want something to change, change something", is a commonly known motivational phrase. I use it all the time, it makes sense. Every change requires action, in one form or another. But, don't we need inspiration, motivation and passion to take action? Isn't there a need for inner motivation? If you need inspiration to take action and inspiration *comes* from action, then where do you start? It sounds like a catch 22, and it *is*. This is when you *do* something. By moving the energy, you move towards an outcome. By simply doing, you are creating a flow of new opportunities and understandings about yourself and your path. Finding your purpose is a search that requires you to be active and awake, honest and true. You cannot think your way to your purpose, you've got to act your way to it.

---

[12] https://markmanson.net/do-something

> Your purpose is what makes you tick. It is what triggers your bliss, your enthusiasm and your love for life. When you find it, you feel at home. We all have one, but it might not be what you expect. It can be very different from what you have been living your whole life. Believe me, I know.

"Here is the test to find whether your mission on earth is finished. If you're alive, it isn't." - Richard Bach

If you are not living a life filled with passion and direction, enthusiasm and meaning, you are not living your purpose. If you are looking forward to vacations months ahead, believing that work is something you do for money only, you are way off target. When the weekends are looking like candy, while week days are simply dragging you along, you are not living it. You might like what you do, but there is no real passion and purpose. Do we all have to be so passionate you might ask? The short answer is yes. It is natural to be healthy, enthusiastic, happy, passionate and loving life. Most people are not, but that does not mean it is not our true mission. What makes us feel purposeful and full of life, is very different, yet the feeling is the same. It does not matter what it is, but there is something that will spark your inner fuse, and light that fire. If you never felt what I am describing, keep working towards it, as it is there. Some of us go through half our lives sleeping, not having a clue that there is a way to live that fuels you every single day. Many will live their whole lives without ever even thinking there is such a thing as a life purpose. The subconscious false beliefs, the clutter, drama and stress, is a complete deal breaker. When we're fear driven, ego driven and power driven, no purpose will show itself. It will *try* to, but our vision is too blurred to notice.

Purpose gives a sense off meaning, a sense of understanding a small part of what this magnificent creation is all about. When there is meaning, there is less confusion, frustration, fear and overall negativity. When we feel meaningful, we feel safer and more content. A hole has been filled and a thirst has been quenched. From being prisoners by our subconscious beliefs, our constant thinking, ego based, disconnected lives, we hunger for that deep meaning of life. The constant search of reason and fulfillment. The hunger is valid, as the lies and deceptions we have lived through have starved our soul from being able to fully express itself. Any lack of expression will harvest a sense of constipation, imprisonment and unhappiness. We need to fully live our truth to be able to embrace all of life. It is not supposed to be complicated at all, quite the opposite. It is supposed to be life, living, creating and experiencing. Nothing we do, say, think or believe can mess up anything, really, but we can absolutely step up our game by owning our true purpose.

Follow the voice of your inner child:

Children are honest about their interests and passions. Until we hold them back by trying to make them all fit into the same box, they are proud of their every endeavor. Until we pour our insecurities and false beliefs over them, they express their true purpose. Willingly and freely they show us what makes them shine and blossom, when we let them. So long as they feel safe, they will unfold their soul's mission. Remember when you were a small child. What did you like to do? What made you happy, and what did you want to do when you grew up? Children will often follow in the footsteps of a parent, uncle or family member when they show honest interest in their profession. The learning has begun. They are open and teachable. Not that a child cannot have the same passion as a parent, but often the admiration of the adult as a role model will play a large role in the motivation.

Look back and observe how your life unfolded and changed. Did your interests shift suddenly? Did someone tell you something about what you liked to do that made you stop? Some may have loved to dance, but stopped because someone told them they were too fat. Maybe you wanted to sing, until your sister and her friends laughed at you. Most of those who have followed their dream, their passion and their longings, have done so despite what others have said, not because of.

Your purpose can be multiple:

There is not a sign or a tablet in the heavens with your name on it, that has one single purpose named "jackpot." You are not singled out for one particular task and nothing else. I believe we have many potentials, and for some even multiple purposes at the same time. The search should never be for any one single purpose, but rather for *it*, whatever it is. If you are good at several things, you are blessed, if you love to multitask and have a passion for a series of activities, you are blessed also. Never try to single out, and thereby discern anything that brings you joy and enthusiasm, and never override the language of the soul.

Be open to everything that gives you joy and inspiration. Embrace all of it. If you love to sing, sing more and louder, and if you love to ride your bike, ride more and longer. The rest will unfold as you follow the lead. You will notice that you are not the only one effected by your enthusiasm. When we touch upon others, and lift them in any way, we are on the path of truth. Confirmed by our surroundings.

> "As we cleanse our entire being from useless and disempowering nonsense, it becomes easier to hear what we have to say." – Hilde Larsen

Lead from the heart:

Listen carefully to your life. It speaks to you through your emotions, your thoughts and your feelings. We are never clueless, always guided by our inner compass. By staying in our brain, by thinking and analyzing with our mind, it gets harder to hear the answer. It comes from the heart. Although we need our brain to write down our lists, to remember and to resonate, the less we think, the closer we get to the truth. Your brain will try to play some tricks on you, to discourage you. The subconscious might have some unfinished business, and remember some untrue beliefs. It is not trustworthy like the heart. Meditate every day to open your heart space and at the same time quiet the mind. Listening to the heart is the same as listening to passion

Our heart will lead us to guiding and helping others, and I believe this is a part of any true purpose. People that have found their place in this world are often known as givers. They happily share what they know because they also know that assisting a fellow human is a part of the whole mission. Together we grow, and there is enough to go around. By reaching out to someone you are showing gratefulness and appreciation. That itself, will create more to be grateful for. We are not separated, only detached. By paying it forward you are stepping into the energy of pure intent, and nothing will be more fulfilling. Giving really is receiving.

Stepping outside the drama:

Be the observer. Step out of your own head, your everyday life, and take a critical look at what is going on. How are you spending your time? What pisses you off, and why. Who pushes your buttons, and why are you involved in any drama? Try to see a larger picture, patterns and beliefs. Sometimes it can be a good thing to simply hit pause and step outside for a minute. Sit down, detach yourself and observe. Do it every day. Practice not getting emotionally involved in your day. Not alone, not around people. Life is not happening *to you*. You are creating it.

Give yourself the permission to search behind the scenes. Your purpose might not be far from where you are. Sometimes all that is needed is some de-cluttering and some reorganizing, and everything falls into place. Perhaps you are doing what you really love, but with the wrong people, or you need to redefine some or your boundaries. You might believe that what you already know to be your path is not sustainable. That it's not something you can support yourself and your family doing. If that is the case, work on releasing those false beliefs, and look for those who have already done it. If you can't find anyone, search for those who have done something similar, and be a pioneer. It takes dedication and work, so give yourself time to work yourself into the new and fulfilling path. If it were easy, everybody would do it. Easy is overrated, and sometimes confused with effortlessness. No real effort is needed when you are in the flow of your heart and soul, but it might not be defined as easy.

Once you follow your truth, life becomes effortless.

Ask and it is given:

Find your journal, and claim it for your life purpose. The most important book *in* your life, and *about* your life. Write down these headlines and do some freestyle writing. Don't use your brain too much, but let the pen do the work. Write from your heart. There is no right or wrong. Nothing has to be politically correct or parent or spouse approved. Everything is allowed, sensor free. Step out of your thinking and let it flow freely and instantly. For each topic, write the first three sentences that comes to you. Repeat every day for one whole week. Let your inner knowing come forth, as you force the subconscious mind to reveal the hidden truth. Let your heart and soul connect with your true self.

- **What are you good at?** We are all good at something. You don't have to see yourself as a master or an expert, yet, but find something that you know within your heart that you are good at.

- **Do you have a hobby?** If you don't have one now, you might have had one as a child, or a young adult. Maybe you have had an interest that never amounted to any real hobby, but you still have a secret passion for the topic. Maybe even more than one.
- **What makes time stand still?** Have you experienced losing yourself in something to the point where time vanished and nothing else mattered? When we are in our zone, we block out everything else, due to a deep focus and engagement.
- **How can you serve?** How would you be able to help others? What do you have to offer that would benefit someone in need? Is there anything the world needs right now that you believe is important and interesting?
- **If you had all the money in the world, what would you do**? If money was not an issue, what would you spend your time doing?
- **What would you do the last year of your life?** This is a typical question, and will of course reflect on the need to spend time with our loved ones, but some interesting things might come forth from asking yourself this.
- **What did you dream about doing as a child?** Write down anything that comes to mind. Small, big, no limits.

Listen to your life, it is bigger than yourself. Listen to your dissatisfaction, and what others tell you about you. Your life has purpose for others, why is that? Get to know yourself, and listen closely.

Our purpose is to find our purpose, to
live it and to share it with others.

Let it flow:

Here is another exercise for you to have fun with. Let your purpose come forth. Get your journal and set the alarm on 3 minutes. That is all you need. Sit comfortably and write nonstop. No thinking allowed. This is called intuitive writing. Write down everything you would do if you could start all over. If you got a whole new lease on life, from early childhood, what would it look like. What would you do, where would you be, and who would you be with. There are no limits here. Not on money, time, age, gender or family. Use your imagination freely. Nothing is too small and nothing is too extravagant or large. This is your dream world. Focus on you, on what you would do, what you would spend your time doing. Do this for ten executive days, then read and see what you find. Maybe every day you write something similar, and maybe there are some things that stay the same. Look for the common thread, you will find your clue.

I will not "work" another day in my life:

When I found my mission, my purpose, my whole life changed. I pursued a trait that reflected what I was good at, or one of the things I was good at. At least that is what I was told growing up. Without having one true passion, I believed that since I had the skill, it would have to be my path. My heart was never consulted. I had several interests and paths I could have chosen. I was a decent piano player, loved everything about music, and danced for years. I was also a gymnast, but ended up as an Interior architect with great success. Success that contributed to stress and ill health. I worked hard, not passionately. I stepped up to my responsibilities, from being determined, well taught and proud, not because of my inner drive. I used my stubbornness, skills and ability to persevere to succeed as we often see it. I was not a complete stranger to my passions, I just never followed them from my heart. I never prioritized my hearts callings, they were always cluttered by my life's teachings. When my life was turned upside down by illness and pain, it was very clear that what I was doing was not supporting my soul purpose. My whole life was not supporting my true mission.

From true purpose comes balance, not stress and disease. No sickness can live in an alkaline passionate and enthusiastic environment. Self-love and compassion will not allow it. My whole life fell apart, and from the ashes I found my true path, and all the blessings that come with it. I was brutally awakened, through losing everything that I knew as my current life. My business and career, my health, my ability to move, my hobbies and my friends. I went through HELL to Inspired, and am now doing what I love, feeling more enthusiastic about life than ever before, and the last thing on my mind is vacation. My job is my passion and my mission. It is my true calling. It fuels me and it inspires me. Sure, there are days that take a lot of effort and determination, and yes - every single day keeps me learning and growing. What it does not do is drain my energy. I am true to myself, and therefore I take care of myself. I do what I love, therefore I love what I do. I follow my heart, as I know what following the mind will do. It is a trap. Don't fall for it.

Chapter 13

Your power and beyond

" The craziest thing just happened to me. I was meeting my mother at this restaurant downtown for and early lunch, and I looked at my watch. It was 11:11. It is not the first time I have seen this, but still. I had just parked my car on the outside, in the shade of some large birch trees, when this woman comes up to me. Out of absolutely nowhere, she is standing there, smiling: "You must be Eva", she said. So crazy! I just moved back to town a few weeks ago! How would she know that I was even here? Ok, so anyways, she then asks me if I know of this large artist event coming up, I just nodded my head. I have been planning to attend the whole week, just to get some inspiration from all the great artists that are featured. In fact, I was thinking about it yesterday. I have been visualizing myself having an exhibition at the event myself in the future. This is part of my reason to move back here, to be closer to the action. She hands me a business card, and says that she got a tip from someone that I would be here, and that she had been looking at some of my work. They had an opening for a few pieces, and she wanted me to meet her to discuss the details.

I am completely freaked out! This is even better than I imagined. I have really been focusing on something like this manifesting, but get out of here. Approaching me on the street? Really?"

Have you noticed that for some, everything seems more easy and effortless? It is like everything flows towards them, and all they have to do is accept the invitations and follow that flow. It seems like everything is already lined up. Like pearls on a string. One event or little happening after the other, fitted perfectly together. From the outside, it might look almost too easy. These people paddle downstream, they don't hustle with the currants, and they let life work *for* them. As if they ordered what they wanted, and now they can follow the downstream towards it. Most of us will initially try to conquer the waves, not seeing that we can be on our own team. Not knowing there *is* a team.

The underlying force of manifestation cannot be seen by the naked eye. For the unaware, being in the flow, in the zone where things line up and manifest, can come across as easy. Even though simplicity is a part of the game, dedication and hard work is required. Do not for one minute believe that living your dream and leaving your shit behind doesn't require persistence, learnability, humility and will.

Our personal perception that certain undertakings and events are no fun, hard, beneath us even, and unbearable, is only the well-known self-sabotage at its best. Even when we know what we want, and what needs to be done, old tricks might re-visit. Let them be short lived. Send them on their way. When you are ready to live a free and purposeful life, roll up your sleeves and get ready to work for it all. The old belief that doing what needs to be done is hard or unwanted is so yesterday. Outdated and never true. Who defined easy, and who decided that focus and dedication was anything but amazingly rewarding and satisfying?

When you have a dream and a passion towards being a farmer, you know that you've got to prepare the soil, plant the seed, nurture it, water it, harvest, distribute, sell and then collect your money. This doesn't mean that you have to do everything on your own, but it means it all has to take place as a part of the action-plan. To be a great farmer, you need to learn from the best, experiment and fail. You need passion for the trait, and the knowledge that is required. It all takes an immense amount time and dedication. You cannot skip one of the steps if you want a beautiful and abundant return on your investment. What you will harvest reflects on your input, your work and your dedication. No matter what you direct your attention towards, the same scenario applies. It all started with a dream, with a thought. First you have to think it, dream it, to ever be able to live and accomplish it though flow and action. Your dream could stay just that, a dream. Until you put some dedication into the project in form of research, learning, support and hard labor, it will not get past the thinking stage. Nothing ever will.

You might want to be a successful designer, which might seem like it has nothing in common with farming. It does. The process is the same. First you have the dream, the idea, the thought, and the willingness to pursue. Then comes the process of preparing yourself through education and studying, conditioning your mind and your creative abilities. The seed is planted by, and nurtured through, your growth and constant sketches, sowing and mending.

You've got to work the field, show up, nurture and engage. Every day you need to water your passion. A crazy amount of time will go into experimenting and failing, late nights working on your designs. Then you need to get it out there, to sell your line and your brand. All with the help of a team. A process and an adventure that will fall together looking easy for those that don't see the process as real work. There is a difference between striving and working. There is also a difference between stressing and being productive. When you find your passion and your purpose, you can find yourself working towards your goal 24/7, and never feeling stressed out. You are in your zone, where nothing seems like hard work. Even the things that you might not love doing right now, you will get done. You are not a victim. You are the creative force. When we follow our truth, aligned with the solution, and are willing to walk towards our vision, it will feel effortless most of the time. And when it doesn't, we keep going anyway.

Everything starts with a thought, and there is a great deal of work and effort put into a synchronized and abundant life.

Nothing can stand in the way of something better than our ego. Nothing can stop the hard work of someone with a true vision. The acknowledgement and the pursuit of any dream, will be rewarded with a lineup of possibilities. The potential is limitless for those who are willing to step up and show up. When you trust your own calling, you are building your fearless strength, and growing your confidence muscles. We always manifest what we believe and hold as true. Not by simply wanting it, or needing it, or even thinking it. That is merely the realization that you have the potential. *You* are the one that can change and steer the direction of the outcome, always *you*. No one else can manifest your reality. The law of manifestation seems to be unprecedented.

> There is no power in calling the bullshit, if you
> are not going to do anything about it.

The law of manifestation:

The power we all hold is beyond comprehension. We are powerful beyond our belief. No science can explain how the universe works, or how we are all creators. We are told we are powerless, that everything happens *to* us, and that we are under the spell of nature, a system, our past and our traumas. We are made believe that we are nothing more than random, half-dumb followers that need to be monitored, controlled and kept an eye on. Criminal by nature, self-destructive, and in need of drugs and restraint. Not much of a starting point for a free and empowering life. This is the reason why the most successful people in this world are free thinkers and bold enthusiast. No matter their success, be it as entrepreneurs, or as globetrotters, living in mansions or in a tree hut. They are all willing to let go of the bullshit, and take back their power. It is what *you* perceive as success that matters, what *you* are here to experience. There is no right or wrong in creation, there only *is*. Doing and living what you are beckoned to do, from the heart, has nothing to do with money, fame, status or the intellect - it has to do with the manifestation of a dream and a calling.

The thought that has all the potential, is often misinterpreted as the end to all manifestation. "Ask and it is given", is not the same as "think and it is given". Even though the thought has a place in planning and problem solving, no brainstorming is going to give you money in the bank, feed you, or put a roof over your head. No thought is going to send you to China or heal your body. The thought by itself is a dormant energy, and it needs to be charged and put into motion to have any significant impact. A thought can even be an obstruction, and a cluttering factor for your project. It can get in the way, get entangled in the need to understand. Suddenly we are overthinking, getting in our own way. The conscious "genius" might not have all the answers, and that itself creates limitations.

Look at it this way: You really want to live in the tropics, and you have no idea how that would ever be possible. What you know, think, see, have been taught, believe and have lived, forms your ability to find a solution. By thinking you would be able to know how it would play out and manifest, is like putting yourself in the position of God. *You* only see a fraction of the real possibilities and opportunities that are available to you. *You* can only see what is already in your bubble of understanding. The possibilities are infinite. The potential is limitless. Thinking is a powerful tool, but it is not enough. The power you hold is way beyond your mind.

By switching your mindset, you are setting the stage for your day and your future. You might have heard that the mindset is everything, and it is, yet it isn't. Without it you are not heading anywhere, and if it`s *all* that you have, you aren't either. Use your mind to map out your strategies, and think when needed, but let it take the back seat to your feelings when you want to expand your horizon. We connect to all our potential paths through our true passion. The brain is needed to open the menu, our intuition and inner knowledge will make the choice, and our energetic feelings and emotions will place the order. It's why passion is so important. Negative or positive, our power is not only present when we decide we would like to turn it on. It is ever present and always at play. When you *think* about how things are not going your way, paired with a heavy dosage of good old negative emotions and frustration, guess what? You are ordering from the menu. We never seem to stop ordering. Our lives are paved one thought, one feeling, and one motion at a time.

Make the list:

Spend time on the drawing table, and make sure you have made that list of goals and passions. Writing anything out with a pen on paper is very powerful. It is action itself, and it makes you feel the words as you write them. Make this list your menu, and get ready to place your order. Expand the power of the list by adding pictures to it, like a scrap book. Get some old fashion-magazines and cut and paste. Make it beautiful and colorful. By not only imagining your life the way you want it, but seeing it with your own eyes, you are creating an unstoppable energy. The action you add from cutting and pasting will act like an amplifier. It will also make you more aware of what you are asking for. This way you can really shop for your wishes. Aim high, meaning let nothing stand in the way of your goal-setting and life creations. If any tiny little thought of insecurity or bullshit tries to enter your mind, call it. Truth and empowering thoughts allowed only. This is private property.

Can you imagine what would happen if we all knew how powerful we really were? If every living soul took back their power and lived their own truth? If we awakened to our original state of self-love, we could never hurt ourselves. How could you hurt someone you love?

The feeling and pure intent connects with the God force, and will open the doors to the flow of solutions. It will send you on a path of small, often subtle signs and opportunistic choices. If you don't follow up on them, or take the bait, new ones will come your way, until you react. If you are not aware of this, you might get frustrated. "Nothing is happening. I have been thinking the right thoughts, really feeling into it, and nothing". Leading us to the powerful tool of actually *doing* something. To take an active part in creating your reality, the most powerful part is action. The power of motion. Nothing moves until you move. You can be shown the way, but *you*'ll have to walk it. You'll have to be mindful and ready to act on the opportunities that is shown to you. Thoughts and feelings are great at creating options and directions, open doors and willingness to achieve.

I love this little story from the movie Pursuit of Happiness:

"Hey dad, you want to hear something funny? There was a man who was about to drown. A boat came, and the captain said "Do you need help?" The man said "God will save me". Then another boat came which also tried to help him, but again the man said "God will save me". The man drowned and went to Heaven. Then the man told God, "God, why didn't you save me?" God said "I sent you two boats, you dummy!"

It reminds us that even though the guidance is there, we still have the free will to act or not. It is still up to us, not only to get off our butt and actually react to our own life, but also to be aware of what is being presented and created for us. We *are* the only one we have been waiting for, everything else has always been there, readily waiting for our move. We have always been there, although disconnected, cluttered, scared shitless and unable to step into our grace. The law of attraction is the law of your own power. Cause and effect. What we send out, comes back to us. What we live reflects how we are conditioned and programed by our thoughts, our genes, our upbringing and our experiences.

Think it, feel it, do it -a simple truth of the universe.

When you know what you want, it is time to call yourself into action. Even when you are *not* one-hundred percent sure what you want, call yourself to action. By taking the first step, you are setting into motion a whole myriad of powerful energies. You don't have to know every step, you'll only have to get started. You'll only have to know in your heart that you are powerful enough to create anything, and go with the flow. Life is not supposed to be serious or fearful. Remember, there is no right or wrong. It is what it is. Your perception is the filter on reality. If you don't like what you see, change your scrap book, and order something else. So long as humans keep bullying each other and keeping a lid on the truth, there will be challenges and obstacles. If we are willing to stay imprisoned by our own mind and the false beliefs we are being fed, we will continue to hurt ourselves. Once we break free, the rollercoaster we are on, is nothing more than life itself.

**When you know what you want, from truth and passion,
the whole Universe lines up to accommodate you.**

Not listening to any more untrue propaganda, any false beliefs from your subconscious programs and follow-up conditioning, is by itself connecting you to your truth. It is letting you live it if you want it. You have been shown the way to a powerful life, if you desire to grab it. Your gift has been given to you, and all you've got to do is open it. It takes courage, oh yes. It takes some boldness and fearlessness, absolutely. It is a lot of hard work, you bet. You'll have to turn off the bullshit channel all together, so you better believe it. The truth is out, and by allowing it in, you signed up for actually living it. It can be quite a challenge, or it can be a simple freedom, depending on your goal, your learnability and your willingness to change.

For some, seeing the truth is very easy, yet living it seems unmanageable. Others would change anything, if they only knew what. Showing up authentically in your life, and walking towards what your heart is showing you, might be very far from what you have imagined it would be like. All we can do is to visualize and let go. Imagine, feel it, be truthful and open to it, and let it go. When you ask for what you want, you *will* get it. How, when, and in which outfit it will appear, you'll have to wait and see. Life will show you. There will be signs for you everywhere. There is a whole chapter on the topic of following your signs coming up. You are not alone, and your fearlessness will awaken you to seeing just how protected you are.

> "I declare to live authentically, true to myself,
> in gratefulness, in service, with my tribe,
> to love myself, to express my truth,
> and to allow myself anything that serves me.
> I declare to honor my life and nature,
> and to walk my talk." - Hilde Larsen

PART THREE

STEPPING INTO
THE GRACE

Chapter 14

Guidance and signs

" *Ever since I started taking those art classes that my friend came across, these amazing little things have happened. I am not sure who to talk to about this, or if I even want to. My journal gets it, I get it. Those dragonflies are everywhere! Like when I first noticed several of them following me to my first class. I've never noticed them around here before, but when my sister brought over a sketching pad with a dragonfly on it later that day, I noticed. It was almost like it was talking to me. Like with what is happening to the radio. Same thing in a way. How is it that every time I turn it on with a question or a pondering in my head, the perfect song comes on. Funny, I know, but it makes me wonder. I am definitively paying more attention to what is going on around me. I am not sleeping through this show. It feels like I am living in a movie that has everything perfectly orchestrated.*

Since I started meditating, my dreams are also changing big time. Like they are turning into some sort of messages. How can that be? I mean, am I not just dreaming random stories?"

Life is always unfolding before our very eyes, and by being more mindful throughout our day, we become aware of the little things that surround us. Look for the subtle signs and messages. Be it a song playing on the radio, a bird or a dragonfly that shows up just as you hold that special thought. Start to notice. The clock, a street sign, or even a number plate could show you some significant numbers and messages. If you are open to the messages, they are everywhere. The more we stay out of our mind, the more open we are to seeing how supported we are. If you are not yet a believer, step into the position of the observer, and be aware of your day. Mind your dreams and your thoughts carefully. There is gold, diamonds and invaluable information there for you. Once the cluttered mind, house, office and life clears its space, the directional and empowering signs will show up in your life. Like small little whispers and confirmations, they might inspire you. When I walked my way back from my Hell, the connection to the direct guiding and my faith in something grander than I could even imagine, kept me on a steady course. I felt safe, protected and encouraged by life:

"There is a calmness that enters my being when I am outside. I have read about grounding, and I know the healing abilities of being grounded, but this was something more. This was me finding a new way to communicate with the divine. I was spoken to, and I was ready to listen. I think it started with the feathers. I call them my feathers. I cannot recall exactly when it first happened, but that's not important. I started to notice them on my daily walks. These were short 10 minute walks, only a few steps from my house, but I needed to get dressed, and I needed to get downstairs. The stairs were a struggle, but remember, I was on a mission. The rest of my days were filled with healing tasks, from diet to enemas. Determination was my strong side, and I was using it for everything it was worth.

Have you heard the quote "When angels are near, feathers appear"? I strongly believe it to be true.

The feathers started to appear on my every day walks. They would be planted in the ground in front of me, hanging on a branch I would have to cross, or simply sitting on my doorstep when I got back. Later, when I was walking in shopping malls and on busy town streets, they still kept appearing in front of me. I read up, and connected with the philosophy. Ever since, I have felt a strong connection with spirit, with the angels, when seeing a feather. I have a beautiful collection in my home, of some of the most special ones that have been given to me.

The feathers symbolize the wings of angels. They do not need wings to fly, so the wings represent their ability to carry out divine will. It is the belief that they will leave a feather when they are near. Many different cultures speak of the spiritual meaning of feathers. In addition to representing the actual feathers from angel wings, they are all referring to spiritual communication, and also the ascension to the higher realms. Doreen Virtue speaks about angels, and has done some amazing work with guided angel meditations. I am the owner of her books and CD`s, and I love how passionate she is about her sharing.

I had read that the ancient Egyptians believed feathers to be a symbol of Ma'at, the goddess of truth, justice, and order. The Native American chiefs wore feathers in their head-dresses to represent their communication with the spirit world. They also believed finding feathers were signs of new beginnings and rebirth from spirit. This to me, made me feel connected to those who had walked before me. The Celtic Druids wore ornately feathered robes to transcend the physical plane and gain celestial knowledge from the realms of spirit. In the Bible, feathers metaphorically represent loving care and protection. As a common dream-symbol, feathers signify the ability to freely move throughout life. Feathers can also represent a fresh start in a spiritual sense, as well as truth, speed, love, lightness, and flight.

This was uplifting and inspirational reading. It rang true with me, and I started to acknowledge the presence of spirit all around me. It was a bridging experience that lead to trust and faith. I knew that I was not alone, and I knew that I was being guided".[13]

The feathers follow me to this day, and they always show me when I am on point, walking my true path. They have become part of my compass. You don't have to look for anything, all you've to do is be aware and open. Ask to be guided if you so wish. Ask to be shown the way, and to be shown the truth.

From being a successful Interior Architect and a fitness studio owner, I felt defined by my accomplishments. My detrimental ill health, proximity to death, and the loss of my business and my friends, pointed me towards a complete new life-path. Once I opened up to the signs around me, I fell into pure awe for nature and creation. My dreams were telling me a new story, and my hours awake were showing me some amazing support from another realm.

"I look at my feet as they walk through the woods. I am barefoot, and the ground is soft. I am walking on moss, surrounded by flowers and herbs. I am busy, and I have little time. Someone stops me, and wants to talk to me. "What are you doing?" They ask. I look down at my hands, and I find myself writing on stones. I am using a leaf as my pen, writing little sentences on each stone. "People are sick", I say, "and I need to write them what they must do. There are so many, and there is so little time."

This experience was short, yet very powerful. At the time, I knew that I had to write it down. Much, much later, I see how great a message this was for me.

Incorporating mindfulness into our lives will make it easy to harvest from our guidance. How can we feel guided if we are too busy and preoccupied to see any signs? It is all up to us to open ourselves to the possibility that we are constantly surrounded by all that is.

---

[13] Hilde Larsen – *From Hell to Inspired, 2016*

To be mindful is also to be humble, and humility lets us step out of our need to know everything. There is no need to understand something that is way beyond our comprehension. It is truly overrated and restrictive. If we would only accept what our brain could perceive and intellectually understand, we would truly be lost in the mind. A sign is not to be understood or believed through science, or proven to man through the intellect. It's got to be felt and known by the heart. It's got to be recognized by our soul and spirit as something significant and precious. It connects us to what we see as the unknown that can only be tapped into through faith and trust. When you have faith in your own power, and you trust the process, you will easily be able to embrace every sign that you see.

The guidance is always there, even though you don't always see it, or acknowledge it as such. The signs are there too, showing you not only when you are in the flow, heading towards your amazing successful true life. Looking back at your life, if or when something happened that threw you off your path, you might notice that you were given several signs that something was about to happen. Me, I got so many signs telling me that I was heading towards disaster with my health and life, but I never listened. I was not only poked, but slapped around more than once. What can I say, some of us are stubborn, clinging to the force of the mind and its programming. So, if you are heading towards rise or fall, it doesn't matter, the force is with you. Trying to give you a heads-up, a chance to redirect. All you've to do is to get your head out of the sand and pay attention. What a blessing!

Guidance through feelings:

Not only by physical signs are we guided through our manifestations. Every feeling and emotion has a message, be it an indication that we are not doing what is serving us best, or a symptom that we need to care for our health in general. Not many are aware that emotions are directly affected by our physical health. An imbalanced thyroid will manifest as depression, and a low adrenal function will show up as anxiety. The liver holds on to anger, and the kidneys represent fear. If you are not in great health, and even if you are, you might have parasites lurking in your body. Most of us do. They can wreck havoc in your physical *and* emotional body. Feeding off you, taking over your ability to think and feel clearly and undisturbed. Everything is connected. Physically, emotionally, mentally and spiritually. For any emotional and physical imbalance or what is called disease, I recommend reading the book *"Know the Truth and Get Healthy"*, to step out of the illusion of disease.

Knowing that you also need to build a strong and healthy physical body, let us look at what your emotions and feelings are telling you about staying tuned in on the truth channel. Minding the feelings that are a part of your awakened state will give you valuable guidance. Notice how you feel when you think about something, or when you meet certain people. When someone asks you something, how does it make you feel? Does it inspire you, or quite the opposite? The absolute short and easy way to let this go down, would be to say; if it is not feeling right, drop it, and most of the time that would be the wise decision.

Only fear will be able to clutter a true inner guidance, and sadly, it often does. That is why using the emotions as a guidance system and a true compass can be tricky. First, we need to make sure that we are clutter-free, of true intentions and able to listen to our heart more than our brain. The feelings that guide us are the passionate ones and the fearful ones. They are both easy to detect, and we are directed by them every day. We shy away from fear, and we love to move towards passion, when the mind allows us to.

Any good love story will tell you that nothing can stop real passion from winning at the end. True love and compassion will ultimately conquer any fear. When you feel passionate about something, truly enthusiastic from your heart, you are on the right path. That is never a maybe or a sometimes. It is always confirmative. It leads to true freedom and joy, happiness and fulfillment. Fear on the other hand, which resides at the other end of an emotional scale, is based on false beliefs, not truth, and cannot be trusted. The feeling might be real, but its message, its meaning, might not be. There is a huge difference. I am not talking about the fear that is triggered by the fight or flight response from standing face to face with a predator, or when looking at any real life-threatening danger. I am referring to the fear that tells you that you are more comfortable where you are, and that change could be dangerous. The fear that arises from having to take a leap of faith, or stepping onto any new ground. That is the one that is holding you back. That is the emotion that most often is trying to trick you and not serve you. And that is why I always look at the more positive feelings as true guidance, and the ones we define as negative as the lurking liars. Although, you could say that not feeling good about a decision or a project is a guidance of such, the lack of enthusiasm is enough, really. If it is missing, you know.

> Every time you feel good, you are on to
> something great. Follow that lead.

Connecting the dots:

Following the guidance that comes from your soul takes faith and a large dose of bravery. We have so many but's and should do's. So much brain, and so little (or less) trust in our own inner knowing. We keep confusing the knowing and the understanding. Think of it as connecting the dots, like your path is already laid out for you. When you have declared what it is you want, that you know where you want to go, approximately, all you have to do is follow the dots there. Step by step, by being aware of your inner and outer compass.

The false beliefs, and the clutter you have standing in the way of your clear sight, will make it harder to connect those dots. Authentic living, and an honest intent is required to be able to go with the flow. Will you recognize truth if you come from anything but real truth?

Sit in stillness, in meditation and ask for guidance. It can show up as anything, from a dove to an old aunt calling you with an important message or insight. A mentor might show up, as a great manifestation of guidance, literally. Showing us we need to be open to learn and to listen. When someone approaches you with information, be sure to listen. Nothing is ever random. You are always surrounded by dots that will connect your whole experience. I remember asking how I could best serve, before I went out for my walk in the forest. What was the key to my own journey of healing and serving others? I connected with nature for clear guidance and signs. As I walked that day, not minding my earlier question, I passed a tree that I often sit by. On one of the branches, right in front of me was a key. A physical key. I took it to heart, that I was on the right path, using nature and my experience to serve and help others. Whatever unfolds for you, take it to *your* heart, and let it inspire you to keep your focus.

You might be looking for a new job, perfect health, or you long for a partner to share your life with. It doesn't matter. So long as you keep following that true passion, you are walking towards it. It will find you.

> The signs are always there, whether we see them or not. We always deserve the best life possible, if we believe it or not. Life will always support us, not matter if we trust in that or not. We can choose to participate or not, to benefit or not. The same way as truth is truth, and it is readily available to us, guidance is always there. Trust, have faith, and keep those eyes wide open.

The emotional scale:

Abraham-Hicks has made an emotional scale that we can use to monitor our emotions, where we are, and where we want to go. The teachings of Abraham suggest that so long as we keep moving up the scale, a little at the time, we are moving towards joy and happiness. The scale has rated the emotions and feelings from complete apathy to bliss. By thinking more positive thoughts that give you the next feeling moving upwards on the scale, you are triggering a positive outcome and manifestation. How about introducing this to our children?

Find your starting point, and work from there. You can use this as a tool of awareness. By being awake to how we really feel, we are acknowledging it, and therefor inviting in more of who we really are. Not that we are not all here, we are, although we often seem to hide away some significant parts. [14]

The Emotional Guidance Scale

1. Joy/Appreciation/Empowered/Freedom/Love
2. Passion
3. Enthusiasm/Eagerness/Happiness
4. Positive Expectation/Belief
5. Optimism
6. Hopefulness
7. Contentment
8. Boredom
9. Pessimism
10. Frustration/Irritation/Impatience
11. Overwhelm
12. Disappointment
13. Doubt

---

[14] Abraham/Hicks – *Ask and it is given, p.114*

14. Worry
15. Blame
16. Discouragement
17. Anger
18. Revenge
19. Hatred/Rage
20. Jealousy
21. Insecurity/Guilt/Unworthiness
22. Fear/Grief/Depression/Despair/Powerlessness

Our emotions and feelings are one of our most apparent guides of where we are at this moment. Not of where we are going, only where we are. A tool for us to use as a compass. Steer your vehicle and attention towards what feels better. Always towards what gives you more joy and passion. It is the truth pendulum. Where it points, you are heading. Use your free will and let the guiding point you in the right direction. You are here to live from your heart, and anything else is bullshit. Claim your life!

> **"My dream is on my side.**
> **My life is on my side.**
> **My path is waiting for me.**
> **The guides are on my side.**
> **When I walk forward, I am always expanding.**
> **I am protected.**
> **The power is within me.**
> **I am strong.**
> **I am free."**

> *"Be bolder than you have ever been, and let your feelings guide you. Freedom awaits those who are willing to cut the cords."* - Hilde Larsen

Chapter 15

Which comfort zone?

" I know I should do it, I know it. I wish I could, but I can't. I have never spoken in front of an audience before. I can't even imagine looking at all those people. They keep asking me, and I wish that I could do it, I really do, but I can't. I would faint, and I would lose my words, go blank, typically. I have no idea how people do that. I wish. I have so much to say, really, and if I keep saying no to events like this, people will stop asking me, and I will never be able to spread my passion. Maybe if I practiced on a smaller crowd. I don't know. What if my face gets all red, and I start to stutter? I would die of embarrassment. I don't know, I wish I could, I might. It would be amazing, like a dream come through."

What we refer to as our comfort zone is the space in which we feel comfortable in terms of less anxiety or uneasiness. When we move outside of it, or push its borders, we feel anxious and unsafe. Imagine the zone having a wall to lean up against, the familiarity of knowing you have your knowledge and your skills to back you up. The feeling of being in control makes us feel safe. You might also call it the control zone. Stepping outside will feel like there is no safety net anymore, and that anything can happen.

It feels unsafe to lose control, to be on rocky ground. The challenge is this: On the outside of this zone, magic happens. So long as we want to grow and learn, we will want a piece of it. Let's call it the learning zone. Being a little anxious will keep you alert and awake, and therefore sharpen all your senses. If you speak to any successful performer, athlete or speaker, they will tell you how they have been pushing this anxiety limit all the way to the top.

How you feel about your entire life will tell you a great deal about how comfortable you are. It might not be what you would expect, but when you are unsatisfied, you are most likely also comfortable. Living a life filled with routines that keep you doing the same thing every day, waiting for Friday to show up, is not a fulfilling one. You might feel comfortable at best, but not fulfilled. To a thriving enthusiast, Friday is just another day of the week, and no week looks the same. Inside the zone, there's order and continuity, repetitions and structure. The safety net is visible.

> Your comfort zone is reflecting your self-image and how you see yourself in this world. It is a self-perceived imaginary boundary, set by a belief and a search for safety. Life will never be safe, nor will it not be. Living is growing and exploring, and you cannot get it right or wrong.

Healthy habits can nevertheless create some great groundwork from operating in safety and comfort. Structure can be a powerful tool. I would not want to step outside my perfectly planned environment for writing any of my books. Nor would I spend the time I set aside for silence and gratitude to be anything but calm and safe. When I am looking for growth and learning, I always challenge myself. It makes perfect sense that a new perspective, a new skill and a new mindset has to come from stretching outside of familiarity and certainty. It makes sense that anything new is to come from a new perspective. The same way, new learning is easier to accomplish where you are more alert and on point.

The zone might sound pleasant enough, and at times it will be, but even though we feel comfortable we might be hurting ourselves. As with the false beliefs and the resistance to change, we can easily be held back by our own pain and addiction to suffering. How sweet it is to wallow in our own sorrow, and to be comfortably able to say no to anything that will take our focus from our truth.

"We cannot become what we want to be by remaining what we are." - Max DePree

The more and longer we stay within our zone, the smaller it tends to get, and the harder it is to step outside. We get even more comfortable, lazy and cluttered with false beliefs. As it shrinks, the further away the magic learning and growing zone will feel. The wall gets higher, and harder to climb. This invisible wall that we have built, with the help from some friends and the good old programming. A lifelong project in the making, from shying away from uncertainty, and believing the crap about not being good enough, smart enough or boss enough. What a hoax. We are all expansion and flowering material. We are all fabulous amazing beings, able to break free from any imaginary zone. If we choose to stay strapped to our comfort, we will never find our true potentials, and never experience what we're capable of achieving. Any learning happens outside that zone. Whenever you start anything new, like a hobby, learn a new language, take up a new sport, or start a new job, you are operating outside your safety zone.

Becoming more of who you really, truthfully are, requires stretching and bending. Limits must be pushed. Comfortable has to step aside for uncomfortable. Uneasy has to do for a while, and the safety net will have to go. This is not about jumping off a cliff, or doing something far from your interest or calling, on the contrary, it is about moving closer to your passions and your purpose. Although stepping somewhat out of character now and then will build some muscle, this is about stretching to grow more into who you already are. Like polishing that diamond, and learning your most hidden potentials. Stretching is most often not extreme, it is more like a widening of the horizon. The comfort zone will grow in the process.

> **"Expand your zone so that you can spread you wings." – Hilde Larsen**

How to break free:

Imagine there not being anything that is holding you back, no fear of the new and unexplored grounds. What if there was no anxiety attached to trying new things? Not the kind of anxiety that is keeping you locked in your place, only a mild spark of eagerness and anticipation. We could argue that this anxiety is what keeps us on our toes, on point and alert, so look at this as the debilitating kind of anxiety. That is where you meet restriction, when your fears are running the show.

An old Chinese proverb says; "A man grows most tired while standing still". Wise words about how we so easily settle for mediocre, when we are created for grandness. How action and stepping into the new will awaken us to a more fulfilled life. How by holding back we are hurting ourselves and our potentials.

- **What do you want that feels out of reach?** As a motivating factor, take a look at what you want to achieve. What has boundaries attached to it, holding you back from doing what needs to be done? Without being motivated, you are not going anywhere. With a strong desire to achieve, more bravery will arise. Do you have a dream that you are not pursuing due to fear of your own abilities? Have you always wanted to sing, but never dared to take those singing lessons? Have you had a secret dream of becoming an entrepreneur, but never trusted your own abilities? Life is too short not to go for it. Take a step outside the zone, and see what is there.

- **How will it benefit you?** What would change in your life if you achieved this goal, and how would you benefit long term? Maybe the reward is larger than *you* even. Maybe many would benefit, and maybe it would only be the start of many endeavors and life goals. Sometimes being clear on why you should push yourself a little will be enough inspiration to actually go for it. It doesn't even have to be what is perceived as a big deal for others. It can be a subtle thing, like meeting new people. How would your life change if you're able to step out and meet likeminded people without feeling like you were going to faint? How about just being able to speak Spanish, which would make it so much easier to communicate with your new colleagues? Sometimes, pushing yourself towards smaller changes, can have an enormous impact on your life and self-esteem.

- **Take risks:** There is no guarantee in life, not for anything. The only sure thing is that we live and we will die. That's about it. Other than that, our lives are pretty much up for grabs by anything that can affect a human being. Life is unpredictable, and yes we will all die, Get over it! You never want to play with your life, or your family's safety. You don't want to take risks that are larger than you are willing to invest, but most of the time, this is not the issue. When we are talking about risks, we are first and foremost talking about the risk of losing your comfortable zone.

- **Baby steps:** If you are not ready to take the leap of faith, take smaller steps. You can stick your toe in the water before you dive in. It is okay to start slow, and do a little at the time. Get the feel of your new ground, get a bit more comfortable, then stretch a little more. We are all different in the sense of what we see as uncomfortable and unsecure. Not everyone is made for the big jump, and not in every situation will it be the most beneficial. Like with everything else, a step-by-step plan works really well. You can take smaller risks along the way, and look back at a fabulous and amazing growth.

- **Have fun, don't be so serious:** Life is not serious, although it is precious. Fun and joy go together with expansion and empowerment. Being uptight and rigid is only feeding your restrictions. A false belief that being serious is the same as being true and successful, will only hold you back. There is no fun in holding back our natural playfulness. Fun-filled activities loosen up the energy of restriction and obstruction. Dare to be more cheerful. It uplifts the soul, and takes away the fear of failure. Go outside your zone with an intent to have more fun doing it. What is the worst that can happen?

- **Failure is learning:** There are no failures, remember? No rejections, only redirection. There are no wrongs, only experiments and learning. Once you really believe this, the game changes. You will find an opportunity for growth in everything you do. Life becomes less serious, and the risks seem lower.

- **Now is the right time:** Procrastination takes us nowhere, and stalling keeps us bonded. The action is needed for anything to move forward, so call this the perfect time to take a step outside your zone. You are not really stepping out of anything, but rather moving the lines a little. Making your zone larger and more eligible for having you as its resident.

Sing a little louder, walk longer, aim higher and dance more often. Smile wider, laugh louder, invest more truthfully and love unconditionally. Step out of any false belief that you are less than magnificent, and stay humble for the opportunities that unfold in front of you. We often care too much, about outcomes, about others, and about our own lack of ability. Care a little less about the things that matter the least. Nothing is standing between you and your ability to just not give a damn.

Reap the benefits of a comfort free zone:

Incorporate a zone-free life where stretching is a part of your growth and bullshit-free living. Play in all areas of your possibilities, and let no anxiety, or perceived zone of the masses, hold you back from your amazingness and extraordinaire. Once the illusion that you have anything to fear by feeling a bit uncomfortable or anxious at times is gone, you are truly free to live. Our lives are not confined by any rules that hold back our creative and passionate exploration. They are all illusionary and false. Take back your boldness and step onto your stage.

- **You will realize that fear is overrated.** The most common statement that follows having done something scary and seemingly risky, is; "Had I known it was going to be this easy or go so well, I would have done it years ago." The fear itself is often what we are most afraid of. The false belief that fear is something we should run from will also change, as you realize that the world did not come to an end, and nobody died.

- **You will grow beyond belief.** Nothing is more empowering than conquering some longs standing obstacles. Be it the resistance to take the leap towards starting a health regime, moving house or starting your own business. Maybe you want to sell everything you own, to start a life journey of travelling the world, or you simply want to ask someone that you really like, out on a date. It does not matter, you will grow, and your horizon will broaden. The first step is always the hardest one, but it will promote the hunger for more. As your comfort zone grows, or as you let go of the zone all together, growth becomes constant. A seed has been panted. Now, all you've got to do is water and nourish it.

- **You will become your own boss.** The position was always ours, although we so easily give it away, or try to give it away. We talk about taking back our power, as if it was ever gone. I don't believe it ever was. It sure does feel like it is taken back, but it was always there, although hidden or suppressed. It becomes easy to hide behind someone else's flaws and shortcomings, when we feel small and inferior in our own lives. Ultimately, you have always been the one that you have been waiting for. You have always been what you have been searching for, but now it will become even clearer to you, and feel more real. How empowering and inspiring!

- **You will get more enthusiastic and lose the regrets.** There are several sayings in this direction of thought. "It is better to have loved and lost than never to have loved at all", or "It is better to have tried and failed, than to regret not trying." I strongly believe in this to be very true. The enthusiasm that arises from stepping onto new ground, while realizing that your life is better for it, is contagious. It will easily encourage you to stretch more, and to get to know yourself even better. We will never regret having tried, once we see the benefits that it will give us.

- **Discomfort becomes a path to success.** The whole concept of comfort changes. Why is it that for some, comfort is the absolute hiding place, yet for others, it is the plague they fear more than anything? There are base jumpers and extreme sport enthusiasts that put their lives on the line every single day. They shy away from what feels like confinement and lack of true feelings. They chase the high from living on the edge. Like a drug, they crave the adrenaline rush that they experience from stretching to their limit. They literally get high. This is the other side of the pendulum, the extreme hunger for more, never seeming to get satisfied. It can become an addiction. While the term discomfort has different meanings for different people, in the light of comfort zones, we know going outside can feel painful. Therefore, the training and practicing of stretching, will condition us to recognize even discomfort as something valuable.

- **You will feel less anxiety and stress:** How can doing something that might push you into anxiety and stress, help you? I was almost paralyzed by anxiety for several years. From being physically debilitated, I suffered greatly on every level. Physical, mental and emotional are all one, connected through our energetics, organs and glands. By walking through your fire, you will break free from the hold that any anxiety has on you. By stepping outside your zone, you will feel empowered to take care of your health on every level. It will benefit the rest of your life. No stressful life is ever a healthy one.

- **You will inspire others.** People are always looking for guidance and direction. By living your truth and growing as a person, you will become a powerful inspiration to those around you. We tend to look towards those who have done what we seek to achieve. Your life will be fulfilled with a new joy from influencing others to also take a leap of faith. To be able to be a way-shower and a mentor. One of the greatest blessings of my life is to be able to inspire others.

- **You will need no one's approval ever again.** You will be done searching for validation. What a relief! You have experienced firsthand that it is all up to you. Not to *do* alone, but to *take charge of* alone. You *know* that you are enough, that you can try anything without being afraid of failure. You *know* that success and magic happens outside the comfort zone. Your zone just took a hike, as you stepped up and claimed your seat. You are limitless and your everyday life will reflect on that.

> **"If you ever want to experience and achieve anything out of the ordinary, that will reflect your true potentials, step outside the zone." – Hilde Larsen**

To expand through your everyday living, start by changing some of your routines. Break a habit, and look for other, and maybe even better ways to do things. If you are usually sedentary, move more. Get away from the computer or the TV, and find some activities to get you moving. If you are very active, always in motion running around, unwind, take a load off. Relax and be more still. Take some *"me"* time. If you are shy, get out more, and if you don't like to be alone, practice. Read more books. Reading what others are saying and have experienced can be uplifting and inspiring. Knowledge is power, and by knowing better we can do better. Go out dancing and shake it up. Be more childish, and tell more jokes. The next time you go to a restaurant, try something you have never had before. Help someone in need, or volunteer at a shelter or a soup kitchen. Count your blessings and serve at the same time.

Chapter 16

Gratitude and the gift of nature

❝ I can't wait to get home to my babies. This plane is packed. So much noise, so much chaos. The Holidays are the worst. Too many people trying to get to wherever they are going. The shopping, the stress. Still, if it weren't for this airplane, I would not get home tonight, so thank you. Thank God, I am able to spend time with my family. Next year I know we will be able to take that vacation together. Thank you for that too. What a blessing. Not everyone gets to spend time with their loved ones. I know that better than anyone. My heart aches for all of them. Can't wait to get back to my babies. It has been so long. What a blessing. The accident changed everything. What was wrong with me? I just couldn't see my own blessings, like I was totally blinded by this chaos. Blind for sure. Not seeing what really matters, the little big things. The magic in a hug and a smile. My heart is full, I am on my way home. All that matters. Thank you.❞

When we strip ourselves of our hurts and our clutter, when we get back to our true balance, gratitude is a part of who we are. The trick is to be able to tap into that naked and honest bliss, even when we are preoccupied with life and its busy schedule. Even when in the middle of what we might see as chaos, we can condition ourselves to feel the grace and the appreciation for all that we have. We can step into it like a state of being, knowing that it is truth. Anything leading us away from gratefulness is a lie. The hardest thing for many, and I know it was for me, is to stop measuring where you are when you are going after a dream. It is easy to get caught up in where you are at this moment, forgetting that every step along the way has value and something to cherish. I was so hungry for health, I often forgot to appreciate how much further I had gotten, or that I was alive and breathing. Keeping the eye on the ball, always looking ahead can also keep us from seeing what is right in front of us. The magic of the *now. Someday, one day, soon, when only*, are outlooks keeping us from seeing that *this* moment is the only one there is.

> **"There are only two ways to live your life. One is as though nothing is a miracle. The other is as though everything is a miracle." - Albert Einstein**

Gratitude doesn't come from the mind. It is not a thought, it is a feeling, a state of being. It is a heartfelt feeling, and it fills the entire body with a nurturing, positive, healing energy. It is very similar to love, but it is directed towards the recognition of all that is. We can be grateful for every single thing in our lives, good, bad and ugly. We can start by being grateful for what is the most obvious to us, what we see around us, and observe how our perception towards life changes. Life has taught us to play the reward game, to do, get paid, feel grateful, or to show gratitude rather. The idea that we need to receive something to be grateful is completely false and in dissonance with nature and who we are. Being alive is a blessing, every breath every potential and every smile. We need to wake up and smell the roses.

Whenever we find ourselves wanting something to change, we must start by being grateful for what we already have. There is always something to be grateful for. Even when we are down, feeling lost and depressed, we can search for the inner feeling of gratitude. Being grateful is the same as ordering more to be grateful for. If we want our health to change, we must embrace and love the work that the body is already doing. Feeling gratitude for our breath, our vision, our hearing etc. If we want a better house to live in, we must be grateful for the home that we already have, or the couch that we are offered by a friend. No matter the status of our current shelter - giving thanks for what is already there, is inviting in more to feel grateful for. Gratitude opens the heart, and it opens the portal for rapid healing and nurturing manifestations. The magic of life will flow towards us, and every cell in our body will align with this vibration.

> "When I started counting my blessings, my
> whole life turned around." - Willie Nelson

Speak that which you want, and let no ungratefulness or feeling of lack throw you off balance. Words are submissions of intent, and even when we are not aware, we are sending out a message to our cells, to the Creation, to God or the Infinite. The energy of gratitude is a pure love energy. It is the vibration of constant positive change.

15

Look at gratefulness as a gateway to freedom. The simplicity is mind blowing. Everybody can do it, feel it, practice it and reap the benefits. The simple yet profound truths are the most powerful there is. We are all capable of tapping into that magical feeling of grace and appreciation that will change our whole lives. Nature reveals it's truth by keeping it simple. Humans want to complicate

---

[15] Hilde Larsen – *Know the Truth and Get Healthy, 2016*

and distort, to break apart and mix up the pieces. By being subjected to control, lies and false beliefs, we have a hard time recognizing every blessing that is already in our lives, just from having one. We are over it, we are back, fully awake and sound of mind and heart. We are in touch with our true essence, and are taking our lives back. Simply by setting ourselves free.

Let nothing take away your gratitude towards the life you are living right now. It is a gift. It is the light that will keep on shining, when everything else seems lost and dark.

When you feel alone, feel grateful
When you feel sad, feel grateful
When you feel hurt, feel grateful
When you feel discouraged, feel grateful
When you feel lost, feel grateful
When you feel defeated, feel grateful
When you feel hopeless, feel grateful

Gratitude and nature:

I believe in nature. It is Creation. It is God. It is truth, and it is a part of who we are. We literally become dirt, our physical body, that is. Our body blends with everything that ever lived. We are that same energy, and turn into the same soil as every plant lives in. We go back to the same state as every other species on this planet. We consume it, and we cannot live without it. We are completely dependent on Mother Earth to exist as we know it, and it is profound when we awaken to the true meaning of that. How can we live in high rises and not eat food from the source, and expect to be healthy and happy? How can we pollute and destroy our homes, our planet and expect to get away with it? Who have bought into the lie that humans are smarter than nature, and that we need a pill, not true healing? The reality in which we live is showing us how far we have strayed from our truth. We are sick, depressed, brain fogged and helpless to show for it. Take a look around and count the vibrant healthy, truthful and truly happy people that you meet. They should all be. They *can* all be, by taking back the ability to change with intent. To feel grateful is natural, being happy is too. So is being healthy and enthusiastic even though life, like nature, has it's seasons.

Every food that is created for man comes from nature. Fresh and toxin free. Feel grateful for every bite. Ultimately all food was wild food. Humans have found ways to cultivate and elevate. The success, or lack thereof, is shown in every supermarket around the world. Humongous stores with boxes and labels. Ingredient lists longer and more complicated than most people care to read. The words are complicated, or at least completely foreign to the average consumer. A mind trick that works like a charm. We generally have no idea what we are putting in our bodies. Until we step into our own control. By feeling grateful for knowing what to eat, what is natural and what is healing, we are honoring not only our bodies, but nature and God. We are saying no to the bullshit being served as food, only to slowly take away our funk. By blessing your food, by giving thanks to every meal, you are inviting even more nourishing elements into your life. Choose wisely and stay educated. Not by the mind only, but by nature itself. Listen to it, to your body, you will know.

Every color imaginable is given to us through nature. We call them the colors of the rainbow. Showing themselves through all the amazingly beautiful flowers, in every raindrop and fallen leaf. Our eyes deliver this joy, and our whole being reacts to them. You might not notice it, but you are picking up every color as a frequency. They all have their own. The colors are blessings from nature that we can eat through the fruits and vegetables. They represent life, our chakras and our emotions. We are blessed by having colorful crystals in our lives, for healing and balancing. Every time you notice a color, give thanks. Your life will be more colorful.

The air that we breathe is what connects us to life. No breath, no life. No one has ever survived without air. It is crucial, and nature has the version that we thrive on. Clean air is not found in cities, it is found in the forest, in nature. Feel blessed for every breath that you take. Give thanks by breathing consciously and deeper. Feel the connection. Breathe in gratitude, exhale love.

The water of life, the pure life giving elixir is another truthful and original natural blessing. Fresh clean water is sadly not for everyone. Be mindful of what you drink, and honor your body with the cleanest water you can get. The juices of fresh organic fruits are also water, and pure nourishment for all our cells. Drink with an attitude of appreciation for every single drop. It brings you life.

The soil that we walk on keeps us grounded and healthy. If you know anything about me, you know that this is a topic that is very dear to my heart. Connecting barefoot to Mother Earth is profound for our whole wellbeing. Most people have no idea that by wearing shoes, they are missing out on one of the most important nourishments there is. Mother Earth is a limitless source of negative ions, the electrons and the energy that we need. They stream into the body when we are grounded. People experience less inflammation and more mental clarity after spending time outside in nature. The longer we stay outside, the more benefits we receive and experience. The Earth is alive, and will never stop emanating the free electrons. Connect the skin of your body with the skin of the Earth, and the flow will not stop. By doing this, every day, the electrons restore, the positive/negative balances, and a natural electrical state in the body is maintained. You now have a natural electrical state in your body. Take this to heart, and see it for what it is: A message to you, about learning and spending more time outside in nature. Free, blessed, grateful and awake.

Nature adapts, it changes with every season. It never makes mistakes, and it never holds on to anything. A tree will keep growing its entire life, following the tide, the natural rhythm. Its newborn leaves during spring, and its fallen leaves during fall. Spreading its seeds, bearing fruits and nuts. All naturally and effortlessly. Every creature has its rhythm, lifespan and season. We are affected by the daylight, by nighttime and by where we are on the planet. Everything is alive, constantly changing, evolving, breathing and expanding. The blessings are more than we could ever count, but let's make sure each day is filled to the rind. Nature is a living organism, like we are.

Everything that we are grateful for is a clue. We can learn something from it. It holds true value. For example, I have yet to meet a person that is not immensely grateful for their children. They are the embodiment of our soul. They represent true love and hope, and we can let them teach us something about life. The children have the innocent view, the simplicity that lets them see through the crap. They don't get entangled in mind games and false beliefs, not at first anyway. They are open and pure, and can show us what matters the most. I am grateful for every child that is born, as they are our hope for the future. Hopefully, they will not fall for anything that is not true for them. Let us hold that intent together. Another example is our health. We all feel blessed by good health, or we will after we have lost it. It reminds us of how vulnerable we are, how short this life is, and how fragile and precious each moment is. Be grateful for your body, for what it can do. Show it appreciation by feeding it well and respecting its boundaries. It is always on your team. Always on your side. It is the one partner you cannot live without. It deserves a great deal of humbleness. I will never let my body down again, and I will never stop thanking it for what it does every single day. Healing itself, letting me express my life through it in every way.

Our elders know how fast life travels by, from firsthand experience. They have knowledge about regrets and gratitude. At the end of our lives we become aware of what mattered and what didn't. We get to the truth, to the core values of our lives, and the interesting part is that we never seem to regret being thankful and grateful. There are no regrets from honoring nature and other beings. The only regrets we might have, are not doing *more* of just that. Let us bring this wisdom to our younger years, and live by it. Value each day as it was something precious, as it *is*.

Every day is a good day to:

Let yourself be surprised
Look around with wonder
Be mindful in every moment
Step outside more
Smile at a stranger
Look at everything like it is the first time
Feel your inner strength
Laugh every single day
Count your blessings

"When you notice the smaller blessings, you are getting the larger picture." - Hilde Larsen

Whenever you feel lost in your own drama or chaos, stop and be still. Take a moment and pull yourself back. This is not your truth, only your play. Connect with everything you are grateful for, and let the rest go. Let it center you and keep you focused on what really matters. Your center comes from a news and propaganda free zone. No fear, no blame, no lies and no bullshit is wanted. Keep it simple and keep it true.

Write of gratitude in your journal. Such a simple and easy tool. To focus on what you already have will fulfill you and help you stay focused on the positive things in your life. Write down five things that you are grateful for, and do it every single day. Focus on what seems like the little things. It can be moments, a feeling or an event. It can simply be the fact that you have a bed to sleep in. Anything that brings you into the focus of content. Feel blessed. You are.

Go for a thankful walk. This is an amazing way to raise your awareness and to help you focus on what is around to be grateful for. Schedule some time every day to go outside for a walk. Set aside at least 20-30 minutes, and longer if you can. Walk in nature or around the block. Step outside. Be aware of everything that you see, hear and smell. Look for things to be grateful for. Stay focused and stay mindful. As you practice you will awaken to the abundance that is all around, and your outlook on life might improve to go with it.

Express your intent. As you keep looking for things to be grateful for, express them, live them, feel them and *be* them. Allow this feeling to come through you as you honor and acknowledge it. Incorporate it in your everyday life. Say hello to every day with the intent that it will be yet another day filled with gratitude and wonder. Your spiritual awakening will lift you and expand your consciousness.

Being grateful is the new strong, the new successful and the new sexy and true way to fulfillment. Not that it is anything new at all. It is the language of God, from pure love. It is the connection to truth, unfiltered. It is not a thought, an idea or a philosophy. It is a state of being. It is a brainless place where we know that there is something so much bigger than us. Something bigger than life.

Saying thank you is not the same as being grateful
Saying I love you is not the same as loving someone
Saying I will, is not the same as doing
Saying I forgive you is not the same as forgiveness

Gratitude cultivates appreciation for all things.
It can be trained, by practicing every day.

To be able to set ourselves free, we need to set everyone else free. Everything that is keeping us from seeing the blessings are hurting our own path and mission. Gratitude for life will make it easy to move into forgiveness. There is no truthful life without it. Forgiving is a gift, to *you*. An opportunity to grow and learn, another blessing. They are countless!

Forgiveness is a blessing:

"Forgive them, for they know not what they do"- Luke 23:34. Choose your battles and step into grace. When you know better you can do better. The power is yours. The heart is yours to fill, and the life is yours to live.

True freedom will always include forgiveness. Gratitude will lead the way. Forgiving is also being grateful, for everything. When we forgive someone, we are putting the energy back where it belongs. By that I mean that we choose to not be the carrier of the event anymore. We refuse to be the one that is emotionally hurting because of what someone else did. The action was not ours, and the hurt or effect of what happened is not ours to keep living. When we are holding on to the memory, we are letting the event continue to hurt us, over and over again. So, you see, forgiving is all about *you*, never about the other person. Once you realize this, letting go becomes so much easier. Every day moving forward has the choice of forgiveness. The blame and anger that comes with holding on will eat you up like any other acid. Just like the acids and alkaline foods, there are alkaline and acidic emotions. The anger, blame, sorrow, hopelessness and despair are all corrosive to our organism, and we need to let them be embraced and set free. Through forgiveness and gratitude – love, compassion, thankfulness, joy and enthusiasm will grow and prosper.

> **"Forgiving is the energy of self-love and compassion. It is also what shall set you free from emotional baggage." – Hilde Larsen**

You might think that forgiving someone is the same as letting them off the hook and that what they did is now ok. That is not the case at all. You might also think that now that everything is forgiven, you will have to be friends with them again, or interact with them even. No, that is not at all what this is about. Forgiveness is not about validating any action or situation. It is not about making anything ok. This is the act of self-freedom and no longer owning the situation. You are no longer allowing it to hurt you. Trust might be broken and relationships might be over, and that is perfectly ok. Forgiveness is your gift to you, and your doorway to moving on.

> The very first step towards forgiveness is acknowledging that it needs to be done. The second step is knowing what it is and what it is not. Once you are ready, give yourself permission to move on with a compassionate heart. That is the heart-felt, true *you*, and you are reclaiming every single bit of it.

What is forgiveness and what is it not?

- *Forgiving is the opposite of victimhood. By stopping the continuing blame and hurt, we are refusing to be a victim. We are reclaiming our power.*

- *We can forgive someone even if we will never see each other again. It is an act of energetic disconnection. By holding on, it does not matter where the other person is, you are still connected by this blame.*

- *Keep walking alongside loving and caring people. Although one can forgive, it does not mean that it is ok to stay in any abusive relationship. Everyone is accountable for their actions.*

- *Forgiveness is knowing that punishment and revenge is not up to you. We are not the ones in charge of justice. Karma is a cosmic law – which means that there is always cause and effect. We do not need to worry about it, it is always taken care of.*

- *The act of forgiving is a choice that is completely yours alone. It is an act of power and sovereignty. You are stepping up to your highest potential.*

- *Forgiving never means that things will stay the same – quite the opposite, it means you will move on without anything holding you down.*

- *No matter what happens, how tragic or seemingly horrible, forgiveness is a process that can start right away. It is ok that it might take time. Grant yourself the time that you need, without indulging in it. There are many meditation- and visualization techniques that can help you during this process.*

- *Forgiveness does not mean that you are denying what happened, not at all. Sometimes the offender does not even know he or she did something to hurt another, and sometimes doing ones best just was not okay at the time.*

- *Forgiveness does not have anything to do with repent. Remember, it is not about them, always about you. We are walking the path of love and healing, which holds no place for degenerating, debilitating anger and despair. It has nothing to do with their attitude, only with yours.*

- *They might be totally unaware that you are going through this process. They might not even know that they need your forgiveness. They do not at all need to be a part of your healing journey, so this is absolutely something that you can do all by yourself.*

- *Withholding forgiveness is like trying to hold on to pain and power at the same time. Holding it back might give a sense of power over the whole situation. It is the kind of perceived power that will eat you up over time, as it is not true power, it is fear of letting go.*

- *We are not looking for the "forgive and forget" – as we are acknowledging the lesson being learned. Forgetting is something that we see as not validating the event, and that is the opposite of what this is about. Forgive and let go, and let every memory be a part of your embraced and loved journey. Any event, perceived as good or bad, holds the opportunity for growth and learning.*

- *You are always ready to forgive - it is not such a big deal really. It is the energy of letting love back into your heart.*

- *Forgiveness is not about covering wounds, that is called suppressing them. No, on the contrary, you are on your way to healing all wounds. No bandage needed.[16]*

---

[16] Hilde Larsen – *Know the Truth and Get Healthy, 2016*

Chapter 17

How can I serve

" *Why am I supposed to do everything? "Do this, help me with that", as if I am a servant or something. Do I look like I have no life of my own? I mean, I get that my mom would need me to do certain things, but how did I end up doing everything? Even my boss seems to think I am a slave. Not that I don't feel appreciated when I am allowed to sit in with her during her talks, I do. And I am the one asking if I can do anything, or help with anything. Sort of my image, always the helping hand. The problem is, it feels like it is all that I am. Like serving and helping everyone is all I do. I am so sick of it. I'm so tired of running around doing other peoples' errands. I am trying to be nice and helpful, but no one seems to care, they only want more. They never give back anything anyway. I would be rich if they did.*

My whole life I was told to be helpful and nice. Still doing my best. Not working. It's not a huge hit. My sisters and brother, well they have their own lives it seems. So, anyway. I better hurry, I need to make sure my neighbor's cat gets to the vet in time. I told him I could drive, although I really have no time for this. I hope he will be happy though"

If you are raised a pleaser, you know this story. If you believe that being a people pleaser will make you a better person, you know it too. I used to believe that I needed to be good at everything, and that failure was not tolerated. I was taught that being a good person was pleasing everybody else. Not serving, pleasing. I was raised to believe that putting myself first was egotistic and selfish, and that setting myself aside to help someone else was expected of me. I believed and did. Program accepted. Don't get me wrong, helping others can be a wonderful thing, but we tend to confuse pleasing and serving.

Pleasing vs serving:

The reason we get this all mixed up is because we are pleasers by nature. It is natural to want to be helpful and pleasing. It is natural to want to serve unconditionally. This whole topic has come forth as a symptom of our imbalanced lives and emotional patterns. We are lost and thrown off balance by our lives and our fears. Our insecurities love to wallow in the realm of pleasing. We almost put ourselves out as martyrs to feel the full benefit of giving. We practice people pleasing, which is something we do to get our own need met. It comes from wanting validation and feeling worthy. People pleasing is something different. It comes from the ego, from wanting something, from insecurity.

- **We please others for validation and for approval.** It can also be used as a means of controlling another person. It is a reflection of not feeling complete and whole. There is the constant longing to be seen and appreciated. As children we tend to please our parents as a mean to be seen and to get praise. The constant search for the outside reason to feel good about ourselves has started. With a lie, it has started this crazy race that one can never win. The longer you are in it, the less validated you will feel. The original intent, bites us in our beautiful behind, over and over again.

- **Serving comes from looking at the bigger picture.** When it comes from the heart, helping someone is natural. Being there for someone, a community or a cause, will lift and empower you. Being able to bring forth joy and inspiration is empowering and giving. You will never expect anything in return, and it will come from free will and excitement.

- **Pleasing takes from your soul.** The battle that goes on inside when a people pleaser gives and gives, leaves a hole of un-fulfillment. We end up disappointed, as there have been expectations attached to the giving and pleasing. Even when they are tired or have to cancel their own tasks, they will show up to help. Resentfully so. Never happy about the service, feeling more and more used, and left with an even bigger hole inside that needs to be filled.

- **Service is given in joy.** Always willingly and from the heart. These people know how to take care of themselves, and that they cannot be of much service if they don't love themselves first. They also know that they can't help everybody, all the time. Being of service is listening to the soul's purpose and living in gratitude and appreciation. It is an honor to be able to serve.

- **When you please, you pay for it.** It comes with a cost, to lose yourself and your boundaries. It often cultivates the victim mentality. You are sorry for yourself for always having to do everything for others, and it builds up resentment and anger. It could also leave you feeling superior, if that is what you need. You are now better than the rest, for putting everybody else's needs before your own. You are the hero, the martyr even. It eats at your soul, your spirit and your sense of freedom. The cost is loss of empowerment. A high price to pay to try to please your way out of your own misery. Heaven forbid you say no. How could you? They would look at you as a terrible person. You would be nothing.

- **When you serve, you gain:** From a sense of connection and spiritual awareness, as a server you feel much obliged and honored to be of service. The joy of being able to give is enough, it is fulfillment in itself. It is chosen and it is done in harmony with your identity. When you serve, you nurture strong relationships and boundaries and are able to act compassionately.

- **As a pleaser you withdraw from your life.** By turning your back on your own needs, you are isolating yourself from the world around you. You have to suppress anything that does not *please* everybody. How authentic is that? Now no one sees the real you, not even you. From years of being a people pleaser, I know firsthand how disconnected from our own needs we can get. Now we feel unseen and like nobody really knows who we are, and they don't.

- **As a server you connect:** Not only to those around you, but to all that is. By being one who listens to yourself and creation, you will feel even more connected by carrying out the divine plan of being in service. As you act from authentic feelings you will draw likeminded people towards you. More situations that are real and true will show up at your doorstep.

> "True giving is receiving. If you cannot see that, you are not truly giving." – Hilde Larsen

Whenever you expect a return on your giving, like an investment, you are off base. Nothing could be farther from the energy of true service. It has no expectations at all. The gift is in the pleasure of being able to contribute. The joy in *that* itself is what fills the heart. When you look at giving as a favor that has to give you something back, you operate from a sense of scarcity, like you will run out of favors to give, or helping hands to offer. Believe me, there is always enough, and you will never run out. Who said that? Your self-worth is not at stake, and you will not get burned out if you take care of yourself. Whenever you feel obligated to do something, and you mask up with your perfect smile to seem helping and sacrificing, stop it!

> A gift is something that always spreads and keeps giving. The ripple-effect is enormous. An act of true kindness will spread like wildfire. The size in value is unseen to the giver. The receiver, by forwarding the empowerment given, is participating in the growth of your gift. A true blessing.

Get rid of your own shit, and serve along the way:

More often than not, we tend to be eager to help others help themselves. It is easy to see fault in others, to want to jump to their rescue. We know better, and all we want is the best for them. We are doing it out of kindness, and we might very well know better, intellectually. We might even be able to guide them towards exactly what they express that they are looking for, but is it any of our business, really? Even though we have the best intent, it is not our place to try to change anyone that has not asked for our help. Even if it doesn't seem that they are choosing the best, smartest, or the most beneficial path, it is their own. All we can do is to offer. All we can do is to let them know we are there. That is all. Everything else is not being of service, it is being a pain and not respecting other people's boundaries. We also tend to project our own baggage onto other people. The "I am cold. Everybody must be freezing" syndrome. Having the need to change others views or behavior comes from a need to control. Let us take back our own control, but not by controlling others. None of our business.

There is an old saying that addresses this topic; "Sweep outside your own front door before you try to clean someone else's." This tells us that we should bring the energy back to ourselves and focus on bettering ourselves first. I would then say to leave the broom at your own door, period. Let people use their own broom, when they see fit. We can all have a broom-party together, if we so choose. By invitation only.

Serving and pleasing, giving and helping. All words that easily get entangled in each other.

The difference lies in the energy behind the word, not in the word itself. We all need help now and then, and we all feel better being able to give back to the world. Through so many different ways, we can all contribute. The bullshit belief that we need something back, a validation or a prize, is not serving any of us. All of us trying to be perfect, while none of us ever will be. There is no such thing, and at the same time we *are* perfect. It doesn't matter. Creation doesn't give a shit. Only we do, and it is holding us back. You might believe that you have to be in a certain place, or be able to hold a special skill to help and guide others. Not so. All you have to do is be you, and there is always someone that will need what you have to offer. You are enough, always. You have a gift, you have an experience that others can benefit from, and you're able to change someone else's life *today*.

> "We can't help everyone, but everyone can
> help someone" – Ronald Reagan

No more people pleasing:

It is time to recover from being a people pleaser, and it starts with *you*. It is always you, me, and *us*. I am sure that we all recognize this trait. Trying to do the right thing, for a series of reasons. To not have to deal with conflict, to not have to worry about someone, or to get some attention and validation.

Practice listening to yourself. Be mindful of your own thoughts and feelings. They indicate how you perceive your life. They also tell you some valuable information about your belief system in general. Let them guide you and be your friends. Emotions and feelings are a natural part of you. Acknowledge them as your friends. Let them speak, and listen.

Be humble and connected. You are a part of the God force, and as long as you stay connected, you will need no validation from others. Stop chasing the outside for what you are looking for. It was always within. Get real with your own shortcomings and strengths. Appreciate, pray and be true to yourself.

Be open and honest. Be authentic and real towards others. Stand your ground by learning how to say no. You have to set your own boundaries. Both *yes* and *no* has a place in your life, although to reject is most often the hardest thing to do. You are allowed to disagree with anyone about anything. Look at why you are not comfortable choosing yourself and your own needs. Let no one tell you what to do, say or feel.

Respect others. Respect other people's feelings and choices, and expect them to do the same. Don't preach over them or tell them what to do. Don't help until asked, and see each person as having their own journey. You are not the lead in their life. You are only the boss of your own. Stay in the service mode towards the world, without having a need to fix anything or anyone. Who gave you the authority to try to change anyone? Allow them the integrity to make their own decisions.

Stay clear of people pleasing. We were never meant to be pleasers. We are givers. We are all our own authorities and equally able to make our own choices. We are not meant to compromise for validation. Through mutual respect and encouragement, we can live in support of each other. You are free. Whatever you thought you had to do, or who you needed to please, you are hereby off the hook. Recap that energy and use it for something that will cultivate growth and happiness.

How can you make a true impact?

Wanting to serve and give is a natural trait in a human being. It is a sign of healthy soul and an inspired spirit. Having a positive impact on the world is a blessing, and something to stretch towards for all of us. With all this crazy, mind-blowing manipulation going on, all givers and awakened spirits needs to step forth. The world needs you, it needs all of us. A small act of kindness and service will make a huge impact. Not only for a person or a family, but on the world in general. I believe we all have that longing to make a difference. We want to matter. We want our lives to matter.

I remember the first time someone wrote me and told me that because of me, they were no longer suicidal. Because of what I had told them and shown them, they were now on their way to a happy healthy life. A woman sent me a message saying that she was no longer diabetic, and that because of this, she had inspired her sister to help herself too. She was now cancer free. We are not all meant to work with people on this level, although we can all do something that will impact the masses. By simply living your truth, you are spreading the light. By simply walking your talk, you are leading others. By simply being loving and caring from your heart, you are helping others open their own hearts. Sharing is caring.

The world needs more fruit trees, more forests, clean water and clean air. Maybe you have a passion for the environment and can contribute to a better world by helping heal Mother Earth. Our children need our attention and our love, to be able to grow up feeling free in a world of chaos and stress filled living. People are suffering, starving, lost and running from war. Animals are suffering, and just by educating yourself, you are raising your awareness and the ability to positively impact a cause that is close to your heart. It will come to you, once you step out of the pleasing mode.

For years I played the phrase in my head: *"How can I serve"*. It revealed itself to me. It became a natural part of my life. When we contribute, we fill our cups. We are charged with love and gratitude.

Expect nothing, give what you can.

Make friends with some new thoughts of abundance. Being able to give comes from the knowing that there is always enough. You are always enough, and you have more than you need. More love, more good intentions, smiles, encouraging words, enthusiastic engagement and authentic interest. Ask yourself these questions every day;

How can I serve?
How can I add value?
How can I make a positive impact?
How can I be my very best while being of service?
What is my true calling?

Be quiet and listen for the answer. It might come right away, or show itself at the right time, as your life changes for the better. It will come from your passion and love for life, never from fear or ego-based thinking. There is no right or wrong way to contribute. While it might seem little or insignificant to you, it can be life-changing to another. You don't have to be perfect to be a mentor or a leader. You just have to be genuine. I stared guiding others long before I was fully educated or healed. People needed my knowledge. They needed someone who were more experienced than they were. There are always people and situations that need what you can give. Chop wood, carry water, smile, show up and power up yourself. Be open and willing. It is a blessing.

By being of service you are also utilizing your gifts. They are given to us, as a service to the world. So, by using them you are blessing others, and by doing so you are blessing yourself. It will transform your whole life to let your talents flow. A musician does the world service with his or her music. Touching souls and raising the vibration.

When you express yourself through enthusiasm you are inspiring others to be of service as well. The ripple-effect is unstoppable. Just by being happy, you are serving. So you see, in term, taking care of *you*, is of great service to humanity. So simple, so profound.

Create through the clarity of your own vibration. Create your desires and let the manifestations that come from them be the service to this world. Being of service does not mean you are going to fill a void of lack. Not at all. It simply means being in your own flow, so that the whole world will benefit. You are unique and the world needs you. Not as a pleaser, but as a contributor of your true self and passion. You are unique, and that in itself is enough. Be true, be real, be loving and be present. You are a gift. Give it!

A life lived with passion willingness to be of service will never let you down. The power of creation will manifest a tenfold return. Not as a means of thank you, but as a natural part of the flow of creation. Let your life expand beyond the daily routines of work and obligation. Let there be room to give back, and to receive. You might feel drawn to donate to a good cause, volunteer at a soup kitchen, an animal shelter or a crises center. A neighbor might need a strong hand. You might feel drawn to charity work in your community or to spend your life travelling the world sharing a message of hope and inspiration. It does not matter. By walking your walk and your own talk, you are always enough. Leave your heart open to new ideas. Be inviting, and watch how life unfolds at a new level. All you have to do is live.

Chapter 18

Letting go of the outcome

" If I only knew how to find the man of my dreams, I would do it. All the lists that I have made, about how he will look, the color of his eyes, how he will be. He must absolutely be highly intelligent. A successful businessman. He also needs to love skiing. I have a long list, as he needs to be perfect. I am so done with those losers. Never treating me right, and always depending on me for everything. Well, not everything, but still. He better be perfect this time. I have been searching for years. I even signed up for this group coaching, all about how to attract the perfect mate. No results. What is wrong with me? Why is he not showing up like I have envisioned? Crap, I feel lonely at times. Sometimes I would settle for someone nice. Someone who made me feel special and loved. Someone who would support me and believe in me. Someone who made me feel good about who I am. Now that would be something. I wish. Oh well, not sure where a guy like that would come from. What would he look like?"

Have you ever had an expectation that wasn't met, or a circumstance that did not reflect how you had envisioned it would be? It will make us feel like we did something wrong, like we didn't do everything the way we should have. Why did this happen? What went wrong? Nothing. Not a thing. It just didn't go *the way* you thought it would, *when* you thought, and *how*. As long as we believe that we know the best outcome for ourselves, we might get disappointed and feel let down. Why didn't the Universe deliver? I planned it all out, in detail. I wanted to be happy, and worked hard at focusing on that scenario. I know what will make me happy, right? Maybe wrong.

I learned this the hard way. When I was bedridden, all I wanted was to get healthy. Of course, right? All I wanted was to get healthy right now. Over night. Just let me get this done and over with. I was asking for healing and happiness. I worked towards that goal every single day. From the moment I opened my eyes, until I went back to sleep, I studied and practiced towards that one goal. "Show me the way, thank you for this healing." I had no idea how grand that wish was. I wanted complete healing, yet I believed that meant to feel symptom free, just like that, and that was it. Not so. I had asked for something that would take eight years to accomplish, even though I am not sure it is ever accomplished. Still, it took me nearly eight years to realize the full extent of my wish, and the perfection in the way that it unfolded. The Universe was guiding me and giving me exactly what I wished for, and more. I didn't know better. How could I know what perfect health and healing would look like? I had never experienced it. I had no perception of the how and the when. All I had was the ego that wanted out of pain, and the control freak inside of me that wanted it to happen in a certain way.

What we need to fulfill our dream and mission might not always be what we believe and expect it to be. Our perception is limited, and our vision is not clear. How would we know? We have never experienced it before. How will we know what is the best way for anything to unfold? We don't. This is why we have trust and faith.

My life was always a blessing, even though I couldn't see it before or during my journey through Hell. My path was always perfect, although I believed otherwise at the time. I was living through what we as humans believe is a nightmare. We cannot embrace the full and clear picture. How could we? The possibilities are infinite, and we are often too caught up in the outcome to notice and appreciate the experience in the *now* moment. Not until I was well into saving my life, back to being able to take some very short walks, fully educated as a health and Wellness Coach, could I see that everything was happening at the perfect time for me. My experience is priceless. My knowledge and firsthand suffering and hopelessness has left me wiser and more capable to spread my message than anything else. I have not only been healed at a physical, emotional and spiritual level. I have been conditioned to help others. I got what I asked for and so much more. I have been shown the way. I have experienced true healing, and I have found my way to serve. Even at my darkest hours, when I did not want to live, I was aware that I was taught to let go of the outcome. I was crazily attached to the outcome. I was a control freak. I had work to do. I couldn't grasp the concept for several years. Not care about the outcome? Should I not give a damn if I got well or not? What was the use in working so diligently and hard, all day every day, with a one-hundred percent focus, if I was not to care if I made it or not? I know, hard to wrap the mind around. The energy is this: There is a big difference between not caring about the outcome and letting go of it. When we let go of any type of control we allow what is best for us to enter. Letting go of the outcome means that we need to surrender to the process and not hold on to any idea or fear about when and how things will happen, but stay in faith and trust that it IS happening. We have to step aside, get out of the way and let spirit work *through* us and *for* us.

There are no rejections, only redirection, remember? Life is never working against us, but *for* us. If you are sick, of ill health, do what you need to do to allow your body to heal, and step aside. Let it happen. Don't get mental about it. You will lose yourself and cling to an outcome that might not even be the one you think it should be. Trust yourself and God. Trust life, and let go. You have set your goal. You have ordered health. You have mapped out a plan, and if not, you need to. Get educated, and get serious. Read up and take charge. Letting go of the outcome is not the same as leaving everything to chance. It is not about not having to actually do what needs to be done. It has everything to do with just that, and then let it go. Now, focus on health only, on healthy thoughts and activities, on happy feelings and what makes you feel good. As long as you stay with it, health will come, at the perfect time for you. As long as you keep your focus on building your business, one day at the time, keeping your schedule, always stretching and advancing, the results you want *will* come. Life has your back, and as we live we learn. As we learn we grow, and as we grow we evolve. If you are in a financial rut, you need to make a plan. You need to take charge and do what you need to do to make the steps needed to change the situation. Once you have the plan at hand, let it go. Spend your time focusing on abundance, while you keep on following your plan. Worries leads nowhere, besides being an open order for more to worry about.

> "What we need, to really get what we want out of life, is not always clear to us. Happiness might come in a different shade than the ones we know."- Hilde Larsen

Even after my crash, my complete disability, I wanted to stay on my current path of ignorance and hunger for validation. I studied journalism while throwing up between classes. I was sure I had the right idea of what the rest of my life would look like, *and* that it was the best view for me and my ego. I was convinced that I could force my destiny if I only used enough strength and persistence. I could not. We cannot. We are too narrow minded, stubborn and out of sync with who we really are. The Universe and God gifted me with a gem larger and brighter than I could have ever imagined. I surrendered to the rest of my life. I let go of the need to attach myself to any outcome. I know that following my passion and working hard will be enough. I know that serving and living with gratefulness and eagerness in my heart will always take me to where I need to go.

We use the phrase "to chase our dream", as if chasing anything is a great idea. Why would we try to run after anything? It will feel like a chase when we hang on to control. Controlling is the opposite of allowing. We cannot forcefully *make* anything happen. It represents trouble. I was a control-freak, bigtime. Not an uncommon trait by those who want a lot out of life. We tend to see letting go, or giving up anything, as a weakness. Now where would such an idea come from? The old conditioning again. The false beliefs we are so dearly attached to.

> Like the weather, our lives will change. It can blow a storm over night, or feel like an endless rainy day. All we can do is to flow with it, change our clothes, be prepared, plan and enjoy. In the same way that we cannot control the weather, we cannot control our lives. We can go with the flow, plan ahead, enjoy every day, and know that there is always sunshine behind every cloud.

Stop being a control freak:

Take a close look at your life, and see how you are trying to control the different aspects of it. Look at how you are pounding on closed doors, stressed out if things don't go your way. How are you handling other's shortcomings or methods of planning and living? How are you trying to ensure what you perceive as success, in every situation? If things are not the way you like them, do you panic? If plans are changed at the last minute, do you freak out? Do you micro-plan everything, every little detail? It makes you feel safe, secure.

- **Control is always rooted in fear.** It represents an addiction to security. What better way to ensure that you are safe than being able to plan every little detail, and to be confident that nothing *"goes wrong".* There is no better way to make sure you look good, feel good and have everything you believe that you need, then by controlling as much as possible. The fear of exposure, of unexpected events are overwhelming for a control freak. They are happy when everything is in order, and when everything is done the right way. *Their* way.

- **You don't have to be Miss or Mr. perfect.** There is no such thing. Get over it. We try to control things because of what we think will happen if we don't. What happens if we fail, if we miss the boat, if not everybody shows up for the event, or if the car is not clean before picking up your boss? What happens if you lose a business deal or a client? What happens if things simply fall apart and get messy? A control freak will feel like a complete failure. They carry every outcome on their shoulders. A heavy load to carry. Imagine being responsible for everything around you, not only in your own business, but in everybody's business. How many businesses can one have? A countless amount. Although a controlling person is mostly concerned with those that affect- and will reflect back on them. It does not all have to do with honor and not wanting to show weakness. It also has to do with order, and not having to be subject to sudden change in plans. You cannot control sudden changes. Let go of the need for everything to look and be perfect, it never will be anyway. And you, if you keep trying, will miss out on all the fun of flowing freely through life.

- **You don't have to be right.** Realize that you don't know what is best all the time. Being right is overrated. Who cares about who is right or not? Even changing your mind is ok. Nothing stays the same. Change is constant. Sometimes what we believed to be right, is not, and a redirection is necessary. Nothing to get stressed out about. It is life. Get used to not knowing it all. You don't.

- **Listen to others, they might have a smart idea or two.** You are not the only one with a brain and a good idea. Let them shine. Practice stepping aside in one area of your life, and observe what happens. You might get anxious at first, but it might also give you some freedom to play. Your way is never the only way. Look at your standards, and surround yourself with people that have similar standards as you. Often, we'll try to compensate, and end up controlling the outcome of any task that is not heading in the direction of our standards. Step aside and let others have a say. Let them come forth with their own opinion and suggestions.

- **You will live.** You don't have to micro manage the whole Universe. Day and night will come, the sun will rise and you will live. No matter what happens around you, even if it's utter chaos, you will live through it. Nothing is more important than your ability to trust life and your path. Connect with your own inner knowing, and surrender to the fact that you have no idea what will happen for the rest of your life. It is uncontrollable. All you can do is direct your visions, thoughts, emotions and actions in the direction that you choose. Then, sit back and allow. Enjoy the ride as you surrender to life.

Loosen up and let go of the outcome. Don't take life so seriously, it is soon over. In the meantime, don't miss out by holding on to holding on.

Don't confuse being a control freak and a semi-crazy; "let me control not only me but everybody's business", with taking charge of your life. You are in charge. That front seat can never be given away, not really. You are always responsible. When you are driving your car you better be in control. You better keep your own hands on that wheel. You better stay focused and alert.

"God, grant me the serenity to accept the things I cannot change,
The courage to change the things I can,
And the wisdom to know the difference."[17]

The art of surrendering:

To surrender means the opposite of resisting. It means you stop fighting and resisting life and its natural flow, and float downstream. Stop paddling upstream against the current. It is much harder. It is exhausting and draining. Creativity is lost, and there is not much time or focus on the surroundings, or the people around you. It takes your entire focus, just to stay afloat. After a while the whole ride becomes nothing but a struggle, and every little rock feels like a mountain. You can never rest, constantly having to be focused on keeping yourself afloat and alive. Surrendering is about letting go of the paddling, letting yourself be carried downstream. Your life automatically shifts. You still have to steer and do some paddling, but you can now enjoy the scenery. You are able to look ahead, and to rest when you need to. You have extra energy and life looks brighter. When you are heading downstream you are always on the right path. You can trust life.

Surrendering is a conscious choice. The key is to accept what is, to recognize that which is here in this moment. We have to completely accept what we are experiencing, and still know that everything will be ok. Having faith is a large part of letting go of control, to surrender.

Ask yourself this question; What is the worst that can happen? Until you are fine with the answer, you cannot surrender fully. So, the worst that can happen is that dinner will not be ready in time. You will live. Or that you will lose your job, or might. A bit tougher. What would happen if you lost your job? No money for a while, losing the house, a scary scenario that could be broken down to being

---

[17] *Serenity Prayer* by Reinhold Niebuhr

homeless and hungry. What could also happen is that you found a better job and ended up making twice the money you did.

Letting go of any outcome through complete surrender is a process that has many layers. By constantly doing better, you will keep recognizing new levels of fear-based, controlling behavior. I believe that as we peel back to what we really fear the most, we end up with the fear of dying. I believe that our core fear of death, is holding us back from completely surrendering to life. For me, everything shifted the day I surrendered to life *and* death. I was so sick and tired of being sick and tired. I was so tired of struggling, trying to get well I was so drained by trying to figure everything out, to want my health so badly, I was exhausted. I had invested my whole existence on the outcome, and I was holding on to it for my dear life. I had to get healthy, I just had to. What would happen if didn't? I would most likely die. As much as I loved life, I surrendered and said; You know what? That is fine, death is okay. I am going to do my very best, every single day. I am going to love the life that I have been given. I am going to keep my focus on healing, without it having to happen in a certain way, at a certain time, or as I see it, not at all. By stating, *show me the way*, I was giving away my control. I could relax and *know* that it would all evolve perfectly, and it has.

> Life is not about trying to put everything into a pre-made form or template. We cannot gather information that will keep us from experiencing unforeseen events. We cannot build a wall to protect us from life, nor can we control every outcome and the way our journey unfolds.

We have been conditioned to be seekers. Always looking for the good life. As if there is a destination and a pot of gold waiting at the end of the rainbow, we continue to search for the good life. Happiness has become something that people of this modern world have as an ultimate life goal. Everything we do and want is connected to outer search. It shall come through something we find, become or accomplish. From the lack of trust in ourselves, and in life, we have become restless seekers of everything we believe we lack or miss within ourselves. The thing is, we miss nothing. We are not missing a link, or a single cell. We are whole, as humans, here to explore and to enjoy the ride. Nothing messes up a fun and educational ride like trying to hang on to the past or present situation. When we spend our time clinging to an outcome, trying to control it, we miss the ride itself. Nothing stays the same - but for now, the sun rises every morning. Have faith in *that*, yourself and the fact that no matter what happens, you did your very best.

> "To the work you own the right, but not to the results thereof." – First Tenant of Karma Yoga[18]

Surrender to your life:

By practicing different meditations and stillness techniques, journaling and mindfulness, you can work on your ability to walk lighter and more fluent through life. The less you hold on to, the lighter your steps will be. The less you are occupied with an outcome, the more capable you will be to expand your perspective. We have been deceived by our lifelong conditioning. We have been falsely led to believe that the more we think, the smarter we get. Our brain has been highly overrated, and we are doing ourselves a great disservice by believing we can think our way through life.

1. **Meditate:** Sit or lie down in a comfortable position and focus on your breath. Simply breathe and let your mind wander. It doesn't matter of you are an experienced meditator, or a freshman, all you've got to do is to be still. When you work on surrendering, work on being nothing. You, breath, and that's it. When the mind comes in, let it pass by. Let every thought become insignificant. Pay as little attention to it as you can. Let it drift past you until you find stillness. If you feel

---

[18] http://upliftconnect.com/something-missing-from-your-spiritual-practice/

you wander into a thought, pull yourself back and connect with your breath. Don't get attached to anything. Just flow and breathe. This is a great practice to let go of your mind- and control-freak tendencies.

2. **Compassionate writing and living:** Gift yourself a new journal for this purpose only. Set aside ten minutes every day to write and contemplate. Shift your focus from your life, to that of others. Write about what you would like to contribute to this world. What would you want to do to change other people's lives for the better? Imagine what that would look like. Write about how their suffering would end, and how the world would look if your visions came true. This is a focus exercise to shift from you to that around you. Once we step outside of our own little lives, we detach from our constant self-focus and therefore control. See how you wish everyone to be happy. Not only yourself. By seeing that we are all dependent on each other, we get less attached and more at ease. Walk through your day with a compassionate heart for everyone. Broadcast live and open your heart.

3. **Observe and expand**: By stepping out of the constant thinking mode, we can observe more. By detaching from the drama in our lives and any current situation, we can more easily see a larger picture. Life is so much grander and colorful than what meets the eye. By pulling back from our daily and weekly situation, the details become less obvious. Notice how your focus on the little things become less important as you expand your vision. Desires and aversions, our typical narrow focus will fade as we expand. Look at every moment as something valuable for all that it is. See how life is larger than yourself. See how you are blessed to be a part of this creation. Spend some time every day to just observe and be grateful. Life is larger than anything you or me can control.

4. **Accept everything**: To be able to fully surrender to the outcome, we must first accept what is. By meditating and expanding, you are already practicing acceptant living, but perhaps not in the way that you think. You are accepting that your life is a part of everybody else's. Your current situation might not be ideal, but it's yours, and it is where your potential lies. Love everything about it. Explore the situation, and know that it is changing from moment to moment. Not through force, but through growth and awareness. Be at peace with what is. Be at peace with your own situation. Walk forward in faith.

> "If we are facing in the right direction, all we have to do is keep on walking." ~Proverb

Chapter 19

From knowledge to wisdom

"*Had I only known that everything didn't have to be this complicated. Had I only listened more to my own voice instead of all that modern medicine's so-called knowledge. Had I only listened to my gut feeling and not my brain and my fear. I would have saved myself years of suffering. All that modern technology, complicating everything. All the books, the knowledge, where is it taking us? Really?*

Shooting off to the moon is one thing, but we are shooting ourselves in the foot at the same time. We think we are so smart. The news drive me crazy sometimes. I mean, hello, spending all those efforts searching for answers in outer space when we cannot even comprehend what is right in front of us. What is the point? I've got all these meds here, and for what? Nearly killed me. Had I only known nature would be all that I needed. My brain got in the way for sure. My intelligence blurred my vision. It is crazy how we are trying to override nature with our highly respected, evolved brains, while killing ourselves in the process. We don't know much about what really matters, it seems. We need to rewire and get in touch with our wisdom. Maybe modern should step aside and listen to ancient teachings? How about that for a change? It might save us from a lot of suffering and misery. I appreciate a great surgeon, believe me, but this medicating, we-know-all mentality, is killing me. Had I only known. I am going to smarten up and do my own research for sure. I am going to listen with more than my ears from now on."

We often mistake knowledge for wisdom. They are related, but not at all the same. You can know all there is about a subject, but still not be a wise person. Knowledge is the accumulation of facts and information. The facts that we see as true at the time. The more knowledge that we seek, the more wisdom we will gain. The search from knowing will awaken our wisdom. Knowledge is the messenger, and it can call on your inner truth, but it is not wisdom. We do not seek wisdom - we meet it. When we least expect it, it will be recognized as kindred. In the world of technology, control and power, we have been conditioned to let our brain take over, and distract us from the wisdom that we all have within. We will be wiser, the more knowledge we acquire, if what we have been seeking is rooted in truth. All knowledge does not support wisdom. As long as we are fed with propaganda, untruths and fictional distorted "facts", we can easily get lost in a world of false knowledge.

You might think you know:

Knowing is a subjective concept, although we base the knowledge itself on truth. Not only on our own truth, but on that of anyone who has a position as a teacher. Be it through reading, observing or vocal communication, knowledge is taken in as a part of our truth. Accumulated and filtered by our ability and capability to understand and comprehend. Because of this, we look for knowledge and facts where it is represented in a way that we can resonate and make some use of it. Filtered through our false beliefs and subconscious programming, it can completely lose its original form or intent. Through our own perception of life, we color our judgments and understanding of anything from religious to political information. As knowledge is gathered from information together with experience, every one of us will have our own personal truth and knowing. Not that there aren't ground rules and laws of the universe, but we color them all. That is what makes each person's input interesting and valuable.

For some, the seeking of knowledge never ends, and for others, it doesn't have such a sexy appeal. They would rather have the solution or the outcome served to them on a silver platter. Seeking knowledge through educating themselves doesn't seem appealing, or so it seems. I believe there is a blockage, a resistance that hinders the natural flow of curiosity. As humans, we are naturally eager to earn, to evolve and to create. Any obstruction of that energy will leave us miserable. Taking the back seat to seeking knowledge often leads to frustration and disappointment.

As knowing is not an absolute, it can lead us to new false beliefs. What you *think* you know might not be so. It will change as you learn and experience life. "If I had known then what I know now," paints a good picture of how we keep learning throughout our entire lives. Look at the young people that believe they know everything. They know what they need to know in that moment in life, some of it will be forgotten, and some will lead to exploring and experiencing. The trouble comes from hanging on to what you think you know. To *think* you know is not to know.

> **"Wisdom is realizing that what you know will change, and that through the gathering of knowledge you will get wiser." – Hilde Larsen**

What you think you know might hurt you:

What you are told to be true, might hurt you. What you don't know might hurt you. As long as you base your knowing on gathered information you can never fully rely on it. We believe, we assume, we think and we have faith. All well and good, although not showing any real leadership energy. You might not feel the need to know everything, or to learn new skills. You might not feel drawn to constantly evolving and exploring. That is a choice.

- **Believing *in* something**, or believing something, from the heart, not from the I-want-to-believe mind, is a true connection to our intuition. Although the word is used loosely, as a disempowering state of "just" having a belief, true belief is anchored in our inner knowing. On the flip-side we believe what our conscious mind is telling us we believe. A mind trap waiting to happen.
- **When we assume anything**, we step aside from our responsibility to do our research and own homework. Assuming is not the same as letting life flow, living by following the currant downstream. It is based upon ignorance and a lack of interest. By assuming, you have handed over your power. Given it away. As children we'd say: *You might make an ass out of* you *and* me.
- **You might *think* this is the only way,** but that is nothing but a thought. When you think, you are being vague. Thinking is often overrated. To resonate and gather information will lead to true knowledge and wisdom. To *think* that you know, is to not connect with your inner knowing. When we know, we know. When we think we know, we don't.
- **Faith is precious.** It connects us to the divine. It keeps us strong when we have no idea what else to hold on to. True faith is the knowing and the inner belief that is anchored in truth. The way we live today has taught us to have faith also in something else. In the outside authorities, marketing, untrue propaganda and hurtful teachings. To have real faith, in you, God, nature and life, you need to be able to discern between truth and agenda. Truth never has one.

When you are a knowledge seeker and a truth seeker, you are on the path of revealing true wisdom. Through awakening to the divine part of who you are, the inner knowing will arise. When your gathered knowledge is in alignment with who you really are, you find wisdom.

What other people believe, becomes a part of your truth.
What you have read becomes a part of your truth.
What you believe becomes your truth.
What you see around you, becomes your truth.
What you feel becomes your truth.
Your experience is your truth.

Ask yourself; What is the source of what I believe to be true? Have I gathered my own knowledge? Have I done my own research? The crazy and sometimes scary wealth of information out there, can be overwhelming, or an asset. As long as you take it upon yourself to seek the knowledge you acquire, you are being a conscious creator. When you leave it to others, in any way shape or form, you are being closer to an unconscious sleep walker.

A knowledge-gatherer, is a truth seeker, and wiser person.

Knowledge is power:

Although we have been told that knowledge is power, it is not necessarily in itself very powerful. It is a tool that can be used for good, bad, or not at all. The beholder of the information, how it has been retrieved, and how it has been processed, holds the key. The ones that are changing this world, making the rules, showing the way, are all seekers of truth and knowledge. They are the ones that find the wisdom and the pot of real gold. The no bullshit, free zone, outside of la-la land. They are givers and free-thinkers. They are the crazy ones, the fearless crowd. They all hold this power over their own lives that allow them to go places, to where others will follow. For the power in them, holds something most people want. I call it freedom.

We have to distinguish between two kinds of power. That of the outer world, and that of our inner world. The knowledge that creates and builds confidence, holds power over how we live our lives. More knowledge, less fear. Be it most of what we fear comes from uncertainty, by harvesting knowledge we feel safer and more confident. We feel stronger and more powerful in general. The outer world looks different when we are informed and growing. Our inner world is greatly affected by our knowledge, as it speaks to our cells. Our whole inner terrain is formed by our beliefs and knowledge. The placebo effect is a great teacher of this point. The term comes from the Latin meaning "I will please". It is used in the medical profession, to show how people react when they believe they are taking a pill for a specific symptom or ailment. The response can be both positive and negative. For instance - symptoms may approve for some, while others may experience side-effects. Side effects of something they are not even taking. They only *believe* they are - or in other words, *they know* they are. The power of the inner knowing. The research has focused on the mind-body connection. How it works, theoretically, intellectually, understandable for the brain, no doctor or scientist has a good answer to. In nature, it is one of the laws. Mind over matter.

> "When you know you know, it becomes true
> power - why? Because you have touched
> upon your wisdom." – Hilde Larsen

A biologist, Bruce Lipton PhD, shows us how our cells are directly affected by our beliefs and inner truths. What we think we know matter to every cell in our body. Through his research, Dr. Lipton and other cutting-edge scientists, mind-blowing discoveries have been made about the interaction between our mind and body. Dr. Lipton shows the process by which cells receive information, and how our genes and DNA do not control our biology. They are controlled by signals from outside the cells. Our mind and our thoughts are in charge! When we look at this information together with the power of the subconscious mind, our false beliefs, our programming and conditioning, you will see where I am going with this. What we have been fed, bullshit or not, is actually controlling our health, and maybe even our genes. That is true power. Careful what you think you know. Does it benefit you? Is it making you wiser, stronger, healthier, happier and more compassionate? If not, keep exploring and growing. [19]

The opposite of a placebo is called nocebo. It is defined as generating the negative outcome, rather than the positive we are looking for in the placebo effect. It has a name, the fact that we are affected by everything we believe, good or bad. A doctor might tell someone they have two months to live, and so it is. They are most often right. Their internal clock is set on what they now believe to be absolute true, and they die, often on the exact day of their predictions. If you think you will die, you most likely will. I have seen people go downhill fast after they have gotten their predicted time of death. "How long do I have doctor"? Come on! No human can tell you how long you are going to live. On the brighter note, when the same doctor tells a patient with the same condition, he has no illness, the story is often very different. They recover. Mind over matter. Careful who you listen to. We believe, and then manifest our truth.

> **"The true sign of intelligence is not knowledge but imagination." - Albert Einstein**

Wisdom, God and nature:

There is wisdom in nature. It teaches us what works and what doesn't. By expanding our knowledge, we will better know how to use nature as our teacher and guide. By looking back on ancient

---

[19] *The biology of belief* – Bruce Lipton Ph.D

cultures, we can learn how they lived and thrived, but most of all we can learn something about ourselves. About how connected to nature we are. From dirt to dirt. All the wisdom comes back to us through closer seeking where we come from. Not only to the beautiful forests and lakes, the ocean and the beaches, but within our own pool of inner nature. The so-called natural. We use this phrase all the time. Like a quality stamp, a label of high ethics and health. Natural. Nothing about us is not natural, not by creation. Nothing in nature, on this earth or from it is anything *but* natural. The further away from it we wander, the more we suffer. By turning to nature for a deeper knowledge and understanding, we awaken to who we are, and find the wisdom that holds truth. Once we see the miracle that we are a part of, that are us, we open our hearts to what is really worth knowing. We become more generous and humble, more compassionate, and ultimately wiser from it. True wisdom is not of the mind.

According to The Essene Gospel of peace, there are three paths leading to Truth. The path of the consciousness, path of nature, and the accumulated experience of past generations.

The path of the consciousness, is that followed by the great mystics. To them, consciousness is the most immediate reality for humans, and also the key to the universe. Through the belief that consciousness is all that is within and around us, it is separated from the material world, and governs different laws of nature. While the laws of mathematics are valid in the material universe, they're not in the realm of consciousness. Our perception of time is believed to seize to exist. Time is not seen as linear as we reflect on it, with our past, present and future. Everything we see as true in this material world, has a different understanding outside this time, space and reality. Consciousness is pure, timeless, space-less and formless. The Essene traditions understands and interprets consciousness as being our source of energy, knowledge and harmony. Therefore, it is the first path to truth.

The path of nature takes us from the inner world to the outer world. As the path of consciousness embodies everything not of a material and physical nature, the second path takes us to the external reality of our world. Through experimenting, scientific research, and other methods of analysis, we now look at measurements and quanta. Through telescopes and space ships, mathematics and what we see as hard evidence, we acknowledge a sense of correlations. Knowledge and wonder about our world and universe becomes evident. We find cause and effect, and we find complexity, yet simplicity. This truth reveals that beyond what any scientist can see, there is something else, something grander. Any scholar or intellectual analysis that uses the truth as their own, has not grasped the bigger picture of creation. Nature and its simplicity is more complex that anything ever created by man. We can merely observe, learn from it and explore its principles and laws.

In nature, we can find absolutely everything. It will reveal to us, the laws of the Universe and the truth to we are a part of. We have read about the masters of the past, the great teachers, like Jesus, Buddha, Moses, and the Essenes. They were all said to have wandered into the mountains, the desert and the wild to acquire real wisdom and truth. From connecting with nature, thus God. From exploring the two connecting paths, consciousness and nature.

The wisdom, experience and knowledge gathered by our ancestors, the masters, and the great thinkers, has left us with the wise and knowledge-based scriptures. Real Universal literature from those who walked before us. This is the basis of our heritage, how we see the world, and what we believe is true. From religious beliefs, to social and tribal conduct, we walk in the footsteps of those who learned and wondered.

The Essenes did not have the technology that we have today, and most likely not the disconnection that we experience from the source. From wandering off our path, we are experiencing symptoms that our forefathers did not. Our path is different as we are very much numbed down by toxins and distractions, yet we can still find teaching in these old writings and understandings. They might even be what we need to study more, to find our way back. If we can let go of dogmatic interpretations and controlled understandings, we might find some hidden gems that will open that floodgate to our inner freedom. We are free to take whatever we want from anything that has been left for us, or tried to be forced on us even. Discernment is our own responsibility, and once we are no longer held captive by our false world views we will know the real message in any text. Any old teaching has to be seen in view of the time in which they were written. Words are also limiting and often insufficient. This is why nature in itself is the greatest teacher. It just *is*. [20]

> The eyes through which you see, tell you what you will know from what you see. By that, I mean that everything you bring with you from your own understanding will be your screen where the movie will be played. The movie of *your* life.

"A wise man knows that he knows nothing." - Hilde

The internet, a blessing and a curse?

Let us take the discussion to this age and time. We are living in the internet era. Around forty-nine percent of the world population has an internet connection today. Back in 1995, it was less than one percent. The first billion was reached in 2005, the second in 2010, and the third in 2014. Today in 2016, we are looking at well over 3,5 billion users. I googled it. From 1999 to 2013 it increased by a tenfold. We are looking at about half of the world's population being able

---

[20] *The Essene Gospel of Peace, Book Two* – Edmond Bordeau Szekely

to google just about anything. Around 90% of all Americans, and more than 70% of Europeans are online daily. [21]

This has a tremendous impact on our ability to exchange information, to seek knowledge and to expand our horizon. We can learn any language, download pictures from every corner of the world, and read articles and books. We can watch videos, make videos, watch movies, documentaries and do online courses. We can enroll in educational programs, find old documents, stay connected with friends, and google the answer for just about anything. If it exists, you will find it on google, or so it seems. There is no end to what you can read up on, find information on and download to your computer, phone or tablet. For a lot of us, it is hard to even remember what life was like without the internet. Instant feedback, and instant knowledge. On-the-spot answers to any question imaginable. Where does all this information and material come from? Is it all valid? Is it accurate and true?

The endless stream of information comes from people like you and me. Everyone who has access to a computer can contribute to the pool of data. Every piece of information ever posted by anyone, in form of an article, a document, a blogpost or an e-book, is out there. A curse and a blessing. Not everything holds water, is valid and trustworthy. Not everything is accurate and true. The internet and its humongous amount of informative writings should not be confused with a database of educational material. It is simply a tool and a constantly changing well that reflects how and what we live. Our symptoms and false beliefs are represented, as well as our accomplishments and successes. You will find the most treasurable pieces of information, and the most disturbing ones. What you decide to do with the opportunity that the internet holds, is up to you. You can leave it alone, you can make it part of your business, and you can use it as a source of connection. What might be valid

---

[21] Internetlivestats.com/ internetworldstats.com

and encouraging to you, might not be for another. From having a handful of TV channels to show us what we believed we needed to know, we now have the choice which data we explore. We can do our own research. It takes more effort, and it can absolutely be confusing and time consuming. You can also choose to turn it off, shut it down, step outside, and disconnect completely.

You can choose to let the internet be a part of your life in any way you see fit. Nothing can reach you, if you don't let it. We do still have a choice, even though it might not be obvious. "I need my computer for work". Well, then you do. If that is not where you want to be, get going on changing what you do for a living.

No computer, google, or any media can decide what you believe and know to be your own truth. Nothing outside of yourself can teach you anything you don't want to be taught. Only you, as the master of your input, can decide what to delete, upload or download. You can connect or disconnect from the physical computer, the same way you can connect and disconnect from the source. The same way we pursue our hunt for knowledge and intellectual brain food and mental understanding, we can seek inner wisdom and ultimate truth.

When the head is clear, and you are able to discern what you can use to grow and evolve, new knowledge is fun and easy. There is no need for skepticism or lie-hunting. You will know what is true and what is not, and everything else will have no interest. Pick your battles, and stay true to yourself first, always. It takes courage and fearlessness to steer through the jungle of life, and a sound, focused mind to step out of the game of manipulation of the masses. It takes an awakening and reconnection to who you really are, to set yourself free. Only *you* know what is true to *you*. Your inner wisdom, the same one our ancestors tapped into, will guide you and grow through you.

> We all seek different levels of knowledge, although at the end of the day we all look for the ultimate truth. The inner wisdom that will lead the way to happiness and fulfillment. To feel at home in our own lives.

Can wisdom be taught?

One can be knowledgeable without wisdom, but not wise without knowledge. The dictionary defines *wisdom* as "the ability to discern or judge what is true, right, or lasting." Knowledge is intellectual, wisdom is divine. The divine does not speak through the mind. One is known, the other one is felt. Knowledge is knowing how to use the computer, wisdom is knowing it is nothing more than a myriad of information, and when to shut it down. A mind can be closed, but wisdom is open. One can use one's wisdom to closely go through so called facts, to examine knowledge, and to keep on the true and divine path.

When we can see and understand for ourselves, listen and examine, discern untruths and lies, be open to new ideas and be awake to our surroundings, we are certainly wise.

When we look to our elders, we find that native knowledge has been handed down to us, and grown into deeply respected wisdom from nature. In the book; *Wisdom of the elders,* the native mind is said to operate from a deep sense or reverence for nature, not from an impulse or any human dominance over it. It sees spirit and connects with the consciousness of all that is. Nature and everything in it is considered sacred. The native mind holds the wisdom to honor Mother Earth, and not use it for financial gain or power. Furthermore, we as humans hold an obligation to balance our health and that of our Mother, the Earth. Quite the opposite of what we are actually doing. Producing toxic chemical medications, for economic gain, is not a wise choice, according to the natives. A native mind does not see progress as something physical or measurable. Words are considered spiritual and generative, and the vocabulary of native knowledge is always gentle towards nature, never manipulative or aggressive. Acceptance is part of the trait, as the unknown is considered a blessing. We find empathy, honoring of the elders and a general teaching of the relationship between man and nature.[22]

The part of you that resonates with the native mind, might be what is called your wisdom. It is revealed through an inner knowing, a feeling. It is not explained. It awakens you to the feeling of magnificence and love for yourself and nature. You don't need to digest or think about it, it just *is*. The life long experience of awakening to more and more wisdom through knowledge, shows us how little we know.

Wisdom comes from knowledge and experiences, synthesized into a deep insight and understanding of life. Wisdom is behind every knowledge that has a bearing in truth and growth. Let's have a look at love. We seek it and we experience it. Intelligently we are aware that it exists, but it is not an intelligent experience. Even though we have yet to feel the deep love for another, we have a knowing that it exists. We have a divine and a soulful longing towards what cannot be taught or thought. It can only be experienced, felt and lived. It is but a concept for the mind, a knowing for the heart.

Be wise, and don't believe you need to know it all. Not everything is within the range of our understanding. Look around and see the magic. Breathe the air, pick a flower, watch a butterfly, and realize that we, all of us, have no way at all to understand any of it, with our mind, that is.

"Wisdom is not a product of schooling but of the lifelong attempt to acquire it."- Albert Einstein

---

[22] *Wisdom of the elders* - Peter Knudtson and David Suzuki

Chapter 20

How dare you?

" *This is not exactly comfortable. I had a feeling I would get this reaction, but not openly like this. – "Who do you think you are? How dare you walk out of here like that? No one quits their job like that!" Well, I just did. Didn't I? Just walk. Keep on walking. I have had enough. I am done. Wow, that was wild. What just happened? I have planned this day for so long, and now, look at me. No steady job, no apartment. Sold most of my things, the rest in storage, money in the bank and freedom ahead. Again, wow! The outside of the office building never looked so sweet. The grass never looked greener, and the air never felt fresher and crisper. This is my lucky day! I feel so light. I feel like I have butterflies in my belly. What will the future bring? Ticket to Paris all booked, then Bali. I just have to do Paris. Meeting my old friend that I never got around to visiting, until now! And Bali, my dream come true! Me, writing my novel, living the simple life. Finding some true purpose, resetting my mojo. Pleasing no one, loving everything and everyone. I know, my family, my friends, but you know what? They will be fine. I am not dead, only ready to live!"*

Life is like a soup of experiences. A pot of everything that you ever thought, looked at, felt, imagined and did. What does it taste like? Sweet, sour, hot? We are not this soup, but we accumulate these bits and pieces, these ingredients as we make our choices, and deal with our reality. Leaving the shit out, inviting the bliss in. Taking off the lid, to let the old and stuffy air out. Breathing! Closing some doors, while opening others. Following the beautiful smell of freedom, and flushing some old habits down the drain. As we keep on going, moving forward towards ourselves and our own true self, we become less concerned with being politically correct, and more focused on doing what is right for *us*. By digging deep into your own longing and inner drive, you will find that your calling might result in some life changing actions. That people around you, might not approve of your new and improved lifestyle. The good news is; they don't have to. The bad news? There are none!

> When you dare to follow your own inner dream and intuition, you will have no one to answer to but yourself and God. When you lead, you follow. All the chains have been broken. You can walk freely.

When your wisdom hits you like fireworks, like a strike of lightening, it cannot be overlooked. There is no way you can continue as if nothing magical happened, without hurting. When that blessing hits, you *know* your life has changed. You have been called. Life is here to take you on a journey. When the feeling of inner knowing settles within, it feels like the seeking is over. From constantly searching for the knowledge, the how's and the what's, stillness comes in and makes it all inferior. The call to action is here. The fear and constant need of validation and security is gone. It doesn't matter anymore. None of what seemed so scary and new matters. The wisdom has come with a feeling of trust and faith in life. Not only that, it has also brought the sense that change is something to celebrate. The eagerness to explore has taken the place of the search for knowledge and intelligent solutions. The mind is no longer the boss, it is degraded to a tool and a friend.

Who do you think you are?

When someone steps outside the norm, breaks the rules of the horde, there will be reactions. How can someone willingly quit their job, without having a new one lined up? It does not make sense for anyone following the common-sense rulebook. It has several chapters on security and how to play it safe. It teaches us everything about using our brain to think everything through, and to make calculated decisions, based on our highly respected intellect. Have you ever looked at someone and thought they might have lost their marbles for not making the same decision you would have? We love to stick our noses in other people's business. We love to validate, condemn, correct and compare. What would we do? How could they? This is crazy. I could never. How dare they! Who do they think they are?

Are we responsible for anyone's actions, their responses, and their feedback? Absolutely not. The most freeing part of any journey from bullshit to wisdom is the freedom in that exactly. The core of the matter is this; When you at any point stop, if only for a nanosecond to look for validation, you are not yet free. We know knowledge can lead to wisdom, but there might not be applause from the crowd. It is a lonely path until you find the value of it. It is an empowering path. As long as it is yours, it leads to "home".

There are certain traits or behavioral patterns that have been appointed unsafe and reckless. How dare you be sexy, bold, crazy and spontaneous? How dare you let go of what I, me, the rest of us has worked so hard to hold on to? How dare you be happier than us, are you better? Are you different? People like to fit in, and when you step out and do what you love, no matter what, they get confused. Those that are not loving their life, get irritated, angry even. At you, for representing what they don't dare to do. Or feel they can, or feel they should, for all the reasons that they can find. It was never about them. It was always about you. Your life was always about you, your values, your goals, your compassion, passion, your mission and love.

What others think of you is none of your business.

Better than what?

Someone who is following their dream, is in reality doing what everybody wants and seeks to be able do. Our search for happiness seems endless. Although it is not a destination, we feel it is something we need to reach, to get to, that "place" of happy and content. We might even believe that we are there, until someone shows us, by their crazy actions, that we are not. How dare they! Do they think they are better than us? We could argue that actually they are. They are closer to living their purpose, and following their own path. They have broken free from what we are still stuck in. How hopeless and helpless that makes us feel. And frustrated. When someone else do their thing, it can look very easy. Especially when they are good at it. As if it didn't take a world of courage and bravery, and weren't the scariest thing ever. It probably was.

The Law of Jante, takes us back to the conscious and subconscious programming that keeps a whole society locked in their place. Danish/Norwegian author Aksel Sandemose wrote these Laws in 1930, as a part of a novel, describing how in a small town, Jante, the attitude towards individuality and success were dismissing. Achievers were not accepted, and discouraged.[23]

There are ten rules in the law as defined by Sandemose's novel. They all lead to the same underlying theme: You should not think you are anyone special or that you are better than us.

---

[23] https://en.wikipedia.org/wiki/Law_of_Jante

The ten rules of Jante:

1. You're not to think *you* are anything special.
2. You're not to think *you* know more than *we* do.
3. You're not to think *you* are more important than *we* are.
4. You're not to think *you* are good at anything.
5. You're not to laugh at *us*.
6. You're not to think *you* are as good as *we* are.
7. You're not to think *you* are smarter than *we* are.
8. You're not to convince yourself that *you* are better than *we* are.
9. You're not to think anyone cares about *you*.
10. You're not to think *you* can teach *us* anything.

It is suggested by Sandemose that by obeying these rules, the community would be more harmonious. Since then, the meaning of Jante's Law, has been extended to refer to any form of personal criticism towards those breaking out of the norm, or reaching higher position in general. When we look at the above statements, it brings us to the reason we might be experiencing a lack of encouragement when we do what is not generally done. Why we might run into envy, eyeballing and even whispers in the hallways. We have been brainwashed for generations to believe that we should and should not. Be careful who you listen to. *Is it true, is it kind, is it necessary?*

We are all family. We are all here together. We are brothers and sisters. We lift each other, and stand on each other's shoulders. Every successful man or woman has climbed and held onto someone else. A word, a poem, a smile or a helping hand. We never do anything completely alone. We are never better than, only different. We are never more, and cannot take away anyone else's mojo. We only have our own to use, and everyone else has their special set of potentials. Let us kick the Law of Jante out the door, and replace it with a set of uplifting affirmations that will serve us, not disconnect us.

My ten rules of empowerment:

1. *Believe* that you are special.
2. *Be confident* about your knowledge.
3. *You matter.*
4. *You are good* at many different things. You are gifted.
5. *Laugh* every day.
6. We are all in this *together.*
7. You are *smart and able.*
8. You are always *enough.*
9. You are *loved* beyond belief.
10. You have *something to bring* to this world.

Feeling empowered and free, is not the same as feeling superior. Okay, so you are taking a leap, finally breaking out of your old ways. Does this mean you are now better than anyone else? No. Simple, not at all. There is no such thing. We are all here on this journey, to learn and to experience. Who are any of us to judge or rate anyone else's path. If that is where we end up, lesson missed. There is nothing to take from an ego that has been elevated and nurtured. There is no wisdom in the eagerness and need to look at others as less evolved. Spiritual superiority is what we see among self-appointed guru's. You don't need it.

"Your life is a gift, and by living it, to the best of your ability, you are honoring creation." – Hilde Larsen

PART FOUR
MASTER YOUR BLESSINGS

Chapter 21

Are you allowing greatness?

"*Look at that woman right there. I need to be more like that. There is something about confident, successful people. They radiate in a way, a good way. I don't mean those sleazy wannabes, I mean truly successful people. Those that people look up to and want to follow. It's like they have something that others want. People want to be around them. Heck, I want to be around them. Well, maybe not everyone for a good reason, I get that, but still. I want to feel that sense of confidence from within. Like my aunt for example. She travels all over the place. Brings the kids even, and looks like she is having fun no matter what she does. She has her own business, loves her work, has this amazing healthy lifestyle, and is always surrounded with the most amazing friends. She so deserves it, though. It wasn't always like that. I have no idea what she did, but it sure changed her life around bigtime! I have to take her up on that invitation. I need to have me some of that. I deserve it too, right? To be happy I mean. Money is not all that for me, I don't think so, but still, it would be more than ok to be able to travel to all my dream-places, and to get that new condo for my mom. Ok, so I am calling my aunt today. It is time.*"

Inspiring people are successful people, and they are like magnets. They draw attention, curiosity and interest. People want some of it to rub off on them, and they might even want a part of their limelight. They are the hot topic of discussion, and they come across as leaders in their field.

What is success?

The word success has many connotations. Webster's dictionary has several definitions; Getting or achieving wealth - respect or fame, and reaching the desired or correct result of an attempt. There are probably as many thoughts and opinions on what success is, as there are people going after- and hungering for it. Success cannot be defined into a single sentence or a word. It is comprised of many different factors, and depends on your goals, your values and your general mindset. In general: To reach a goal would be considered a success, and to feel you have achieved, would be considered being successful.

The way we have been conditioned, and the fact that money has been attached to power, we often link success to riches, to material gains. We look at people who are driving the most expensive cars as the most successful ones. We look at famous people like movie stars as the typical definition of success. They look happy, they have money, they are mostly fit, and they seem to be living their dream. Sure, we know they also experience loss, depression, heartache, weight gain and life crises. They are human. Still we get blinded by the spotlights and the presentation of fame and success. The media has created a false picture, and the further the presented image is from the average life, the more we are distanced from feeling successful ourselves. Us, the average Joe. The more glam and glitter we are presented with, together with happiness and the "good life", the less successful we might feel.

You experience feeling a sense of lack, depending on the size of the gap between what you are presented with, compared to where you are. You might look at where you are as less successful. If you buy into it, that is. So long as you seek outside of yourself, you will find stimuli and picture books, make beliefs and hidden agendas. If you at any point are discouraged by what other people achieve, you need to look at your belief system. Your reaction is in you. Something needs to be let go of.

> "Success consists of going from failure to failure without loss of enthusiasm." - Winston Churchill

Being competitive in life, is a beneficial trait if you want to be a successful athlete, for example. Your primary goal is to win. It is the name of the game. On the arena of any sports, winning is success, losing is not. Not much confusion around the games of competition. Some bring competition to all areas of life, and that can be tricky. Seeing ourselves in comparison with others is not only exhausting, it takes away our feeling of greatness. Being a copy of someone else is never as good as being the best version of ourselves. There is nothing wrong with looking towards those who have done what you want to do, be it in terms of financial gains, or spiritual growth. You do not have to make the same mistakes, or experience the same setbacks. Some things are worth learning from those who have walked the path. We all stand on the shoulders of our forefathers, and all successful people have had their mentors, both in the physical and through books and other media.

> "To be a successful person, you need to validate every step and every goal that you reach." – Hilde Larsen

> The feeling behind true success is the feeling of having accomplished something valuable. Something we are enthusiastic towards. When we are inspired to work and evolve towards something, no matter what it is, we will feel successful when we reach it, or find it. It can be abstract or concrete. It can be an achievement or a spiritual awakening. Love or health.

I see a distinct difference between growth and achievements. What we achieve is linked to outer goals, like career related accomplishments, material gains and physical performances. They are all about tangible objectives. We have an ambition and a destination. When we reach it, we achieve what we wanted, so we succeed. We are successful. When we evolve as humans, by letting go of our old baggage, and by bettering ourselves, we are constantly growing. We are getting closer to who we really are, or experiencing more of it, and as we keep living that truth, we will feel another kind of success. The kind that comes from an open heart. The kind that needs no validation. In my opinion that is *true* success. Creating material riches is not success, growing into your best version is.

What does success mean to you?

I grew up in a typical Western household. Working parents with the understanding that holding a nine to five job, getting a proper education, marrying, owning a house and not doing anything out of the norm was living a successful life. More money, a respected reputation, a higher status - equaled a higher value.

My life, up until it was completely turned upside down by ill health, consisted of striving for accomplishment and validations. Being the best at what you do is not at all a bad thing. Believing that life is evaluated by your ability to achieve, your high speed, your level of fitness, and your strong will, can kill you. I was so stressed out by my beliefs and my need to do what I believed was expected of me, thinking it would make me a successful human being. If I could only hold down my business, take care of my home, my family, my children, the cars, the vacation home and plan our travels, I would be a success. If I could just get this body to feel better, to constantly meet my demands, then maybe it was good enough. I had to reevaluate my beliefs and understandings. My "system" failed. It was not based on truth and greatness. I had to delete most of what I had learned about life and success. I had to start from scratch, or so it felt. I had to rebuild my entire health, recognizing that any financial gain was not on my success list at all. Real success for me is not tied to any trophy or material thing at all, it comes from my willingness to work, strive and stay committed.

For you, success might mean being able to get up in the morning, to get your health back, to be able to walk a mile or two. Another person values his or her family more than anything, and looks at being a good parent as their greatest success. For someone else, taking over a large corporation, buying the dream mansion and having a private jet is success. Simply being alive and breathing can also be defined as a success. Your life, your current situation, your goals if you have any, will define how you look at your own level of success.

Warren Buffet, one of the world's most successful financial people, was asked in an interview that I read online; "What is your definition of success?" His response was; "Success is having what you want and wanting what you have.", and "success is having the people whom you love around you." One of the wealthiest men in the universe doesn't equate success with money.

The thing is, no matter what your beliefs are, the core message is that success can only be measured in who you become. Not what you do, say or believe, but what you become.

251

"What you get by achieving your goals is not as important as what you become by achieving your goals." - Zig Ziglar

Why do we want it?

It is not necessarily the money or what they have achieved that makes us want to be like high achievers and successful people. It doesn't have to be the specific lifestyle or obvious performance that we would like to see happen. The type of person that they have had to be to have done what they did, is inspiring our soul to want to do and be better. Someone who wins the lottery is not successful, or especially great or accomplished. Someone who inherits a lot of money, doesn't necessarily hold a lot of skills. Having a vast amount in your bank account doesn't make you rich. What makes you interesting and a teacher for others is the personality and ability to follow through that others wants to learn and follow.

We all want great health. A basic need that we all strive to experience. Some more vigorously than others, and some with a higher standard and motivation than their fellow beings. Still, health is wealth. Without it, there is not much fun in anything. Successful people know this. You might believe that the obvious health guru's and more spiritually focused part of the population are the only ones that are eating for life, not for death. Not so. Healthy people stay away from junk food, from the standard Western diet. They know better, they are educated, they use their ability to take action on their knowledge. They make better choices, because they know how important health is, *and* they know what makes you and breaks you. When you know that your body and your brain is your tool, you valuate taking care of it. You are not fooled by the industry and the marketing of packaged, processed and toxic foods. You know better. We want the great health that some are able to achieve, and we look up to the strength and endurance of those who are able to achieve it holds.

The most important difference between success and mediocrity is the ability to act, not the knowledge. A lot of people know, *only a few* do.

Our hunger for success comes from the basic needs of fulfillment. To be able to feel our greatness. When we have lived feeling less than, not believing we are worthy of an amazingly fulfilling life, our basic needs have been suppressed.

We want to feel significant
We want to matter
We want our lives to matter
We want to make a difference
We want to be challenged
We want to help others
We want to be the best that we can be
We want to belong
We want to be proud of who we are

Our basic needs will be fulfilled once we allow greatness, and realize that true success is living the grace we have been given. Through honoring our strengths and our ability to learn we succeed in life itself.

> "Don't strive to be a success in the eyes of others, but contribute to growth and value." – Hilde Larsen

Are you conditioned for living your greatness?

Many have put their name on this quote or saying; "There are three kinds of people in this world. Those who make things happen, those who watch things happen, and those who wonder what happened." We are all flesh and blood, yet we all have a different make up. Some carrying more of their own and other peoples bullshit around than others. Some more ready to take responsibility than others, but still, we are all more than able. I like to believe that we all have what it takes to allow ourselves the greatness in our lives. I don't believe that some have it and some don't. What is it that seems to be the difference between those that have the capacity to succeed, and those who don't? Between those living and inviting in their greatness and those who linger in the background? I call them the brave ones. They are the ones changing the world as they move forward. They are the ones showing the way to a better life for all.

1. **Brave people are eager to talk about positive ideas.** They constantly look for solutions and ideas that could improve their lives. Average Joe's engage in gossip and jealousy. They engage in discussions that focuses on goals and aspirations, growth and positive outcomes.

2. **Brave people adapt to the changes of life.** They take advantage of every situation and sees it as an opportunity. They accept the way it is, and look for the best possible alternative path. They see life as half full in every situation. Mr. and Mrs. Joe, on the other hand, will sit down, complain and need to talk about it. They will groan about their problems, not focusing on solutions. Their glass is always half empty.

3. **Brave people not only set goals, but they make an action plan.** While the Joe's will set the goal, maybe even write a list, they will fall of the wagon and not follow through. The more than brave, will use their strength, their motivation and their ability to work hard, to follow the step-by-step plan that they made. They continuously plan and map out their goals and progress.

4. **Brave people are occupied with their own business,** and has no need to judge or criticize others. Even though most people have a tendency to judge and spend time focusing on others, some of us don't. We evaluate ourselves rather, to learn and do better.

5. **Brave people create a better life.** The average person keeps dreaming. While everybody will strive to live the best

life that they can, there is a distinct difference between those that actually create, and those who don't. Some are makers and some are watchers. The brave will strive to better themselves, while Mr. Joe often wants to be better than others.

6. **Brave people read books**, and educate themselves by learning from those that already did what they want to do. While the average Joe's are staring at the TV screen, they are reading uplifting and educational literature. They spend their free time differently. One being outdoors and active, one in front of a screen, a game or something else that adds no real value.

7. **Brave people control their thoughts, and create their own norms.** They are not letting themselves be controlled by anyone or anything. They only need approval from themselves. The rest of the crowd will most often let their thoughts control them, and freak out if they don't feel the support from the masses.

8. **Brave people do not need to hold on to things.** They know there will always be enough. They do not thrive in clutter or overabundance. They know the value of simplicity. They buy value, not things. They invest in health, alone-time and spiritual growth. Striving, less successful people will accumulate possessions and hold on to as much as possible.

9. **Brave, successful people have the ability to simply say no.** They need no special reason or long explanations. They are the boss of their own time and life, and can live free from feeling obligated to do what is not in their own and their family's best interest. Most people have a tendency to say yes. Simply from having been falsely taught to believe that pleasing others was more important than doing what was right for oneself. Being a yes-person, is exhausting and not very brave.

10. **The bravest will look for the long-term rewards.** They are willing to sacrifice. They are willing to do what they need to

do in the now-moment, to be able to harvest in the future. The more average person will keep looking for the instant gratification, it is addictive. Feeding a lack and an emotional imbalance.

"Successful and unsuccessful people do not vary greatly in their abilities. They vary in their desires to reach their potential." – John Maxwell

What is greatness?

Greatness is bravery.

It is beyond success.

It is courage and humbleness.

It is the honest and true ability to serve and grow into more of one's own potential.

It is honoring God and creation.

Greatness has no limitations or egotistic agenda.

It emanates from love and pure intent.

Allowing greatness means accepting all that we are, and loving ourselves enough to honor our purpose and passions. By humbly and truthfully living to the best of our ability, greatness will be a part of everything that we do. Because we are, we are great, and because we have free will, it is our responsibility to honor it. Through the pure intent to keep seeking expansion and compassion for everything, we will fill our shoes more and more.

Realize that learning from the best, honoring their knowledge and wisdom is not only smart, but it shows humility. By being humble, we are allowing our greatness to come forth. We must see ourselves as worthy and able. We must be humble, teachable and free from comparison to others. By staying true to our own path, our own truth, and our own strengths and mission, we are celebrating every step of the way. There is no end goal in life, only bits and pieces of accomplishments and growth. When we see how unique and special we are, and are willing to use it for something good, by stretching and creating, I believe we have found true success and greatness.

> "No man is an island, but every man is within himself greatness." - Hilde Larsen

Chapter 22

Spread your wings

" I feel so blessed. What a ride this has been, and what a blessing my life is. Looking back, I can't even believe how much everything has changed over the last few years. It all started the day I walked out of that office building. Wow, was I scared. And excited I guess, deep down, somewhere. I was so done doing what I didn't like doing. I was so ready for change. This, I could have never even imagined! Me, ready to go on stage, in front of all these people, totally crazy. To be able to live my dream through writing is one thing, but to receive a prize for best newcomer, and to have my book made into a movie, again, WOW! Who would have thought? Not me. Dreamed of, sure, but actually believed? A long stretch to even imagine. That day, standing on the sidewalk, with my stuff, no job, with a novel that wanted to come through me, turned out to be one of the best, most blessed days of my life. I had no idea choosing myself and trusting life would pay off like this. Sure, I have worked hard, and sure not all the days have been amazing. Looking back, I wouldn't have it any other way. I am nervous, so many people. Wow again! So nice to feel appreciated for doing what I love. I won't "work" another day in my life. This is too much fun!"

When we have not been told how awesome and fabulous we are, there is a tendency to hold back. We go slow, testing the ground. Will it hold? Will it be ok? Am I good enough? Am I doing the right thing? Whenever we dive into something new, from living our greatness, and daring to seek success and truth, we lose our safety net. The zone is pretty much gone. Comfort is not always the nominator and guiding force of action. We *take* action. We *do* instead of reading about, we become the kind of person that lives instead of dreaming. We no longer wonder what happened, we *make it* happen. Not forcefully, but through following the current, flowing downstream while working hard and focused towards our goals. Life is no longer overwhelming or filled with drama and complaints. Everything happens *for* us, not *too* us.

It is not advisable for anyone to jump off a cliff before you can swim, or to drive across country the first time you sit behind a wheel. To jump into any task that you are not at all prepared for is like trying to write a book before you can write. It makes no sense, and it doesn't set the stage for success. It is closer to the recipe for failure. Call it experimenting, as there *will* be something to learn from it. Smart? No. There is a large difference between taking blind risks, being unconditioned and undereducated, and stepping up the game. By skipping the steps of preparation, you are missing the whole process of growth. By letting yourself grow more confident, you are nurturing your outcome. You are so amazingly capable, and once you feel it at the core of your being, no bullshit can ever touch you again. Become untouchable. Hold on to every moment of any process. It is your life. Every breath, every heartbeat. Life.

"Do the difficult things while they are easy and do the great things while they are small. A journey of a thousand miles must begin with a single step." - Lao Tzu

Prepare for the best.

Study hard. Read more books, or at least start to read. If you think you know everything, get over yourself. If you believe you already have all the knowledge, you need a reality check. Be open and know that there is always something to learn. A wise person knows that learning never stops, and an even wiser one knows that the more they know, the more they realize they do *not* know. Remember, there is no failure, only growth and experiments. No rejection, only redirection.

The preparation for anything grand, anything with a true purpose, often hurts. Look at any great teacher of health. They have been very ill themselves as a part of their learning. A teacher of how to successfully grow a business from absolutely nothing, most likely has gone through some devastating economic times. Great teachers might come from broken and miserable lives. The best relationship counselors have been through the most heart-wrecking break ups. Through painful and trying experiences, growth will happen. This is what makes them experts. They have learned from firsthand experience, the best method of learning there is. Coupled with the words of those who have done it before them, they have prepared for their life as way-showers to others. A successful author has spent hours and hours practicing his writing. A dancer has been working with his or her body for more hours than they can remember. Sweat and frustration, mentors and long hours. Diligently focused in preparation of fulfilling their dream and passion. They all conditioned themselves for their mission. Not by thinking only, but by doing. Not by doing a little every other day, but by stepping on it, and freeing themselves from the fear of failure. They could smell greatness as a part of them. They were ready to own it, and to honor it by taking honest action.

"He who would learn to fly one day must first learn
to stand and walk and run and climb and dance;
one cannot fly into flying." - Friedrich Nietzsche

Let yourself shine.

The internal gas pedal, the action button, it works! By living and breathing, we are always moving. Slowly moving forward by letting go and preparing. Even if it feels like you are sliding backwards, there really is no such thing. Life is never moving backwards. In reality, it's not moving forward either. It feels like it, as we use the terms of "leaving things behind", and "moving forward". It is what it is, and we live in the now-moment only. Keep this in mind, when looking at life as a whole. We evolve through every single experience, no matter what it is. Our perception of life is created by our unconscious and conscious mind, and has not been trustworthy. There is a clear path ahead for those who are ready to step on it, to hit the pedal. There is freedom ahead for anyone willing to take a chance. Feel the air.

> The reality that reveals itself when we step out of our imaginable hiding place, has a whole new set of rules. There are signs saying; "Take whatever turn you like. Exit here or anywhere else. Stop and pause whenever. No speeding if you don't want to. Turn off the radio. Sing while driving, but keep your eyes on the journey ahead."

- **Speak up.** Silence is golden, but not all the time. It is important to know when to hold your thoughts and opinions to yourself, and it is equally important to know when to open your mouth. To be the observer and keeping distance from drama is great. To be humble and teachable is important also. Then, when you are ready to go, you go. You have prepared, saddled up and set your destination by direction. Now it is time to be bold and determined. Take a stand, cut the cord to the old, and unleash the power within you. Be fearless and honest. Truth will always get you there. Throw in some fabulousness and pure awesomeness, and you are in it for the win. You can be strong and vulnerable at the same time. You can speak your mind, write your truth, freely live your dream.

- **Fly now.** Over-preparing is called procrastination. Waiting for the right moment to get going can be fatal. When is ever the right time? You learn how to fly by spreading your wings. When you have done what you needed to do, when your enthusiasm and eagerness to move ahead is ready, *you* are ready. Practice, practice, practice. Prepare and jump. Get ready and go, but don't get stuck in preparation mode. For some, jumping sooner, preparing and researching later, gives them the kick-start they need to get going. Take the leap and let your feet lift from the ground. I know the "both feet on the ground" saying. Let me tell you this: With both feet on the ground, you are not going anywhere, anytime, not sooner, not later. To live on the "free" side of life, you need to spread them, and learn how to fly. On your own.

- **Follow no one.** Stop staring at someone else's back. They might not be heading your way, *and* they are blocking the beautiful view. At the same time, keep observing what they are doing, you will learn something new. Be the driver, the pilot. Feel the power from that, the freedom. It will give you strength when you need it. You are never alone. You are just heading your own way, making friends and finding new partners-in-crime along the way. Take the new ride for a spin by trying out everything that you have learned, free from everything you have deleted. At this point in your life you are ready to actually make a difference. No matter if you want to be the best caregiver or a farmer, do something that has your name on it. You are unique, and have something to offer that no one else does.

- **Schedule your life.** Back to the calendar that keeps you organized. It doesn't have to be filled with every little task. That would leave no room for impulse and change. A calendar can have open spaces, intently left for winging it. We tend to write down the major events in our lives, that and business appointments and events. What about your life schedule? How will you get organized and on top of your game? Schedule some dates with yourself. Tasks that are less than your favorites; stop worrying and schedule them. Write it down, and keep your appointment. Once on paper, the brain is off the hook. You are free to use it on something other than remembering and trying to juggle what needs to be done and when. Your schedule will also allow you to see what- and how much time you spend on what. That in itself is worth it. Reality check on why you feel you have too little time.

- **Discipline for the win.** Without the follow through, action is nothing. How many times have you started something, and not followed through? How many times have you set that goal, made the list, walked those first couple of steps, only to find yourself back where you used to be? When you condition yourself for a powerful life, you are toughening up all your senses. Your self-discipline is a powerful muscle. It will take you from lift-off to the landing place. Everything in between preparing, scheduling and lift-off, to getting to where you want to go, requires this tough, on-point discipline. Anything worth working towards is worth disciplining yourself for. This is your life; you are worth the efforts.

"Never has there been a map, however carefully executed to detail and scale, which carried its owner over even one inch of ground." – Og Mandino

Bring yourself only.

Leave no one behind unforgiven. Bring nothing with you except what will benefit your journey. Take inventory and let no bad blood or unfinished business drag along when you hit the start button. The weight that is lifted when you finally let go of everything, will alone make you want to fly. Most often it is not even the large issues or things that keeps us on stand still. It is the *number* of little things. The need to pack them, at least some of them. Let's hold on, just in case we need them. They feel so familiar. Who will we be without just a few little grudges to hold, a bad conscience maybe? A little blaming of oneself for the ride? Such a party pooper, the self-blame. No fun at all. Realize that you did the best that you could, with what you had, at the time, and that is that. It is done, life is now, and you know better. We all do what we believe is best, and even when we screw up, and do something that leaves us with regret, we have learned something. By forgiving yourself you are setting yourself free to learn from the event or situation. By forgiving and letting go of everything else that weighs you down:

- You are letting everyone else be their own driver. They will make their own mistakes.
- You will get over everything that is already done. You have no room for it.
- You will realize that none of it really matters anymore.
- You can take the leap and follow through.
- You will wonder why you didn't do this years ago!

Taking action is spiritual.

When life gives you lemons, make lemonade. When life serves you all your potentials, live fully. Nothing is ever stagnant, as everything is energy. Therefore, everything moves. Action through a physical expression, takes you places in the physical world. When you move your body, it reflects on your achievements and your material gain.

When working on your spiritual side, you move your whole being closer to your potentials. Through meditation and compassion, mindfulness and love, the spirit world opens itself and our consciousness expands. We can move through time and awareness, through different realms of creation and reality. Action is a term that signals intentional driven force of movement. A planned shift that is done to gain an outcome. Being focused on the physical work only, might leave you missing an important part of the action plan. Leave nothing behind. Clear your head and dig deeper into your bullshit-free subconscious mind. Let spirit come forth. Let magic work through you. Best copilot there is.

> We have the capacity and the ability to go where we have never been before. Not only by working harder, but by tapping into the infinite pool of possibilities. Through raising our consciousness, our true intelligence will say; hey, there is nothing you cannot do.

"Never confuse movement with action." – Ernest Hemingway

Chapter 23

Spiritual awakening.

"My heart is racing. It's hard to breathe, so dark. I am trying to think. I am soaking wet. I hate this. Nightmares from hell, I absolutely hate them. Dear body, it was just a bad dream. No need to sweat and shiver. We've got this. Back to reality please. What time is it? I don't care, I am not going back to sleep anyway. The sun will be up soon enough, and I'll be ready. I need a shower. Wow, that shook me up. What was I dreaming? I always seem to forget, as if it doesn't really matter. Not pleasant, that's for sure. Something about being lost, not knowing where to go. Something about having forgotten who I was. Wandering around searching. Constantly searching. Not feeling at home, like some sort of prison. Yes, that's it, some sort of prison. Glad to be awake. Hello new day, no more bad dreams please. Geez."

The journey called life is in large part about waking up. Seeing the truth is like opening your eyes after sleeping. A bit confusing, but freeing after a while. When the stress and uneasiness settles, it is such a pleasure to be able to rest in the life that feels so much closer to home.

You are not the avatar that you have created of yourself. You are not the persona that holds all these traits and talents. You are not your body, and you are not your mind. You are the spirit, consciousness, love and peace. You are everything that you have been seeking. This, your life, is nothing but a way your soul is expressing itself, and the more you step away from that pure understanding, the further into dream-land you will drift. From being a small child, following the guidance of an adult or an older sibling, we become adults, with the power to change everything. We are given the choice to wake up to what our lives can hold and be. Can a child not awaken? Is it not powerful? Beyond belief! I would say that a child *is* awake. Only to be put to sleep by society and life. Nevertheless, there are no absolutes, and not all parts of this world hold the same values and lack thereof. In the Western world, we fall asleep during our childhood, not willingly, but steadily.

Our lives are molded like a piece of clay. Day by day, thought by thought, we are conditioned to lead a life that fits our outer world. A dream is created. We play and re-play, until we either wake up, or leave this body. As spirit, I believe we are immortal. Our eternal self is what we connect with when we feel the most powerful and invincible. The pure energy behind our thoughts. Our essence that enables us to open our eyes, despite the false beliefs we have been holding on to.

> Don't believe what your eyes are telling you. Look deeper within. Look towards where your mental reasoning and understanding cannot go, to your inner knowing. There, you will find no limitations.

Start an inner revolution:

Take a closer look around you. What do you see? Are you living a conscious life? Are you mindful and present as your day unfolds, and are you aware of how you live? Are you aware of your values and your contributions? While juggling every part of a typical modern lifestyle, it is hard to stay fully present. Mindfulness is a rare trait amongst those who drift through life in stress and accomplishment mode. Is it possible to be mindful, enthusiastic, hard-working, focused and success-minded at the same time? I absolutely believe it is. You can set your goals, get out of your own way, and be aware of everything you live, from breathing to smelling the well-known roses. Can you smell them on a daily basis? If not, start a revolution. Be a quiet and compassionate rebel, and allow your spiritual side to enter your life.

Our spirit is always free, and it is always there, which makes spiritual awakening hard to define. How can we define something that is beyond words? We mix in terms like enlightenment, which is defined as losing one's perception of self, of identity with the ego. With this standard, not many humans qualify as enlightened. To be awake or not, that is the question. If we are not, then how do we wake up?

We are living in a world full of boundaries, on the outside as well as the inside. The awakening to the spirit world shows us a place where there are none. No boundaries at all. Complete freedom and bliss. Time ceases to exist, and the weight of the body diminishes. All our expectations, our rules, our restrictions and our limitations, all gone in a flash. We no longer feel overwhelmed or anxious. The feeling of abundance and unconditional love is all that exists. We are used to having love attached to some type of conditions and rules, while awakening to the spiritual world leaves us with the opposite. The feeling of nothing and everything, the feeling of unconditional love. A bit airy fairy for some, but a life-changer for those who experience it. Once you have felt and seen what spirit is, your life is changed, for the better.

The challenge is to live in both worlds at the same time. To be an awakened human, living in this world of so much tragedy and pain. How can we find peace and tranquility in such a world?

To be able see with more than the physical eye will open a different perspective on life. The truth, the wisdom and the knowing all comes together as one. From a perspective of living our dream and purpose her on planet earth, the spiritual connection is for many the missing link. They will realize that everything is within them, the whole of creation. There is no separation, nothing outside of themselves. Every experience is different. Some might meet their spirit guides, others experience seeing their spirit family and angels. Some find what feels like wisdom and infinite and innate knowing. Once the seed has been planted in our aware consciousness, it is forever with us. The expansion and continuous awakening becomes part of our lives. We have been introduced to our awareness in its natural state. A blessing that will open our hearts as we continue on our path. Eternity is a mighty large concept to discover. It blows the roof right off any earthly medium-sized "problem". Our obstacles don't quite seem as significant when we awaken to the larger picture.

Nothing is as humbling as the truth about who we really are. It changes how we look at everything. – Hilde Larsen

Know yourself:

Whether or not we are spiritually aware in our daily routines, we are spiritual beings. Through practicing meditation and stillness, we will continuously keep reaching for that connection with ourselves, our spirit. To turn inward is to turn connected. By doing so we are reminded of our soul, our true purpose and our truth. For some, practicing simple meditation techniques will give them a glimpse of the spiritual world. It will inspire to keep on practicing. The sweetness of peace and love will do that.

Celebrate your life by going on a silent retreat or a meditation and yoga retreat. Taking a few days by yourself in nature is a great alternative. Anything that takes you away from your other world, takes you closer to the inner and awakened one.

Get to know yourself from your inner most vulnerable place. Look for your most sensitive and private chambers, behind all the veils and shadows. Look for everything that makes your life what it is today, what forms your thoughts and your ideas. This is not about knowing your limitations or your material goals. It is not about your wants and regrets. It is about knowing who *you* are, besides pure consciousness.

- What are your core values?
- What are your pure and honest dreams?
- What are your strengths and weaknesses?

Get to know your body. It is an extension of your life. It is created by your every breath, emotion, thought and physical nurturing. It is one out of many bodies, and most often the forgotten one. Wait a minute, how can we forget the body? It is so physical. Indeed, it is, and yet often seen as completely separate from who we are. Like a lonely mechanism, running its own show, without any connection to our spiritual being. It can do amazing things, get to know it, this amazing vehicle of ours.

> The Tao says: "One who knows other people is wise. One who knows himself is enlightened."

Love everything:

Love beyond the self, the people you care for, the things you cherish and the places you are captured by. Love beyond your mind and comprehension. Your love is like the air, and will sweep through any nation. It is like the water that will penetrate the smallest of spaces.

It has no limits, no boundaries or restrictions. True love is limitless and unconditional. Nothing can defeat or break it. No true love will ever get old or boring. Love for life itself is an expansion of the love we hold for ourselves and others. It holds the *all-that-is-I* form of God and spirit. The language of creation is love and compassion, expressed through passion and purpose.

It becomes easy to be true to oneself and one's life when we realize the amazing creation that we are a part of. The awakening is an ultimate bullshit killer. Going back to sleep is not an option. Being awake and aware is too much fun, and the impression left from feeling the touch of heaven is ever lasting. We are here for this split time in creation, to make a difference. We are here to find our way, through this veil of misinformation. Sometimes fully asleep, sometimes awake. An experimental journey of faith and courage. Trial and error through living and evolving.

How can a man, with his limited mind, ever find the reason behind his existence and his behavioral patterns? Only through touching upon spirit will we glimpse a heaven and a deeper understanding of where we come from. We are the blessings. We are the manifestations of true love. Hard to believe when we look around, yet behind the veil we can find our way back to our spiritual self. Living is not only a blessing, but a challenge. For a brief moment we are here, surrounded by beauty and suffering, with a free will to change how we interact and contribute to all of it. The simplest things can have a profound outcome. I believe we can ripple this world into a new vibration. We can consciously choose to raise our vibration, hence that which of everything around us. Simply and mindfully.

What we can all do right now is simple:

- Pick a flower
- Admire a child

- Make a difference
- Walk barefoot
- Show up
- Be rebels
- Stay strong
- Live like we mean it
- Cut the crap.

"This is love: to fly toward a secret sky, to cause a hundred veils to fall each moment. First to let go of life. Finally, to take a step without feet." – Rumi

Chapter 24

True abundance

" *Every time I pass someone who seems to be in pain, or someone suffering in any way, my heart bleeds. I am literally hurt from seeing how much agony is out there. I am praying people will wake up. I know the road they are on. Not a fun one. People keep asking me what I missed the most while I was bedridden. Did I miss going to a party? Not being able to travel, drive my car, wear nice shoes? I know, you would think, right? That I missed all that like crazy. Sure, depending on how sick I was at the moment, but most of the time, no to all of the above. Miss anything? Heck yes, but most of all I missed having any kind of health. Being sick speaks louder than absolutely anything else, and until you have been there, you will never know just how loud. Sometimes I wish people had been there, just to be able to feel the difference themselves.*

Although, that wouldn't be good either, forget it. Never go there. Never find out. Stay on top of the health game. It is the most unsexy, devastating experience, to feel like crap, not being able to enjoy any part of life. My life perspective flipped completely. Nothing else mattered.

I have to pinch myself. Now, my blessings are as many as there are minutes in a day. The air smells better, the colors are brighter, and my heart is filled with gratitude as I look forward to every single day with anticipation and love.

If people only knew how amazing life will feel when the body is actually functioning like it should! Oh, how I wish they knew. I am blessed"

If all of us knew that true abundance is connected with the physical body as well as the spiritual connection, and that it is there for all of us. Would we then live differently? Without our health and body, life is no fun. Pain is no fun. Suffering is all-consuming. It is suffocating our creative force. Health is true wealth, believe me. Now, after recreating and re-claiming my health, I feel rich, from my core. From the inside out. A different kind of riches. The kind that grows from giving and spreading the word. It has become my mission, my true purpose.

Truth is truth, and there is nothing that an empowered mind and being cannot do. One step at the time, as I did - anyone can.

Cut through all the crap, all the lies and false beliefs, and this is where we end up. In front of the mirror. Staring at ourselves, up-close. What are we doing that is hindering this amazing, true health-abundance to come alive? How are we not valuing our most precious asset? Why are we not even acknowledging that it is? Ignorance and disconnection. Take a close look in that mirror. What do you see? Are you taking care of the most precious and most valuable asset that you have? Are you honoring it as your number one investment?

Your body is your temple:

How much would you invest in your body if you knew the ROI was one-thousand percent? I bet you would throw in all that you have.

I bet you would sell out all your other investments to focus on the sure thing. Most of us would, yet we don't. The most challenging aspect of the return in form of health is the fact that most people don't even make the investment. Why? They don't see the value until it is close to shut down time for the whole business. Even then, depending on the level of awareness and connection to the true self, seeing health as the number one pool of wealth can be hard.

By ignoring our temple, we are ignoring life. We came here in a physical body, and we leave when it is no longer functioning, when we are no longer breathing through it. Every physical experience we have on earth, is through this body. Suffering and poverty are contraction, abundance and riches are expansion.

I was almost dead before I realized, not that I would simply have no life without my body, but that it was up to me to take care of it. It was easy to notice that life was no fun when pain was overwhelming my every experience, but it took time before I could see how blessed I still was. I had been given the opportunity to live in abundance. It was handed to me through birth. I had been given a choice, a power, and ability to choose wealth. I was not a victim, I was capable. I was brainwashed, numbed down and ignorant, but always able, always blessed, always abundant. My life was my wealth. As long as I was breathing, there was something to invest in, and I invested. I went all in, and received everything in return. Not in form of money or assets, but in form of truth and love.

> I was shown the truth about our bodies, how we can let them restore and rejuvenate. They are designed to self-heal. It is a mechanism beyond our comprehension. We are designed to eat raw, living, vibrant, healing, amazing, beautiful food. Every bite will be an investment. Every meal is reflecting growth and abundance.

When we don't eat optimally, we will know it. I know it, and you know it. Food is supposed to be fuel, and not a burden. Most of what we eat today in the Western world is actually a burden to the human body. Every time we eat something that is outside of our natural diet, it becomes a burden. I remember heavy dinners as well as you do. You know, when you just wanted to lie down afterwards, completely drained of energy. Food is supposed to be fuel, not drain your energy. This only shows that the body has a hard time with what it has been fed. There is no way we can eat what is not good for us and not know it at one level or another. The problem is that we are surrounded with so much toxic waste that our pineal gland is clouded. Because of this, it is hard for us to see truth. When we detoxify our bodies, this changes. We regain our awareness and our natural instincts.

Eating raw is important for our vitality and rejuvenation, and to live at the level of health that we were designed to do. Most importantly though, as we have fallen into the trap of social conditioning and programming, we need to go back to raw to be able to detoxify our bodies. Detoxification simply means cleansing, something that the body does naturally when given a chance. Every day it works to clean and restore, but because of what we are feeding this amazing organism, it is working to survive, not to thrive. So, in that sense, you might say that without raw, living foods there will be no real health, or wealth, because only when introducing the vibrancy and the healing effect of our natural food, will the body be able to clean and restore.

I was led to raw foods, as I was seeking truth. I was seeking true health and vitality. I was shown the simple way, the easy way, and the natural way. Maybe not easy to do, but truly the way to magic and true abundance.

Raw food is simply natural foods, straight from nature. There is no labeling or list of ingredients necessary. There is no complicated list of additives of fillers. The body will be able to digest it with ease, and not be harmed or intoxicated. It is the real fast-food, pure and simple. The foods we eat are secondary to all the other things that feed us; our relationships, career, spirituality, and exercise routines to name a few. At the same time, they are the key to everything, as you will no longer harm what you now love. Raw living foods will raise the vibration and the awareness, and also magnify the feeling of love and compassion.

We are primates. What we are witnessing is what happens when we really, I mean *really* move away from that, and feed our bodies dead altered chemistry. All animals that are taken off their diet get sick. Animals in the care of humans often get diseased. Wild animals do not, and how could they? Nature is perfect and no species will get sick, fat, and unhealthy from eating the foods intended for them. We, the humans, tend to believe we can outsmart nature. That we are more intelligent, and that our will can override the simple laws of the Universe. It is not so, and we are being told this and shown this, every single day, symptom by symptom. What we are eating is killing us, and it is about time we know it, and really own it. It is about time we realized that we are sitting on a gold mine of potentials, all in our God given creation.[24]

To me, abundance has a whole new meaning. Health has a whole new meaning. Healing and rejuvenation is a natural part of our lives if we let it. Abundance is given to us for free. It will never cost us a single dime. Not a cent. Only awakening and acceptance. Allow it. You are worth it. Own it, and pay it forward.

It was never about the money:

The cliché "Money cannot buy happiness", is not far from the truth. Money can certainly bring us closer to our goals and provide the most necessary necessities for comfort. It can also increase our

---

[24] Hilde Larsen – *Know the Truth and Get Healthy, 2016*

overall satisfaction, but in itself, it can never buy us happiness. Therefore, it cannot buy us true wealth, or make us wealthy and abundant in the way that our heart seeks.

> **"Not what we have but what we enjoy constitutes our abundance." - Epicurus**

We chase the money-trap as if it will buy us feelings and emotions. We keep chasing pride and status as if it will ever define who we are, or our worth in any way, shape or form. To assume that money will make us feel more accomplished, happy, free or respected, is a dead-end in the pursuit of an abundant life. Happiness does not require more. Gathering and saving up for a rainy day, might end up being a trap, robbing you from the now moment, and the abundance that is already here. Yes, we should strive for our goals, and yes money is great, convenient and all that. If you recognize everything that is already here, what you work towards will seem like an even larger accomplishment and joy.

When you recognize the true abundance in your life, you will end up giving away more. Authentic abundance requires balance. Holding on to anything is, as we know, not the energy of allowing more to come our way, be it physical, mental, emotional or financial. Greed is a sign of disconnect and fear. Step out of it.

- True abundance is being able to recognize your riches regardless of your financial wealth.
- True abundance is loving yourself, with all your strengths and weaknesses.
- True wealth is true health.
- True abundance is doing what you are passionate about.
- True abundance is being able to eat fresh, living, organic food.
- True wealth is loving and being loved.
- True wealth is feeling free and peaceful.

Once you follow your passion and honor your abundant life, money will always flow towards you as you need them. It is not the abundance in itself, only a byproduct of your creations.

Knowing is growing:

Our lives represent a full circle of actions and reactions. A full and complete round of living, giving and receiving. Be it while sleepwalking like zombie's, or awakened brave humans, we still create what we live. Our subconscious and conscious mind travels with us on this journey of joy and heart aches. We experience ups and downs, highs and lows. Nothing is constant. Duality is a part of our reality. It is what makes us learn and grow. It is what makes us push our limits. We seek abundance, and everything that comes with it, as it is our natural state. We *are* abundant beings. Blessed beyond belief.

In a world that seems to require a tough and strong constitution, we eagerly look for the crutch and the validation that life is hard. That abundance is something for the few and lucky ones. We tend to take ourselves out of the race, from looking at those who seem unreachable. Believing that wealth comes with a dollar sign on it, and that it is a result of true success. Surely one that has made millions of dollars, doing what he or she loves, spreading love and joy, is by definition a success. By him or her own means, and by the means of the eyes of others. They are the inspiration and the passionate people that move the energy forward. Those are the souls that are way-showers for many. On the other hand, the level of success is never measured by the number on a bank account, but by the size of the smile, the inner happiness, the compassion and the true health and joy.

Chapter 25

Your life manifesto

❝ I can see it now, the whole picture. Me, my life, my future, why the past was perfect, everything. I can see how amazing my life is and will be. I am manifesting every part of it, through my intent and my focus. I am true to myself, I am honest. I am enthusiastic and I am no longer a sucker for drama and media hype. No more photoshopping in my life. No false pretends or me wearing any masks. I feel free! I feel blessed. I failed, I learned, I move on. I made mistakes, I discovered myself and I found faith and greatness. I fell in love with my life and it fell in love with me. I found my bravery and my fearlessness. I am proud to always stand up for what I believe in. I am proud to walk my talk. No more bullshit!"

Failure is a part of creation.
Mistakes are discoveries and experiments.
Endings are always new beginnings.
Rejections are redirections.

As we walk through life, it is easy to drift off towards everything and anything that calls for our attention. It can be challenging to keep our energy where it is most needed. We can easily get distracted and side-tracked in life. Writing a personal life manifesto is like anchoring your visions and values. You are forced to take inventory, to open your heart, to dream big and to evaluate what your goals are. How do you see your life? What do you believe in, and what will you spend this lifetime accomplishing or being? Your personal manifesto will bring you back to your own reality and purpose. It is an amazing tool for any conscious living human. It is your living declaration of truth, and it will change as you grow and evolve.

> A manifesto is a personal declaration of one's intentions, beliefs, truths and opinions. The word traces back to the Latin; manifestum. It means conscious or clear. It is a document, well organized, with one person's writings on her or his life. It is a declaration that holds everything that is important to them, for the future. It includes values and commitments.

The power of writing and intent is beyond intellectual comprehension. Words are powerful, they are energy. Although you will find words in books that will ring true for you, from other people's manifestos, nothing is as powerful as writing your own. You true words, from your soul and wisdom. It can be short, long, specific or more in general. You can write about the topic that you are most enthusiastic about, or compose a full life manifesto. You can start, and add to it later. It functions both as a call to action and a statement of principles.

Look at your written manifesto as:

- Your compass and directional guide.
- Your general frame for your life and how you live it.
- Your reminder to keep striving and achieving your goals.
- Your source of motivation.

- Your inspiration to always do better.
- A reminder of your priorities.
- A reminder to live your purpose more fully.
- Your go-to- reading when things get rough.
- Your foundation for building your life
- A new start on your new bullshit-free, true life.

"A written statement to publicly declare your intentions, motives, or beliefs."- From the Latin manifestum

Write your own life manifesto:

This is a practice that will change your entire life. The process in itself is revealing, freeing and has a great learning curve. I recommend you write it on your computer. That way you can edit it and add to it as your life unfolds. It is work in progress, and a wonderful way to keep yourself on track. That being said; if you are willing to take the time of writing it with pen and paper, nothing is more powerful. The mind is even more receptive to the words when they are strengthened by the signals from the physical writing. I am a strong believer in pen and paper, however, sometimes it is not the most practical. You choose.

Read it as often as you like. Some read it every day, some look at it every week, or every month. There is no right or wrong. It is your document, and only you can decide what you want it to consist of, how long it should be, or how many topics it should include. Some like to make sure everything is included, in detail, and some simply want some easy to read sentences that represent their future life and values. The most important step is to actually *write* one. To get started.

First, write a short introduction: What is your intent for the manifesto? What do you want it to help you accomplish? Keep it simple and clean. The intent is the most important, not the fancy words. Use words that give meaning to *you*. Find a quiet place, breathe deeply, and tap into your own space. Write when you are in a good and hopeful place. Use positive words and phrases. This will be an uplifting document, made for you to further grow and manifest your dreams and values. It declares your vision. It lets you tap into your dreams. Once you have written down the intent, you can always go back and take a second and a third look later. Pour it from your heart, and try to bypass the brain. What is it really that you want this declaration of how you will live your life to read back at you? This is private if you wish it to be, and no-one but you have to read it. Be direct and authentic.

You can write your personal manifesto in many different ways. Short or long, simple or more complex. It can define all areas of your life, or only a few. It can focus on goals, or more general live-by guidelines. You might want it to be written in the form of short single sentences, or more like a story.

Here are some suggestions:

Keeping it simple manifesto: You can start off with three basic components: Wisdom, goals and beliefs. You can make is as simple as that. Write a header for each of the three topics, and let the pen do the rest. Write down what wisdom is to you, what you know to be true, what your beliefs are, then write down what your goals are and so forth. Keep it on point. Limit each topic to one page. For example: I know how valuable I am. My life is beautiful. Nature is perfect.

Defining the areas of your life manifesto: You can make a list of the areas of your life that you want to address. It can be your love life, your relationships, your work life, your financial goals and your health. For example, you can write how you would like your health to grow and manifest. What do you want it to look like, and what do you want to be able to do physically? Each area gets its own section, where you can put in writing everything that rings true to you about the topic. This is all about what you want to leave behind. What you want to look back at when this life comes to an end. Your core beliefs, but also your victories and successes. You might include areas as:

- How will you deal with failures and mistakes?
- How will you interact with others?
- How you will treat your body
- How you will deal with risks and opportunities
- How you will spend your money
- How you will serve
- How you will spend your free time
- How you will approach life in general
- What are your business goals?
- What does your living space look like?
- Where do you want to travel?

The specific goal setting manifesto: Write out exactly what it is that you want to do. Be specific. Start with your overall plan, and break it down to specifics. What is your desired outcome? How much money do you want to make, or who do you want to meet? Where do you want to travel, or what other dream do you long to accomplish? It can be related to any aspect of your life, as long as you know exactly what you want.

- What are you willing to do to get it? Write down exactly what you are willing to do and sacrifice. You might have to put other projects on hold. You might have to live on a low and fixed income for a while, and you might have to live in a less desirable environment for a period. Put it in writing, the specifics.
- Map out every step you've got to take to get there. Be specific. What do you need to do? Follow them and be persistent. Write down your route towards your success.

- Give it a timeline. Make deadlines and guidelines. Keep yourself accountable. Look forward and trace your steps. Vision it already done, achieved. Schedule everything. Plan one, three or ten years ahead. Whatever looks right for reaching your specific goals.

The values and personal power manifesto: Write down the answer to some simple yet profound questions. Do some deep soul searching and write a general declaration of your core beliefs, wisdom and understanding. Use the answers to each of these or similar questions as an outline for your written statements.

- What am I willing to die for?
- What do I believe in?
- What do I need to change in my life?
- How do I define myself?
- What do I value the most in my life?
- How do I want to live my life?
- What excites me?
- What is my true purpose?
- What do I stand for?
- What makes me truly happy?

> *"Just trust yourself, then you will know how to live." – Johann Wolfgang von Goethe*

General guidelines:

Use a language that is firm and positive. Make it uplifting. Bring out your positive notes, and dig deep for those inspiring words. While reading them, they should not only uplift and give *you* a boost. They should fire up the whole universe. Be direct and to the point. You do not want to be reading your declaration, wondering what exactly it is that you mean. Too many fancy words will only clutter the message.

Use affirmative and strong language. Be precise and speak in a tone of solution and success. Never use the negatives. For example: "I will never be sick again." Instead always affirm what you want to see happen: "I will stay healthy and strong." Kick it up a notch and say" I am healthy." Be firm in your statements.

Don't make it longer than you need to. Remember, you are going to keep reading it. Start simple and add on as needed. I have both added and subtracted from my manifesto. It is a tool that will give *you* more and more as you give *it* more, by reading and rewriting.

Write in the present tense. When you write about the future, it will stay in the future. All there really is, is the *now*, and so writing in the present tense is the most powerful. It is confirming that it is already done. As you write, also envision it with your inner eye. See it as done. It has a very powerful energy.

Take your time. Don't rush it. Let your personal manifesto be an honoring of your life. By writing it you are acknowledging its significance, and that it is worth spending some quality time on. If you choose to find your pen and paper, it will automatically take more time. On the computer, we are more prone to multitask. Make sure you don't. The creation of it in itself is very powerful. Imagine you are writing a letter to the Creator, declaring your life purpose and willingness to better yourself and to be more aware and mindful.

Let it all come forth. Let the inner most beliefs and motives surface on each of the topics that you choose. We are after the core values. That which makes it all true for *you*. This is an opportunity for you to do some deep digging within. All the cards on the table please. You might be surprised at what you mean and feel on certain subject. What you see as your future, and how you relate to friends and family.

The amazing values of a personal manifesto:

Your manifesto should be something you will find strength and support in reading. For optimal value, go back and read it every single day. It will remind you of why you are doing what you are doing.

Keep it positive. Once you have written your own, you can find strength and support in reading it over and over again. Reading it every single day will give you direction and keep you focused on your goals and your purpose. Life is a flowing journey, and every single day we need to remind ourselves of our values. To be able to deal consciously with the outside world, we need to stand our ground on the inside, within our own space. Balance on the inside, can conquer any upheaval on the outside.

Writing your manifesto, and reading it every day will change your life. A bold statement, I know. How could it not? Once you tap in to your truth with the purpose of intentions, you *are* change. It will help you remember why you are here, and why you are doing what you are doing. Keeping you sane when things go a little crazy, and whispering in your ear when people feed you their insecurities and fear. The manifesto is a representative of your standard, your pure intentions. As there is no right or wrong, how you write is up to you. I am certain you will want to change it along the way. As you evolve and secure your grounds, you will see even more clearly what your values and powers are. Your life will show you more to want to manifest, and more to be appreciative of.

"To hell with circumstances; I create
opportunities." – Bruce Lee

My Personal Manifesto:

I wrote my first life manifesto many years ago. While I was in bed, sicker than I care to even remember. I was hanging on to anything that was keeping me focused on life and healing. I was conditioning my brain and cells to grow free and healthy. I was literally full of shit, and almost completely numbed down by my subconscious programming. My whole life I had been walking towards this point of disaster, and only by treating my life like a warzone could I drag myself back up. At least that is what it felt like. I went through the *Dark night of the soul.*

The term goes back a very long time, always used to describe the collapse of the perceived meaning of life. The feeling of complete meaninglessness and loss of self. In the modern world we might confuse this experience with what we call depression, but it is not. There is no meaning to anything, and everything feels meaningless. The dark night can be triggered by an event in your life. You might lose your job, someone close to you, or have in some way a life-altering experience. A severe trauma in any way can trigger a reason to embark on such a journey. It will feel like everything is collapsing. It is like we are shaken out of what we perceive as our reality, and the experience is changing our concept of life and the meaning that it has been given. There is an awakening happening. The one living the experience will most often not be aware of what he or she is going through. For me, it was profound. It was shredding me to pieces. I was being stripped of everything.

I became completely naked.

I was nothing.

I was NO thing!

This is the awakening to something deeper, a sense of real purpose, to true and real passion. It is like a death and a rebirth, where everything that *was* has now left, and new meanings, new concepts, and a new sense of existence arise. There is a death of the ego, yet nothing really dies except the ego's own sense of self. A very painful death, and the experience is that of death itself, even though nothing real died, and never will. It will feel like endless despair and darkness.

This is often a part of an awakening process, leaving us stronger and more true to ourselves than before. Once we have gone through the dark night of the soul, and have been "reborn", we can see that what was let go of was the false sense of self. What dies was never real, but we were clinging to it as a part of the illusion of ego. I remember the time as being completely heart breaking and mind scattering, yet it has been my most important learning experience as I see it. [25]

From that point, I rebuilt my whole existence, my whole perception of who I was, where I came from and why I was here. My life manifesto helped me define my inner most solid beliefs, and my own sacred truth. I have since then written several, on different areas of my life, and I want to share with you an example of what a simple 33 point life-value declaration can look like:

1. I choose to be happy. I know it's a choice.
2. When I lead, I follow. I trust myself and my inner voice.
3. I am able to change my thoughts, change my mind, and change my life.
4. I am authentic. I allow myself to be true to myself and others.
5. I forgive easily.
6. My purpose is to inspire others to live their full potentials.
7. What others think of me is none of my business.
8. I breathe, live and talk health and prosperity.

[25] Hilde Larsen – *From Hell to Inspired*

9. I am a creator in my life. I take responsibility and action towards my goals.
10. Every day I strive to do better.
11. I focus on the positive side of life, and know that there is no failure, only learning.
12. I treat my body like a temple. With love, respect and honor.
13. I nourish my body with raw living food. I always have enough.
14. I walk in nature and honor all of creation.
15. I walk lightly on this earth by being conscious about the planet and it`s earthlings.
16. I live in gratitude for all that is. Every day I count my blessings.
17. Every opportunity that comes my way, is gratefully accepted and explored.
18. I am tough, strong and disciplined.
19. I never give up. I persevere until I reach my goals.
20. I walk mindful through the day.
21. I meditate every day.
22. My finances are always I order, and I am provided for. I am abundant in every way.
23. I spend time with people that uplift and strengthen me.
24. I am confident in what I do. I am brave and diligent.
25. I remain open to try new things.
26. I create and grow an honest and prosperous business.
27. I value my time and other's.
28. My words are spoken from a place of truth. Is it kind, is it true, and is it necessary?
29. I serve where I can, with joy and gratitude. Giving is one of life's greatest gifts.
30. My family is loving and supporting.
31. I honor my gifts through pursuing them.
32. My home is a sacred place. I keep it neat and clean.
33. I honor God, Creation, truth and my life.

"You are braver than you believe, stronger than you seem, and smarter than you think." - Winne the Pooh

After writing your own manifesto, feel proud! Not many people do this, and actually know what their values and core beliefs are. Play with it. Write a manifesto on single topics, like your health. What will it look like? Remember to write in present tense. Write it like a full description story. What do you see, how do you feel and what do you do? What does a typical day in your healthy life look like? How will you live according to your values? What good will you do, and how will you spend your time on this earth? This is you creating your life. The bullshit-free, amazingly mind-blowing, fantastic life. You are the captain, the driver, the boss and the humble observer.

Read your declaration every day if you wish. It will nurture your soul. When truth is spoken, your cells dance. Let it include all of your dreams, and as you read, you will believe even more. Your whole life will change in accordance to your wishes and statements. It is a mission statement, a living evolving document that you can change as you explore further. This is your owner's manual, your self-appointed set of rules that will help you grow into your very best version of yourself. Make several copies of it. Keep it in your purse. Hang it in your office, and let it inspire you every day.

We can all contribute to make this world a better place, through striving to become the best version of ourselves. We can always do better, learn and grow. Together we are stronger, and our united truth is more powerful. When we say no to lies, we honor our lives.

"To be yourself in a world that is constantly trying to make you something else is the greatest accomplishment."– Ralph Waldo Emerson

AFTERWORD

No matter what life serves us, we have the power to adjust, grow and change our path. No matter where you are today, the free will and innate wisdom handed down to you from your ancestors will guide you towards your true path. No matter how long ago it has been since you felt powerful and strong, you still *are.*

Nothing can distort or tear down the real you. Nothing can get in the way of your true powerful self, if you don't let it. No one can manipulate you or keep you down if you don't let them. Nothing can hold you back if you decide to break free.

Your truth is stronger than any lie.
Your passion is stronger than any disbelief
Your mission is here weather you recognize it or not.
Your strengths are unbreakable.
Your ability to change is obsolete.

Although the World we live in seems like a terrible place at times. Although we are witnessing war and suffering. Although disaster and fear is upon us. Although love and peace can seem like it went missing. Your life is yours to love. Your experiences are yours to claim and to mold. This is it, and when we wake up to the amount of glory and possibilities that has been handed to us, everything changes. You, me, them, all of us, here to do good. We are all here to make a difference. Let's cut the crap and own it, that responsibility. The world would change in a heartbeat. Suffering would end, and peace would reign. Love is everywhere. Look for it.

Push the easy button:

Claim your life
Show up
Stop trying
Be a warrior
Be a rebel
Stay strong
Freak out more
Aim higher
You are ready
Get real
Cut the crap

No more bullshit!

NOTES AND READING SUGGESTIONS.

Bibliography
(Listed chronologically)

Freud, S. (1915) - *The unconscious*, standard edition, Vol. 14
Larsen, Hilde (2016) – *From Hell to Inspired*
Larsen, Hilde (2016) – *Know the Truth and Get healthy*
Chopra, Deepak (1994) - *Ageless Body, Timeless Mind: The Quantum Alternative to Growing Old*
Fisher, Louis (1982) - *Gandhi, his life and message for the world*
Abraham/Hicks (2006) – *Ask and it is given*
Lipton, Bruce Ph.D (2005) - *The biology of belief*
Bordeau Szekely, Edmond (1981) - *The Essene Gospel of Peace, Book Two*
Knudtson/Suzuki (1993) - *Wisdom of the elders*

Articles

Shapiro, Fred R. - *Who Wrote the Serenity Prayer*, Yale Alumni Magazine (July/Aug. 2008)

Webpages

"The Emperor's New Clothes":
https://en.wikipedia.org/wiki/The_Emperor's_New_Clothes

NAIC: National Vaccine Information Center:
www.nvic.org

The Stockholm Syndrome:
http://medical-dictionary.thefreedictionary.com/
Stockholm+syndrome

Feng Shui:
http://fengshui.about.com/od/glossaryofterms/ss/What-is-Feng-Shui.htm

Return of Investment (ROI):
http://www.investopedia.com/terms/r/returnoninvestment.asp

Mark Manson:
https://markmanson.net/do-something

Karma Yoga:
http://upliftconnect.com/
something-missing-from-your-spiritual-practice/

Internet Statistics:
www.internetlivestats.com / www.internetworldstats.com

Law of Jante:
https://en.wikipedia.org/wiki/Law_of_Jante

Made in the USA
San Bernardino, CA
22 January 2019